T0274338

BARTLEBY
AND ME

BARTLEBY AND ME

Reflections of an Old Scrivener

GAY TALESE

MARINER BOOKS

New York   Boston

The Mariner flag design is a registered trademark
of HarperCollins Publishers LLC.

HarperCollins books may be purchased for educational, business,
or sales promotional use. For information, please email the
Special Markets Department at SPsales@harpercollins.com.

A hardcover edition of this book was published
in 2023 by Mariner Books.

FIRST MARINER BOOKS PAPERBACK EDITION
PUBLISHED 2024.

Designed by Renata DiBiase
Frontispiece photograph by Catherine Talese
Illustrations by Joel Holland

Library of Congress Cataloging-in-Publication Data has been applied for.

ISBN 978-0-06-335064-9

24 25 26 27 28 LBC 5 4 3 2 1

For Nan:
who helped to chart our serendipiter's journey
sixty-six years ago and is still at it

CONTENTS

BARTLEBY
AND ME

PART I

A Story of Wall Street

Chapter 1

New York is a city of things unnoticed. It is a city with cats sleeping under parked cars, two stone armadillos crawling up St. Patrick's Cathedral, and thousands of ants creeping on top of the Empire State Building. The ants probably were carried up there by wind or birds, but nobody is sure; nobody in New York knows any more about the ants than they do about the panhandler who takes taxis to the Bowery; or the dapper man who picks trash out of Sixth Avenue trash cans; or the medium in the West Seventies who claims, "I am clairvoyant, clairaudient, and clairsensuous."

New York is a city for eccentrics and a center for odd bits of information. New Yorkers blink twenty-eight times a minute, but forty when tense. Most popcorn chewers at Yankee Stadium stop chewing momentarily just before the pitch. Gum chewers on Macy's escalators stop chewing momentarily just before they get off—to concentrate on the last step. Coins, paperclips, ballpoint pens, and little girls' pocketbooks are found by workmen when they clean the sea lions' pool at the Bronx Zoo . . .

In New York from dawn to dusk to dawn, day after day, you can hear the steady rumble of tires against the concrete span of the George Washington Bridge. The bridge is never completely still. It trembles with traffic. It moves in the wind. Its great veins of steel swell when hot and contract when cold; its span often is ten feet closer to the Hudson River in summer than in winter. It is an almost restless structure

of graceful beauty which, like an irresistible seductress, with-
holds secrets from the romantics who gaze upon it, the es-
capists who jump off it, the chubby girl who lumbers across
its 3,500-foot span trying to reduce, and the 100,000 motor-
ists who each day cross it, smash into it, short-change it, get
jammed up on it . . .

These words were written more than sixty years ago when I was a young reporter at the *New York Times*. Growing up in a small town on the Jersey Shore in the late 1940s, I dreamed of someday working for a great newspaper. But I did not necessarily want to write news. News was ephemeral and it accentuated the negative. It was largely concerned with what went wrong yesterday rather than what went right. Much of it was, in Bob Dylan's words, "good-for-nothing news." Or it was Gotcha Journalism, in which reporters with tape recorders often got public figures to make fools of themselves trying to answer tricky questions.

Nevertheless, news continues to be made every day based on the statements and activities of newsworthy people—politicians, bankers, business leaders, artists, entertainers, and athletes. Other people are ignored unless involved in a crime, or a scandal, or had suffered an accidental or violent death. If they had lived lawfully and uneventfully, and had died of natural causes, obituary editors would not assign reporters to write about them. They were not newsworthy. They were essentially nobodies. When I joined the *Times* in the mid-1950s, I wanted to specialize in writing about nobodies.

As a reader I was always drawn to fiction writers who could make ordinary people seem extraordinary. Out of a nobody they could create a memorable somebody. Among the writers who achieved this was Herman Melville, whose great short story about a nobody is called "Bartleby, the Scrivener."

Appearing in *Putnam's Magazine* in 1853, two years after the publication of Melville's novel *Moby-Dick*, the story takes place within a small and dreary law office on the second floor of a building on Wall Street. The first-person narrator is an elderly lawyer who is not given a name but is described as a mild-mannered individual lacking vanity and unabashed professional ambition. Instead of arguing cases in court and seeking public recognition, he serenely conducts "a snug business among rich men's bonds and mortgages and title-deeds."

In this era when legal documents are copied by hand, with pen and ink, the lawyer delegates this tedious and exacting task to a newly hired scrivener named Bartleby. Whether this is his first or last name is the reader's guess, but in any case Bartleby— "pallidly neat, pitiably respectful, incurably forlorn"—makes a fine early impression as he sits quietly throughout the day, head bent, pen in hand, scribbling prodigiously at a corner desk hidden behind a high green folding screen that the lawyer placed there to provide some privacy for both the new man and himself.

The lawyer's desk is on the same side of the room as Bartleby's, while two veteran scriveners and an office boy (the latter a barely pubescent but purposeful youth who earns a dollar a week running errands and sweeping the uncarpeted floor) sit on the opposite side of the room. Bartleby never initiates conversation with his fellow scriveners or the lawyer, but he briefly exchanges a few words behind his screen once a day with the office boy—who then, jingling coins, leaves the office and goes out to purchase a handful of ginger-nut biscuits for Bartleby, retaining a couple for himself. Bartleby seems to eat little more than ginger nuts. He never goes out to lunch. When the lawyer and the others depart from the premises in the evening, they always leave Bartleby behind, working at his desk by candlelight.

Eventually, however, the lawyer alters his high opinion of Bartleby. This happens when, for the first time, he asks Bartleby to assist him in checking a legal document. Up to this point Bartleby has spent all of his time writing alone behind the screen and not joining the others when they partner to compare documents, making sure that the duplicates match the original word for word. On busy days even the lawyer, together with the astute office boy—who aspires to becoming a lawyer—lends a helping hand.

While Melville's story portrays the lawyer as a reasonable man, it also makes clear that he has not forgotten that he is the boss—one with "a natural expectancy of instant compliance" from his underlings—and so on this particular occasion, after he calls out to Bartleby by name and explains what he wants Bartleby to do, the lawyer does not anticipate hearing from behind the screen Bartleby's soft-spoken voice telling him: "I would prefer not to."

Assuming that he had not been clearly heard, the lawyer again beckons his assistant to emerge from behind the screen, carrying his chair with him, and come forth to participate in verifying the document. But again, politely but emphatically, and without moving an inch, Bartleby responds: "I would prefer not to."

This time the lawyer quickly rises from his own desk, strides past the screen, and, staring down at Bartleby, echoes: "I would prefer not to!"—adding: "What do you mean? Are you moonstuck? I want you to help me compare this sheet here. Take it!"

"I prefer not to," Bartleby answers, once more in such a gentle and deferential tone that it leaves his boss speechless, mesmerized, and confused.

I looked at him steadfastly. His face was leanly composed; his gray eye dimply calm. Not a wrinkle of agitation rippled him. Had there been the least uneasiness, anger, impatience or impertinence in his manner; in other words, had there been anything ordinarily human about him, doubtless I should have violently dismissed him from the premises.

Literary scholars and critics who have studied "Bartleby, the Scrivener" and have conducted countless seminars through the years pondering its meaning see much significance in the subtitle that Melville attaches to it: "A Story of Wall Street." It is suggested that the lawyer's walled-in office with its limited sunlight reflects Melville's dark view of the financial community, and that Bartleby alternatively serves as capitalism's opponent, its victim, and an example of "white-collar Marxist alienation." Among the wide-ranging comments are the following: "Bartleby is like a laboratory subject trapped in a maze with no exit" / "He fights by refusing to fight" / "I Prefer Not To becomes the mantra of the dispossessed and dislocated" / "This story belongs to a narrator who, like his money-driven society, ironically drains Bartleby's life of energy even while mouthing pious concern for him" / "Bartleby shows no emotion throughout the story."

This last remark is not entirely true. Near the end of the story, with Bartleby arrested and imprisoned due to his refusal to vacate the old building after he had been dismissed from his job and the firm had moved elsewhere, he becomes uncharacteristically peevish toward the lawyer when the latter comes to visit him one day in the prison yard.

Rejecting the lawyer's greetings, he declares: "I know you, and I want nothing to say to you." As silence ensues and the lawyer realizes that it is pointless to remain, he makes his exit— but not before a final gesture of goodwill. He offers money to a jailhouse kitchen worker who promises to keep Bartleby well fed. But this too proves to be pointless, because Bartleby goes on a hunger strike and dies in prison of starvation.

The story ends with the grieving lawyer mentioning that he later received a vague report claiming that Bartleby, prior to being hired as the lawyer's scrivener, had served as a subordinate clerk in the Dead Letter Office in Washington, a position he lost following a change in the administration. Although the lawyer cannot confirm the accuracy of this report, he nonetheless pauses to imagine how depressing and demoralizing this experience might have been for Bartleby, this job of "continually handling these dead letters, and assorting them for the flames."

But again, the lawyer concedes that he is not sure that Bartleby ever held such a position, and furthermore, during the entire length of Melville's lengthy tale, the reader learns nothing about Bartleby's private life and what might have motivated him.

Chapter 2

During my writing assignments and my longtime residency in New York City, I have met many people who, in one way or another, remind me of Bartleby. These are people whom I might see regularly but whose private lives remain private. I might know them by one name, or no name, or by little more than a nod, and yet I continually cross paths with them as they perform their duties as doormen, bank tellers, receptionists, waiters, mail carriers, handymen, cleaning women, and counter clerks at the hardware store, dry cleaner, pharmacy, or other places employing people who might meet an obituary editor's definition of a nobody.

When I was hired by the *Times*—I began as a twenty-one-year-old copyboy in the summer of 1953, earning $38 a week—the first thing I noticed as I entered the vast third-floor newsroom within the old Gothic-style office building on 43rd Street off Broadway were the horseshoe-shaped desks around which sat the bent-over bodies of dozens of copyreaders. Nearly all of them were men who wore green plastic eyeshades and, with pencils poised, were reading, correcting, and revising the typed pages of the articles that lay in front of them and were scheduled to be published in the next day's paper.

The copyreaders' names were unknown to the newspaper's general readership and also to most of the bylined reporters whose work they were editing. Like Bartleby, the copyreaders were physically close to their fellow employees while remaining socially and emotionally distant. Huddled for hours around the rims of the curved desks in the middle of the newsroom, with a minimum of movement and little conversation even among themselves, they were private, pensive, and pondering individuals who were entirely focused on reading and evaluating what might be fit to print in the next edition and what might eventually be preserved eternally in the paper of record.

After their final editing had been checked and approved by the chief copyreader and a few senior editors, the articles were relayed via an air-chute conveyer up to the composing room on the floor above. There the reporters' words were transposed by linotype operators into metal type that was later placed in trays and hammered to fit precisely within page frames by teams of printers—individuals whose names were rarely known and whose voices were rarely heard. A substantial number of printers at the *Times*, and at publications elsewhere, were deaf mutes.

What might be deemed a handicap in other occupations might be regarded as an asset if one were working in proximity to the noisy intonations of the composing room, and more so when close to the gigantic and clamorous high-speed press machines located within the basement and subbasement of the fourteen-story Times Building. Here, after the machines began to roll each evening, the sound became so ear-splitting that few people with normal hearing capacities could tolerate it; and, in addition, the vibrations were so pronounced as to be felt within the second floor's advertising department, the third floor's newsroom, and even the fourth floor's composing room.

When the night's work was done, and while many thousands of printed copies were wire-wrapped in bundles and packed into the delivery trucks, some of the printers would walk across the street to Gough's Chop House, at 212 West 43rd Street, for a beer and whiskey chaser. The printers were distinguished for wearing ink-stained, box-shaped, four-cornered folded news- paper hats, and, although they used sign language when ordering drinks, the bartenders at Gough's seemed to understand them.

While I was never personally acquainted with a printer or a copyreader, I regularly had a close-up view of them when I and other copyboys spent our off-hours at Gough's, where the burgers cost thirty cents and where on weekends we returned to cash our salary checks. The printers usually confined them- selves to the bar, while the copyreaders would likely be found at one of the booths in the back, seated close to, but not social- izing with, the reporters who might also be having a late-night dinner there.

This sense of separateness was in no way an indication of dis- respect between the two but rather an understanding, tacitly supported by higher management, that the interests of the paper were probably better served when reporters and copyreaders avoided close personal association. Yes, they worked for the same newspaper, but their priorities were different. Reporters were fact-gatherers. Copyreaders were fact-checkers. Report- ers were natural seducers who tried to convince their outside sources to be more forthcoming, whereas the copyreaders were the paper's guardians, rectifiers, standard bearers. They were trained to trim stories, to check the grammar, to clarify what was unclear; by not befriending reporters, they could more easily resist whatever entreaties might come from reporters desiring more space for their stories or for the restoration of a favorite phrase that the copyreader might have marked as purple prose and eliminated.

If reporters were unhappy with the editing, they were not to complain directly to a copyreader but rather consult with the city editor—a risky option, however, since the latter, disliking confrontations, might view the reporter as a whiner and reduce his assignments. In any case, the floor space around the horseshoe-shaped desks was all but forbidden territory to reporters in those days. As a copyboy, I often ran errands for the chief copyreader, who occupied the open space within the horseshoe—he was referred to as the "slot man"—but in later years, during my decade as a reporter, I deliberately stayed away from that area and consequently never became well acquainted with copyreaders.

Still, I was always curious about them. I believed they had interesting stories to tell and led fuller lives than was evident from what was seen of them. I was thinking this one night when I noticed a copyreader leaving the newsroom after work with a violin case under his arm.

Chapter 3

During this period I did get to know one of the *Times* electricians, and, before going to my copyboy job one afternoon, I interviewed him for a short piece that I later deposited in the city editor's mailbox. This resulted in my first published words in the *New York Times*, on November 2, 1953. It appeared on the editorial page, which did not carry bylines then, but an extra $10 was added to my paycheck the next week.

The electrician I wrote about was a stocky, bespectacled, and affable gentleman in his late fifties named James Torpey. Sometimes with an assistant or two, Mr. Torpey operated the paper's famous electromechanical moving-letter news sign that was illuminated by nearly fifteen thousand twenty-watt bulbs and spelled out the latest headlines in five-foot-tall gold lettering that rotated around the fourth-floor cornice of the slender wedge-shaped twenty-five-story Times Tower. This ornate building, near the corner of Broadway and 42nd Street—also the site of the annual "ball drop" festivity on New Year's Eve—was constructed in 1903 and served as the newspaper's headquarters until the paper outgrew it and moved less than a block away, in 1913, into vastly more spacious quarters at 229 West 43rd Street.

Still, for mainly sentimental reasons, the paper's owning Sulzberger family was reluctant to sell the Tower building. The cornerstone had been laid in 1904 by an eleven-year-old schoolgirl who was currently the paper's aging matriarch, Iphigene Ochs Sulzberger—the only child of the paper's owner, Adolph S. Ochs, who died in 1935. Ochs was then succeeded as publisher by Iphigene's husband, Arthur Hays Sulzberger. In young Iphigene's speech in 1904 she dedicated the Tower building to "the welfare of mankind." It was then the second tallest building in New York, topped only by a twenty-nine-story skyscraper at 15 Park Row, near City Hall, owned by a syndicate headed by a financier and horse fancier named August Belmont, who in 1905 established the Belmont Park racetrack in Long Island.

Mr. Belmont, who was also quite friendly with Adolph Ochs, tipped off the *Times* owner about a new subway station being planned for 42nd Street, and this certainly influenced Ochs's decision to move uptown from his 41 Park Row headquarters and construct his Tower building within what was then called Longacre Square, a name of London lineage. Three months after Iphigene had laid the cornerstone for the Tower, Longacre Square was renamed Times Square in honor of its new journalistic neighbor.

When I joined the paper in 1953, eight years before younger and less sentimental members of the Sulzberger family would sell the Tower to an advertising executive and sign designer named Douglas Leigh, the only *Times* employees still working in the building were in the classified advertising department, located on the ground floor, and the electric-sign operators on the fourth floor. The rest of the space within this narrow and odd-shaped quadrilateral structure was occupied by a dwindling number of commercial tenants. The sidewalk steps leading up to the building's main entrance served as the daily dropping-off spot for truck drivers unloading newly printed copies of the *New York Daily News*, *New York Mirror*, and other newspapers that I fetched each night as part of my job before carrying them back to the newsroom on 43rd Street, where various editors quickly scanned them in the hope of finding no worthwhile information of which the *Times* was not already aware.

On one occasion I arrived at the Tower well in advance of the truck drivers, and, indulging my curiosity, ventured up the Tower's staircase to the fourth floor and paused at the open door of a room cluttered with machinery and component parts whose purposes and designs confounded me. My attention was immediately drawn to a heavyset man standing on a ladder with his back to me, reaching with his right hand up toward the highest level of a large wall cupboard. There the shelving was lined with rows and rows of thin brown slats of an early form of plastic called Bakelite that in size and shape resembled paperback books. Also high above, but away from the cupboard, was a slow-moving chain conveyor with a pair of crawling rubber belts that traversed almost the full length of the ceiling before looping down to link and ride along the edges of a perhaps thirty-foot-long cast-iron industrial conveyor track that rose about three or four feet from the floor.

I watched quietly for a while, and, after the man had stepped down from the ladder and turned in my direction, I politely greeted him, adding that I was a copyboy and was very interested in what he was doing. With a friendly nod and a smile, he introduced himself as James Torpey, the chief operator of the news sign. After a pause, he handed me one of the slats he was carrying, identifying it as an electrical contact plate. It consisted of a five-and-a-half-inch silver metal letter mounted on Bakelite. There were many hundreds of such plates in the room, he said, and on each was imprinted a single letter from the alphabet. On the contact plate he gave me was the letter C.

Mr. Torpey went on to say that after he received a headline via teletype from the newsroom on 43rd Street, it was his job to quickly spell it out, letter by letter and then word by word, utilizing the contact plates in a manner similar to that of a compositor setting manual type. After the plated words of the headline were in order, then secured within a long and narrow metal frame, the frame was placed on one end of the lengthy conveyor track and, when activated, moved forward to make contact with electrical brushes that stimulated the many thousands of light bulbs that studded the news sign outside, instantaneously spelling out, in sparkling letters, the five-foot-high words of the headline.

Mr. Torpey said that the 380-foot-long sign that girdled the four sides of the building, and rotated headlined words from right to left, could be read by most pedestrians from a distance of several city blocks. He went on to say that he and the paper's owners joined in inaugurating the sign on November 6, 1928, with Torpey's first headline signaling Herbert Hoover's victory over Al Smith in the presidential election.

Torpey's "scoops" included being the first to announce the discovery and death in 1932 of the missing twenty-month-old son of aviator Charles Lindbergh and Anne Morrow Lindbergh. The child had been removed earlier from the nursery of his parents' home near Hopewell, New Jersey. Later, Torpey also led with the news that a jury in New Jersey had convicted Bruno Richard Hauptmann of the kidnapping and murder of the baby, the crime for which Hauptmann would be executed in 1936. The most gratifying headline that James Torpey ever copied was posted on the evening of August 14, 1945, in the aftermath of the Japanese surrender and the termination of World War II.

Despite my limited experience in journalism, I knew immediately that Torpey's story was a good one—and it was my kind of story. Here was a Bartleby-related character, an obscure scrivener working largely unnoticed, copying words that radiated light. Here in the Theater District was a kind of choreographer who created a chorus line of letters that shimmered and dazzled. And here, more important, was my opportunity to call attention to a headline-making man whose name had never appeared in print.

Below is part of what was published on the *Times* editorial page on November 2, 1953:

The electric news sign in Times Square will be twenty-five years old this week. Making its debut on Nov. 6, 1928, the night of the Hoover-Smith election, the sign has been a Broadway hit ever since as it rotates in five-foot golden letters around The Times Tower . . . from twilight to midnight . . . with only three interruptions — all due to wartime "dim-out" regulations.

And as we mark this silver anniversary of the electric sign it is fitting to acknowledge the service performed by James J. Torpey, a genial gentleman who, as head electrician, has been putting the news in lights since the debut . . .

Often in the past twenty-five years his service in the Tower has been far beyond the call of duty. On V-J Day in 1945, for example, Mr. Torpey remained at his post for twenty-three and a half consecutive hours awaiting the green light from The New York Times news department to give the tremendous crowd in the square what it had been waiting for: the official announcement of the end of the war.

Chapter 4

Another obscure individual whom I befriended during my rounds as a copyboy was Isaac Newton Falk, a sixty-year-old, diminutive file clerk who worked down the hall from the newsroom in the archival department, which was commonly called "the morgue."

The space there was dominated by multiple rows of tall steel cabinets filled with cardboard packets containing tens of millions of newspaper clippings—some of which, yellowed and brittle, dated back to the early 1900s and beyond. Also stored in the morgue were many advance obituaries awaiting the demise of newsmakers that were written by reporters no longer alive. On entering the morgue I often thought of Melville's reference to Bartleby and the Dead Letter Office.

The first time I was sent to the morgue was to obtain background information about the city's subway system for the transportation editor, and it was Isaac Newton Falk who assisted me. Only his head and shoulders were visible as he stood behind the counter and handed me the material. He was less than five feet tall. He had bushy eyebrows, and his wire-rimmed glasses were peppered with dandruff. His hair, gray and unkempt, protruded over, under, and through the green eyeshades he wore. He seemed to be shy and a bit awkward, but as I later got to know him I was impressed with his willingness, efficiency, and intelligence.

During a coffee break he once told me that his mother, a devotee of classical music, frequently took him as a boy to operas and concerts, and along the way he'd acquired massive amounts of knowledge about the great composers and their music. Consequently, whenever the *Times* telephone operators received outside calls requesting information—calls that were routinely directed to the morgue—Falk was always consulted if the inquiry concerned classical music. Initially, other employees in the morgue were unconvinced about the accuracy of his spontaneous responses; but, after checking with the paper's chief music critic, it was found that Falk was close to infallible.

He began working in the morgue in 1924, no doubt benefiting from the fact that his maternal grandfather, Michael B. Abrahams, had previously served the *Times* as an assistant city editor. When Falk was not working at the morgue's counter, he sat in the rear with other scissor-bearing employees, clipping articles from laid-out newspapers. Almost forty copies of the *Times*, and more than half that number of other publications, were set aside daily for such purposes. After each article had been cut out, it was neatly trimmed at the margins and labeled either by name or subject matter. It was then folded and tucked into a string-tied thin cardboard packet measuring seven-by-five inches, then filed alphabetically within one of the rolling drawers of the steel cabinets.

In addition to his knowledge of music, Falk's other main interest was baseball, especially regarding his favorite New York Giants baseball team—until it broke his heart by moving to San Francisco in 1957. The Giants home field was in Upper Manhattan at the Polo Grounds, and, whenever he was off duty during the baseball season, he could usually be found in the grandstands of the Polo Grounds watching a game, along with the paraphernalia he always carried: a rubber razzer and two cowbells.

If a Giants player struck out or made an error, Falk would blast the razzer. If a Giant got a hit, Falk would ring the small cowbell. When a Giant homered, Falk would not only ring the larger bell but sometimes throw it up in the air and let it drop with a loud clatter in the aisle near his seat. This feat often upset the attendants and nearby fans, but Falk was never evicted because he held a special pass issued by Ford Frick, president of the National League.

In early 1936, during his lunch break at the morgue and while reading the sports section, he noticed a scheduling error regarding the coming baseball season. Both the Giants and the New York Yankees were playing at home on August 20 of that year. Since both local clubs never played at home on the same day, Falk immediately telephoned the sports desk at the *Times*, and other papers as well, alerting them of the mistake. But in dismissing his calls, most people told him that he had read the schedule incorrectly or that what he had read was a typo. The only person who took the time to listen to him carefully was a sportswriter who was deaf. He was John Drebinger, who covered the Yankees for the *Times*, and he ultimately contacted the Major League scheduling officials and prompted them to correct their error. One result was a season-long gift awarded to "Isaac Newton Falk and One," providing free tickets to all National League games, a privilege that was renewed for the rest of his life.

I wanted to write an article about Falk, describing him as an interesting if contradictory figure—at times a quiet man in the morgue clipping articles, at other times a crazy fan tossing cowbells. I hoped the piece would be printed in the "*Times* Talk," the paper's slick twelve-page house organ that was published monthly for not only the five thousand employees within the building but was mailed out to several hundred retirees, foreign correspondents, privileged subscribers, and college journalism departments.

After writing a one-page outline for the article, I delivered it to the "*Times* Talk" receptionist on the twelfth floor. But I was disappointed a few days later when I received a polite rejection slip. As a subject, Falk was considered a bit too eccentric for "*Times* Talk," it was explained.

A week later, however, my spirits were lifted when I received a note from the travel editor, on the eighth floor, saying that he was interested in another idea I had: a piece about the men who made their living pushing passengers up and down the Atlantic City boardwalk in reed-covered, three-wheeled rolling chairs. Atlantic City was about to mark its hundredth anniversary—it was incorporated in 1854—and the "baskets on wheels" business began on the boardwalk about thirty years later.

As a boy growing up in Ocean City, approximately ten miles south of Atlantic City, I was familiar with the rolling chairs, and I had once received a ride as part of a birthday gift. The cost was a dollar per hour for one or two persons, and an extra fifty cents for three. The talkative Black man who vigorously pushed my chair said I was his tenth customer that day. On average, he walked twenty-five to thirty miles daily and claimed never to be tired. There were about four thousand chairs and men involved in the business. The founder was a partially crippled Philadelphian named Harry D. Shill, who, during the 1880s, in addition to renting baby carriages on the boardwalk, soon added invalid chairs for the many convalescents who vacationed in Atlantic City. When the trade began catering to the general public, one of its best-known patrons, while on weekend visits from Washington, was Charles Curtis, vice president under Herbert Hoover.

The article I wrote was published in the travel section of the Sunday *Times* on February 21, 1954. It was illustrated by a photo of a couple being pushed in a chair near one of the boardwalk's finest hotels, the classically designed Marlborough-Blenheim. The headline over my article read: "Famous Rolling Chairs Beside the Sea." Displaying my first byline in the *Times*, it began:

A sizeable number of the 10,000,000 visitors here each year consider their vacations incomplete until they have ridden in one of the three-wheeled over-sized perambulators which, along with saltwater taffy and public auctions, comprise the good life on this popular sand bar now celebrating its 100th anniversary . . .

Chapter 5

Some months later, during my final weeks as a copyboy, I had a story idea that was accepted by the Sunday *New York Times Magazine*. I proposed writing about a silent-screen actress named Nita Naldi, who, during the 1920s, had been one of movie idol Rudolph Valentino's leading ladies in Hollywood. Before that, after working as an artist's model, a vaudeville performer, and a chorus girl, she had been cast as an exotic figure in Paramount's 1920 film *Dr. Jekyll and Mr. Hyde*, starring John Barrymore, who had initially spotted her as a dancer.

But in 1954, decades after Nita Naldi's retirement as a vampish attraction in the film business, it was announced that a new musical called *The Vamp*, inspired by Naldi's career and starring Carol Channing, was scheduled for Broadway. I had read this item in a tabloid's theater column one day while riding the subway to work. The column mentioned that Nita Naldi was then living as a recluse in a small Broadway hotel, but the hotel was not named.

New York then had close to three hundred hotels in the Broadway area. I spent hours looking in the yellow pages in the *Times* newsroom when I was not otherwise occupied; I jotted down the hotel numbers and later began placing calls from one of the rear phones that copyboys were allowed to use. I phoned about eighty hotels over a four-day period, asking each time to be connected to Nita Naldi's room, speaking always in a presumptive tone that I hoped might give the impression that I knew she was staying there.

But none of the hotel people had ever heard of her. Then I called the Hotel Wentworth, at 57 West 46th Street, and, to my amazement, I heard the gruff voice of a man at the reception desk respond: "Yeah, she's here—who wants her?" I hung up. I did not want to speak to her over the telephone. It was not only late in the evening, but I had already been warned by a veteran reporter at the *Times*: "Young man, never interview anyone over the phone if you can help it."

He explained that the telephone was an inadequate instrument for interviewing people because, among other things, it prevents your learning a great deal from observing a person's face and manner, to say nothing of the surrounding ambience. I also came to agree that people will reveal more of themselves if you are physically present; and the more convincing you are in conveying your genuine interest, the better will be your chances of obtaining that person's cooperation.

On the following afternoon, two hours before reporting to work, I walked across the Wentworth's lobby to the house phone in the corner and firmly asked the operator to connect me directly with Miss Naldi—thus avoiding the assistance, and perhaps the unwanted questions, of one of the desk clerks. It also seemed to me that using the house phone was less invasive, more direct, and more likely productive than calling in from the outside, because, after all, I was now calling her from her own address—I was already there, manifestly present.

"Good afternoon, Miss Naldi," I began. "I'm a young assistant at the *Times*, and I'm downstairs in your lobby, and I'd like to meet you for a few minutes and talk about doing an article about you."

"You're downstairs!" she said, in a dramatic voice of mild alarm. "How did you know where I live?"

"I just called all the Broadway hotels I could."

"You must have spent a lot of money," she said, in a calmer voice. "Anyway, I don't have much time."

"May I just come up to introduce myself, Miss Naldi?"

After a pause, she said: "Well, give me five minutes, then come up. Oh, the place is a perfect mess!"

I immediately took the elevator to the fifth floor, then paused a little longer than five minutes in the hall before knocking. When she opened the door, she stared at me silently for a moment; then, after I had introduced myself, she smiled broadly and waved me in. Quite tall and striking, she presented herself in a way that had probably been filmed thirty years ago in a scene with Valentino. She had dark arched eyebrows and long earrings, a black gown, and jet-black hair that I guessed she dyed often. Her gestures, revealed as soon as she began to speak, were very exaggerated, as in the silent-screen era they had to be.

She shared her small suite with four parrots, and her parlor could have passed for a turn-of-the-century movie set—wall tapestries, crown molding, and Art Deco furniture, although now quite worn and scratched. The parrots, who did no talking, were paired off in two cages, and overlooking the center of the room was a small dusty chandelier.

I began the interview with questions about her early years, her elevation from being a Ziegfeld Follies girl in 1919 to her 1922 co-starring role with Valentino in *Blood and Sand*. She was not hesitant about discussing the downside of her career, conceding that her last film with Valentino, *Cobra* in 1925, was not very successful, nor was the one she did a year later, *The Mountain Eagle*, which marked Alfred Hitchcock's second venture as a director. She added that some bad investments, her own mismanagement, and the fact that she was no longer getting good parts in films led to her bankruptcy in 1932.

She did later appear from time to time in television shows and secondary roles in plays and musicals on Broadway, but her financial struggles continued. She admitted to me that she needed help from the Actors Fund in order to pay for her room at the Wentworth.

While she was grateful in 1954 when the producers of *The Vamp* hired her to help prepare Carol Channing for the leading role, she did tell me that she herself would have been a far better choice for the part. After all, she had lived the part, she explained, adding that she had a strong and rich voice and much stage experience in musicals. But then she asked that I not quote her on that subject. And I did not.

After spending almost two hours taking notes, I thanked her for her help and then spent the next three or four days writing the piece during my off-hours at my apartment. Finally, I folded the ten-page typed final version into an envelope and left it with the editor's secretary in the Sunday department.

A week later, the articles editor called to tell me that he planned to use the piece. His decision marked one of the happiest days of my life. But its publication had to coincide with the opening of *The Vamp*, he went on to say, and, since the musical was in an early production stage, opening night was still unknown and might be far away.

Whenever it was, I knew I would undoubtedly not be in New York. In late June, I was scheduled to begin a two-year tour with the army, reporting first to the Armor School at Fort Knox, Kentucky. When I told this to the editor, he told me not to worry: Whenever the musical announced its opening night, he would insert that information into my piece, then mail an advance copy to my unit. The story finally appeared in the Sunday *Magazine* of October 16, 1955.

It began:

In order that Carol Channing be flawlessly vampish, beguiling and pleasantly unwholesome as the star of the musical on the silent movie era which comes to Broadway Nov. 10 and is called, not unexpectedly, "The Vamp," she has had as a kind of adviser, aide de camp, critic and coach, that exotic former siren named Nita Naldi. When it comes to vamping roles, no one is a more qualified instructor than Miss Naldi. In her heyday, in the Twenties, Nita Naldi was the symbol of everything passionate and evil on the silent screen.

It ended:

Still very dark and buxom, Miss Naldi is recognized surprisingly often as she travels about.

"Women don't seem to hate me anymore," she says with satisfaction. She is often stopped in the street and asked, "What was it really like kissing Valentino?" Young people will remark, "Oh, Miss Naldi, my father has told me so-o-o much about you!" to which the actress manages to respond graciously. Not too long ago a man approached her on the corner of Forty-sixth Street and Broadway and exclaimed in wonder. "You're Nita Naldi, the Vampire!" It was as if he had turned the clock back, restoring Miss Naldi to the world she had inhabited thirty years ago. Eager to live in the present, the actress replied in a tone that mixed resentment and resignation. "Yes, do you mind?"

Chapter 6

I had long known that the United States stored vast amounts of gold in a vault at Fort Knox, but, until I received my military orders, I had no idea that Fort Knox also served as the home base for several thousand troops being trained in the use of tank warfare. Prominently located on the base, about thirty miles south of Louisville, was the General George Patton Museum, honoring the most famous tank commander of World War II; and, not long after I arrived there, it was announced that Fort Knox's new chief of staff, recently returned from Korea, would be Colonel Creighton W. Abrams, who had served heroically under Patton in Europe before and during the Battle of the Bulge.

As a journalism student at the University of Alabama—having enrolled there in 1949 at the suggestion of our Birmingham-born family doctor in Ocean City, NJ—I invested some of my extracurricular time with the Reserve Officers' Training Corps, a campus program available to students across the nation who, upon induction into the military, would enter as commissioned officers. In my case, since I was assigned to Fort Knox, I would begin as a second lieutenant in a tank unit. But first, I had to pass the Armor School's sixteen-week basic training course, where the challenges included learning to drive a tank up and down hills, learning how to change a tank's caterpillar tracks, loading and firing a cannon from the turret, and, while bivouacking at night in a tank with three other men, trying to get some sleep. The latter was by far the most difficult.

In November, after about five months of tank training, I was transferred to the headquarters building to assist the public information officer in writing stories about Fort Knox activities for the base newspaper, *Inside the Turret*, and also prepare press releases that might be published in journals around the state, especially in the prominent daily in nearby Louisville, the *Courier-Journal*.

Thousands of troops spent their weekends in Louisville, contributing greatly to the city's economy, and therefore I had a receptive audience for many of my ideas from the editors at the *Courier-Journal* and also the *Louisville Times*, an evening paper. The social page editor at the *Courier-Journal* printed my story about the many globe-trotting, multi-lingual students attending grade school at Fort Knox, and on another occasion the *Courier-Journal*'s Sunday magazine published my interview with a Bangkok-born lieutenant who had been my classmate at the Armor School.

I followed up with another *Courier-Journal* magazine piece about a Fort Knox–based twenty-year-old paratrooper, Private Stanley A. Melczak, who, while on a training mission in Alaska six months earlier, had jumped from a C-119 transport aircraft about a thousand feet above the ground, and, although both of his parachutes failed to open, he lived to tell me about it.

The fortunate Private Melczak survived because he fell into a forty-foot snowbank. It happened on January 29, 1955. He and about thirty troops from the Eleventh Airborne Division were supposed to be gaining experience in harsh climate conditions, but, after everyone had jumped, only Melczak's parachutes failed to open, and so he came down the hard way.

After being released from the hospital, and being assigned to temporary duty at Ford Knox, he told me that he'd landed feet first in the snowbank, with his hips and knees flexed 90 degrees. His body was a sort of shock absorber. "The medics and chaplains were the first to me," he said. "They cut my equipment, got me on a stretcher, gave me some shots, and soon I was on a helicopter to an army hospital. My arms and back felt broken, but it was only three fractured vertebrae."

After the *Courier-Journal* published my story on Melczak—"The Luckiest Man Alive"—it was picked up by the Associated Press news features syndicate and reprinted in dozens of newspapers around the nation and overseas. Since I was on the army's payroll, I accepted no fee for this or any of my other newspaper articles. I did receive bylines, however, nearly all of them identifying me as a second lieutenant and an assistant to the public information officer at Fort Knox.

My boss, the PIO, was an elderly cigar-smoking lieutenant colonel from Texas with a fondness for Kentucky bourbon, who, after decades of service, was eagerly anticipating his retirement in the coming year. Welcoming every opportunity to make his job less demanding and stressful, he often passed on to me responsibilities that were properly his, such as accompanying the chief of staff, Colonel Creighton Abrams, to social occasions and speaking events.

Abrams, soon to be promoted to brigadier general, was a heavy cigar smoker, and sometimes while I sat next to him in the back of the staff car, he would share one with me. This was a time of unhealthy bliss. Cigar smoking was even permitted on commercial airliners, and it is likely that Abrams's love of cigars contributed to his early death. He died at age fifty-nine, in 1974, as a four-star general in the Pentagon while the army's chief of staff. He had been undergoing surgery at the Walter Reed Army Medical Center in an effort to remove a cancerous lung. Some years after his death the army named its new main battle tank the M1 Abrams.

I was separated from the army at the end of June in 1956. Four months before that, I accompanied the Third Armored Division from Fort Knox to Frankfurt, Germany, to write stories highlighting the arrival of thousands of troops dedicated to winning the Cold War. But nothing that I saw in Germany convinced me that I was not part of a peacetime army. Yes, many big buildings in Frankfurt were still leveled as a result of bombs dropped more than a decade before, but otherwise the economy seemed to be flourishing, no doubt due to the many dollars coming out of the pockets of American soldiers. Being here in Frankfurt was not much different from being in Louisville, it seemed to me, except here the Americans went shopping every day for Leica cameras, became connoisseurs of Bavarian beer steins, and were winked at in the streets by prostitutes sitting behind the wheels of slow-moving Mercedes-Benz convertibles.

One day I traveled about twenty miles north of Frankfurt to Butzbach, to interview a young Third Armored Division officer from Marietta, Ohio, who had just taken command of a seventeenth-century castle and was quickly making it ready for occupancy by a few dozen troops from his unit. The land on which the castle stood was part of eight strongholds in West Germany overseen by the Third Armored Division, and the castle itself would provide living quarters as well as parking space for jeeps (in what had been a knight's stable) and a consolidated mess hall.

The story I wrote about the castle-commandeering lieutenant was published in mid-April in the Louisville *Courier-Journal*. Had I remained with the army two years longer, I would have had a far better story to tell: about a newly recruited private in the Third Armored Division named Elvis Presley.

Chapter 7

When I returned to the *Times* in midsummer of 1956, I was promoted from copyboy to reporter in the sports department. Although I would have preferred writing general news, the only staff opening then was in sports, so I accepted the position immediately while knowing it might also mark me as a member of the newspaper's "toy department."

This trivializing reference to sports journalism came from Jimmy Cannon, a sports columnist at the *New York Post*, but it failed to mention that many distinguished authors began their careers writing about sports; and furthermore, as a high-school contributor to my hometown weekly, the *Ocean City Sentinel-Ledger*, and later as an Alabama campus correspondent for the daily *Birmingham Post-Herald*, I had always been influenced and inspired by the works of literary writers dealing with sporting activities.

There was Ernest Hemingway on bullfighting and fishing, and John O'Hara on the esoteric game of court tennis, and also Irwin Shaw's story "The Eighty-Yard Run," about a Midwestern college halfback whose high point in life occurs during a practice session when he eludes all tacklers and dashes untouched into the end zone. Sadly, nothing thereafter will ever match that one magical moment on the football field, and in a follow-up scene outside the stadium, his wealthy girlfriend is waiting for him in her convertible, with the top down.

"Were you good today?" she asked.

"Pretty good," he said. He climbed in, sank luxuriously into the soft leather, stretched his legs far out. He smiled, thinking of the eighty yards. "Pretty damn good."

There was also F. Scott Fitzgerald's story "Winter Dreams," about a status-conscious caddie who carries bags at a club in Minnesota, where the members hit red-and-black golf balls because they are easier to see than white ones when hit into patches of snow along the fairways and the rough. On the course one day, the caddie sees a beautiful girl who will later befriend him and then cause him heartbreak. This story is a prelude to *The Great Gatsby*.

When I myself began writing sports pieces for the *Times* about caddies, football players, and other athletes, I tried to emulate Fitzgerald, Irwin Shaw, and my other favorite writers' storytelling techniques and their attention to detail—such details as Carson McCullers illustrated in her story "The Jockey": "If he eats a lamb chop, you can see the shape of it in his stomach an hour afterward."

I initially doubted the possibility of anyone being able to see the shape of a lamb chop in a jockey's stomach, but then one day the *Times* sports editor assigned me to interview an ex-jockey named Harry Roble, who had once been the top jockey in the United States, and I made a reference to Carson McCullers' story.

Roble had not been aware of it, but after I quoted her line about the lamb chop, he nodded. "Yes, that's possible," he said, then added: "I never liked lamb chops, but I'd sometimes sneak in a steak afterwards and I could feel the damned steak pressed against my skin. In those days, when I was weighing 98 pounds and struggling to keep it at that, I'd even put on two pounds with each bowl of soup."

When I wrote about Roble for the *Times*, my lede, privately dedicated to the memory of Carson McCullers, began:

> Harry Roble was one of those jockeys who gained two pounds after every bowl of soup and, if he ate a steak, you could sometimes see its lumpy outline lodged in his stomach.

During my years in the sports department, from mid-1956 until the beginning of 1959, I had many opportunities to indulge my interests and write about minor characters in major-league settings—people on the sidelines of stadiums, individuals who are part of the game but rarely written about, such as the referee in a boxing ring, the grass cutters at the ball park, the teenaged retrievers of tennis balls at tournaments, and such providers of services as Dr. Walter H. Jacobs, a dentist specializing in mouthpieces; Mike Gillan, "the Capezio of horseshoe makers"; and Hal Ott, who produced false hair pieces, goatees, and mustaches for the heavyweight fighter Floyd Patterson, who, shamed in defeat, wished to exit the arena in disguise. And there was also George Bannon, a seventy-eight-year-old grandfather's clock of a man whose job was ringing the bell between rounds at Madison Square Garden. When I interviewed Bannon, he said he had attended seven thousand fights and rung the bell more than a hundred thousand times. Before he became the Bartleby of bell ringing, he had made his living tuning pianos in the Bronx.

When I was not working in the sports department, I was pitching ideas for offbeat articles to other sections of the paper. For the drama editor, I wrote about a stage-lighting technician on Broadway. For the national news editor, after the Russians in 1957 had launched a dog named Laika into orbit, I wrote about other headline-making dogs in history—such as Balto, the sled dog who led a serum run in Alaska in 1925; and Chinook, who accompanied Admiral Richard E. Byrd's expedition to the South Pole in 1927; and Franklin D. Roosevelt's rakish little black Scottie, Fala, who became an issue in the 1944 presidential campaign.

Some Republicans charged that a destroyer had been sent to pick up Fala in the Aleutian Islands, at considerable cost to taxpayers, after he had allegedly been left behind on a presidential trip. The charge was nipped in a speech in which President Roosevelt said the Republicans were "even wanting to make war on Fala."

In 1957 I wrote in the Sunday *Magazine* about the many lives of New York's estimated four hundred thousand alley cats, and then followed that year and the next with magazine pieces about bus drivers, telephone operators, ferry boat captains, fortune tellers, tattoo artists, helicopter cops, iron-ball demolition crews, marriage brokers, cockfight promoters, and the designers of mannequins that adorn department-store windows.

After being transferred to the news department in 1959, I continued to concentrate my reporting on the lives of non-newsworthy people: doormen, bootblacks, dog walkers, scissor grinders, the late-night tile cleaners in the Lincoln and Holland tunnels, the clerks sitting in subway booths, the pushboys in the Garment Center, the carriage drivers in Central Park, a hay dealer posted in the city's freight yard, a prideful builder of pushcarts at 541 East 11th Street, a busy printer of traffic tickets at 111 West 19th Street, and, during Manhattan's power failure in mid-August of 1959, a stationery shop at Broadway and 72nd Street that sold thirty-five hundred candles in two hours. During the same blackout, within a four-story building at 62nd Street near Broadway that housed the New York Guild for the Jewish Blind, two hundred blind workers led seventy sighted workers down the dark steps safely to the sidewalk.

During this year I also wrote about a wealthy Manhattan chauffeur named Roosevelt Zanders, who had his own chauffeur. The forty-three-year-old Mr. Zanders, born in Youngstown, Ohio, actually operated a deluxe car service that employed five New York City chauffeurs for his five Cadillacs, while he himself drove, and was sometimes driven in, his custom-built Rolls-Royce that had wall-to-wall fur rugs, two separate hi-fidelity sets, and a jack almost the size of a midget wrestler.

At the 1959 St. Patrick's Day parade, after securing a seat in a reviewing stand at Fifth Avenue and 64th that offered an un-obstructed view of the eighty-nine bands and 130,000 march-ers, my attention soon drifted away from marshals and other dignitaries that were featured in front and I wondered: Who is bringing up the rear?

I left my seat and strolled several blocks downtown along Fifth Avenue until I located the parade's last marcher, a sixteen-year-old horn player wearing the peaked cap and striped uniform of the Holy Cross High School band, located in Flushing, Queens. His name was Richard Kryston. I found him on 49th Street, marching ahead as majestically as he could within the encumbering shape and weight of his large instrument—a sousaphone, which is a kind of tuba with curves. He had been standing in line for two hours awaiting his turn, and when his chance to march finally came, at 5:15 p.m., Fifth Avenue began to darken, and rain and snow began to trickle down his big golden horn.

At 5:18 he was striding toward St. Patrick's Cathedral. Watching from the steps were Cardinal Spellman and his retinue. But just before the horn player arrived, the cardinal and the others left their viewing spot for the dry indoors.

On he went past Peck & Peck, then past Bonwit Teller, then past Bergdorf Goodman—seemingly unnoticed by all but a window mannequin waving with fixed sophistication.

The crowd, which had jammed the sidewalk an hour earlier, had disappeared by 5:25 when Richard Kryston passed the reviewing stand on 64th Street. Mayor Wagner, his hat dripping, was signing autographs and waving to people who were calling "Hi, Bob," "Hi, Mr. Mayor." The mayor did not notice the horn player.

At 5:30 the policemen began to go home. People were yelling for taxicabs. It was raining harder. The city's cleanup crews were dismantling the wooden bleachers. Behind them came the sweepers, men in light uniforms sweeping brisky, as Charlie Chaplin used to do in the movies. At 5:45, when the sousaphone player was last seen, he was tooting in the 80s, but it was almost too dark to see him.

Chapter 8

During my almost seven years as a reporter in the news department, it was not often—maybe three or four times a year—that I was assigned to cover stories many miles outside the city; and, as in New York City, I always tried to interview people who might add a different perspective to the story, people who were unaccustomed to being consulted or paid attention to—in other words, people in step with the marcher bringing up the rear of a parade.

On October 22, 1962, in an alarming speech delivered from the White House, President John F. Kennedy declared that U.S. reconnaissance planes had discovered Soviet missile bases in Cuba and, if they were not promptly removed, a major war with Russia was upon us. I was not part of the *Times* coverage of this story, having been dispatched to the Wooster college campus in Ohio to report on the arrival of a diminutive, white-haired New Englander named Sherman Adams, who had accepted an invitation from the political science department to deliver a series of lectures on the American political system.

Mr. Adams had been the governor of New Hampshire from 1949 to 1953, and between 1953 and 1958 he had served in the White House as chief of staff for President Dwight D. Eisenhower. But he had been forced to resign in September 1958 following reports that he had accepted an expensive vicuña overcoat among other gifts from a Boston textile manufacturer who had business dealings with the federal government.

Still, after Mr. Adams had arrived on the Wooster campus, there was no mention of this by his faculty hosts, and the students with whom I talked had never heard of Sherman Adams—so fleeting, apparently, his fame and notoriety. And besides, the students were no doubt distracted by their own issues and also petrified after watching President Kennedy's address on television. In this fearful time, they asked, how could they concentrate on midterm examinations, and, even worse, what if they were forced out of school and drafted into the army?

While I was conversing with a Wooster faculty member named William I. Schreiber, and expressing horror over the prospects of atomic war and annihilation, he suggested that I might find temporary relief from anxiety by visiting the horse-and-buggy Amish farming community that existed just eight miles from Wooster. Yes, many of us on campus were worrying about the end of the world, he said, but the Amish people next door dwelled spiritually in another world, one in which tranquility prevailed, and this might be worth my attention.

Professor Schreiber, in addition to directing the college's German department, was the author of a new book, *Our Amish Neighbors*—and his closest neighbors, about a thousand of them, lived in the adjacent village of Apple Creek, in Wayne County. To the south, in Holmes County, were four thousand other adult churchgoing members, while there were forty-five other congregations around the state. There were more Amish settlers in Ohio than anywhere else in the United States, surpassing Pennsylvania and Indiana; and, since each family had seven children on average, it was estimated that within a half century the Amish population would exceed three hundred thousand.

Originally from Germany, the Amish began moving into Ohio in the early 1800s, Professor Schreiber said, and they currently operated some of the finest farms seen anywhere in the country. They grew corn, wheat, oats, alfalfa, potatoes, and were associated in cooperative cheese production in twenty-seven Swiss cheese factories in Ohio.

In Apple Creek, and in Amish settlements throughout the country, the people lived without electricity, eschewed automobiles, traveled by horse and buggy, and hung plain blue curtains on their windows, never silk. The men's beards were long and untrimmed, and they wore coats without lapels, shirts without neckties, pants without belts or cuffs, and their clothing was fastened not by buttons but by hooks and eyes. The women wore black ankle-length dresses, low-heeled black shoes, and black bonnets.

"The Amish are the only group in America that has kept to its old ways of eating and living and thinking and loving and marrying and burying," Professor Schreiber said, adding: "They are peace-loving farmers. They don't fight wars. They don't lock their doors. Some time ago here, some kids stole cattle and money from the Amish, but when the sheriff recovered it, the Amish refused to take it back. This was 'sin money,' and so the sheriff, not knowing what else to do with it, gave it to county welfare."

I drove my rental car with power steering into the Amish settlement on the following day, moving along dirt roads through acres of farmland with fenced-in cows and horses and busily engaged workers in dark outer attire. I parked the vehicle and received friendly greetings from the Amish elders, then as I approached and was shown where and how they lived, my first thought was not that I was among a backward or eccentric people but rather a unique gathering of religious white Americans who were a minority by choice. They were rooted to the agrarian ways of their ancestors, and, rather than assimilate and modernize, they exercised their constitutional right to retain their old traditions and values—to be different in dress and manner and from what worried most people around the nation and world.

That they have been able to exist for so long on their own terms was not only a tribute to their perseverance but perhaps as well to the egalitarian policies of a democratic republic, even though the latter frequently failed to protect vulnerable minorities from hate groups. Still, here in Apple Creek, the system seemed to be working, and it was oddly comforting for me to be interviewing people who were not fixated on the Bomb, who did not watch television, and who did not say "no comment" to reporters.

With courtesy and patience, they attempted to respond to my questions, but they often seemed to have no idea what I was talking about. This was true of a senior member of the community named Levi Hershberger. He had been working in his barn next to his immaculate white home that he shared with his wife, and he unhesitatingly put his tools aside when I approached and introduced myself.

"Mr. Hershberger," I asked, "what did you think of President Kennedy's speech last night?

He raised his inquiring eyebrows, paused for a moment, and replied: "I know of no speech."

I followed up by explaining that an important speech had been made and that war might be near.

"Mister," he said, firmly but not ruefully, "the happenings of the world, as far as I am concerned, are on the other side of the fence."

Chapter 9

When I left the *Times* in 1965, it was not really a departure from the paper but, rather, an opportunity to return to it as a freelancer and write about what I could not have done as a member of the staff. I wanted to do a series of articles for *Esquire* magazine based on interviews I would have with certain reporters, copyreaders, and editors with whom I had worked in the newsroom.

The term "media" was not yet such a popular part of the lexicon as it would become later, sparked by Watergate, and so except for book-length biographies on such newspaper publishers as Joseph Pulitzer and William Randolph Hearst, plus the press columns in the rear of newsweeklies and critiques in the *New Yorker* by A. J. Liebling, it was generally assumed that there was not a great deal of general interest in, nor much of a market for, lengthy stories about journalistic endeavors and personalities.

Indeed, journalists were not supposed to have personalities. They were trained not to become part of a story. Who they were, what they thought, how they felt, was deemed irrelevant. They were hired to cover the news for the paper of record. They were coverers, copyists, and the scriveners of other people's doings and deeds.

Yet, knowing them as I did, I believed that they had personal and professional stories to tell that were as worthy of attention as were the stories of the so-called newsmakers whose names and photographs appeared every day in the paper. Equally important to me was that *Esquire*'s editor, Harold Hayes, shared some of my sentiments, and in September of 1965, he offered me a contract to write about my *Times* people, as well as other subjects of his choosing, while being guaranteed an annual salary of $15,000 that matched what I had been making at the newspaper.

My decision to join *Esquire* in no way signified dissatisfaction with my superiors at the *Times*. Not only had they accepted most of my story ideas, but when they themselves selected my assignments I was rarely disappointed, particularly during my later years, when higher management decided it wanted not only fair and accurate reporting but well-written stories as well.

One of my last major assignments at the *Times* was to help cover the civil rights march in Selma, Alabama, that would culminate in a massacre known later in the history books as "Bloody Sunday." It happened on the mild Sunday afternoon of March 7, 1965.

Earlier in the day, in front of a redbrick church in the Black quarter of the city, five hundred peaceful Black Americans, carrying cloth satchels filled with extra clothing and shoes, lined up along the sidewalk, planning a five-day fifty-four-mile walk to the state capital of Montgomery to protest Selma's efforts to prevent Blacks from becoming registered voters. In this onetime plantation town, where more than half of the 28,775 population were the descendants of slaves, only 325 Black residents were registered to vote.

But after the demonstrators, walking two abreast, had proceeded downtown through the business district and crossed the Alabama River via a steel arched bridge named in honor of a Confederate general named Edmund Pettus, they were un-expectedly attacked along the highway by a charging wedge of state troopers equipped with billy clubs and gas grenades. I was standing with other journalists and TV crews, about thirty feet away from the front line of marchers, and none of us expected to witness what we suddenly would: the explosion of trooper-tossed gas grenades hitting the ground, the rising clouds of toxic smoke burning and blurring the marchers' vision, the moans and cries of those pummeled repeatedly by the law-men's clubs and rifle butts, the sight of other victims stumbling backward, half blinded and frantic, seeking to escape and run back across the bridge to their church, leaving along the highway their hats, umbrellas, toothbrushes, handkerchiefs, satchels, and blood.

Seventeen of the nearly seventy injured ended up in the town's segregated hospital, transported there by ambulances owned by Black undertakers. One of the lead marchers, the twenty-five-year-old ex–Freedom Rider and future member of Congress John Lewis, suffered a skull fracture from the club-bing, and the scars on his head would be forever visible. (The Reverend Martin Luther King Jr. had been at his headquarters in Atlanta when all of this happened, but he would be in Selma on the following day.)

As I and the other journalists retreated through the ex-cruciating smoke, trying to elude the arrival of the sheriff's posse on horseback swinging long leather whips and electric cattle prods, I continued to hear along the highway the click-ing sounds of television cameras that had filmed the gruesome scenes and were continuing to focus on what occurred as a result—including Martin Luther King's anguished nation-wide call for volunteers to come to Selma and join the walk to Montgomery.

His request would draw a total of twenty-five thousand followers by March 21, when—after overcoming court-ordered delays and White House timidity about protecting the expedition with federalized National Guard troops—the King-led procession finally entered the Alabama capital and petitioned the racist governor, George Wallace, for voter-registration reform. There is little doubt that this large gathering of out-of-state white and Black sympathizers had traveled to Alabama because they had been sickened by the depictions of inhumanity shown again and again on network television.

These events proved how persuasive television news reporting had become in projecting imagery and attitudes in ways that could immediately mold and mobilize public opinion. Indeed, the film clips of Bloody Sunday would soon inspire Congress to pass the Voting Rights Act that President Lyndon Johnson signed into law on August 6, 1965.

I remained in Selma for a week and a half after Bloody Sunday, writing several pieces for the daily paper, and a month later I returned for a follow-up article that the paper's Sunday *Magazine* published on May 30. What I wrote was based on not only interviews with some of the marchers but with the white people who had joined them in Selma from all parts of the nation in response to Dr. King's appeal. I also did not neglect to mention that great numbers of these white supporters dwelled in segregated neighborhoods up north and elsewhere, and they were now condemning Selma for racist practices that they quietly tolerated back home.

Unlike most of the out-of-state reporters who covered Bloody Sunday, I had been to Selma a few times before, beginning during my student days at the University of Alabama; and, in an essay published decades later in the *Times*, I recalled the rampant racism that marked my youth in Ocean City, New Jersey, a politically and socially conservative island resort founded during the 1800s by Methodist ministers.

Although Black students attended school with whites in my hometown, it was otherwise a largely segregated community. At the boardwalk's Village Theater, Black students as well as Blacks of all ages sat by themselves in the balcony while whites gathered below in the orchestra. I recalled seeing groups of white-sheeted Klansmen holding meetings occasionally on our campgrounds, within a few blocks of the business district, where my Italian-born Catholic father owned and operated a tailor shop.

When I first became part of the University of Alabama's all-white campus in 1949, I saw nothing so different from what I had observed during my New Jersey boyhood.

In June of 1963, as a reporter at the *Times*, I had an interview in New York with Alabama's governor, George C. Wallace, who had flown in to appear on NBC's *Meet the Press*. He stayed in a large suite at the Pierre hotel on Fifth Avenue, where our talk took place.

The interview had been going well for the first ten minutes, but then Governor Wallace suddenly rose from his chair, took me by the arm, and led me to one of the windows overlooking Central Park and the row of expensive buildings that line Fifth Avenue.

"Here we have the citadel of hypocrisy in America," he said, pointing down to the street and declaring that hardly any Black people, even those who could afford it, could hope to share living space with whites in this area because of the long-standing, if unacknowledged, practices of real-estate segregation in New York and other northern cities.

And still, he went on, they come down to the South and rant about equal rights!

I quoted him at length in the next day's paper, but I left the interview without mentioning to Governor Wallace that I myself had an apartment a few blocks away from the Pierre—and I did not have then, nor do I have to this day, an African American neighbor on my block.

Chapter 10

Having left the newspaper on good terms to join *Esquire* in September of 1965, I had no difficulty in getting permission from the *Times* managing editor, Clifton Daniel, to revisit the building and conduct interviews with my selected list of *Times* people, including himself. He was one of four *Times* figures that *Esquire*'s editor, Harold Hayes, had agreed to let me portray in full-length articles, ranging in length from four thousand to seven thousand words or more. Accustomed as I was to a twenty-five-hundred-word limit at the Sunday *Times Magazine*, I greatly welcomed the space increase as well as having more time for research and writing, since *Esquire* was a monthly magazine.

On the downside, however, was my having to please Harold Hayes occasionally by interviewing a movie star or other celebrity. When he proposed that I write about Frank Sinatra, I tried to talk him out of it, and, while resisting the temptation of using Bartleby's refrain—"I would prefer not to"—I did emphatically remind Hayes that there had already been several recently published pieces about Sinatra and I wondered what more could be said about him. I preferred to not write about celebrities because I knew from experience that few of them had much respect for writers, they were often late for interviews (if they showed up at all), and regularly insisted that their press agents or attorneys sit in on interviews and review the articles prior to publication.

I would never agree to this, nor would any newspaper or magazine of which I was aware, including *Esquire*, but Hayes still desired a big piece about Sinatra in his magazine and wanted me to do it. He reasoned that it was only fair that I sometimes try to help him increase newsstand sales with celebrity covers since he was allowing me to publish stories about journalists of whom few *Esquire* readers had ever heard.

In reviewing the four newspaper people on my proposed list, Hayes acknowledged being familiar with the Pulitzer Prize–winning foreign correspondent Harrison Salisbury, who had covered Russia during the Stalin years; but he knew little about the managing editor, Clifton Daniel, except that he was married to the daughter of the former president Harry Truman. And Hayes said he had no idea who my other two choices were: a young general assignment reporter, John Corry, and a veteran copyreader named Alden Whitman, who had recently become the *Times* chief obituary writer.

Rather than begin my contract at *Esquire* by further sparring with my new boss, I agreed to do a profile on Sinatra, but first I wanted Hayes to publish one of my *Times* stories. He consented, and so I told him that my first piece would be about Alden Whitman. I had never before had a conversation with Whitman, or any copyreader, but I remembered seeing him at work and at Gough's Chop House when I was on the paper, and, near the end of my time there, I once sat close enough to him in the *Times* cafeteria to get a good look at him.

He was a short, stout man who walked in smoking a pipe and bearing a serious, if not dour, expression that contrasted with his sprightly attire. He was wearing a red polka dot bowtie, a yellow pinstriped shirt, and a rakish double-vented tan hacking jacket. Though middle aged, he had a full head of brown hair without a trace of gray, a thick reddish mustache, and, after selecting his food at the counter, he walked with quick spry steps across the room toward an unoccupied corner table. In his right hand he held a plastic tray on which was a bowl of soup and a salad, while in his left hand was a folded copy of the *New Statesman*.

He then spent the next half hour by himself, reading while eating, carefully feeding himself with one hand while holding his newspaper with the other, positioning it within an inch or two of his nose and then squinting at it through his horn-rimmed glasses. I assumed that he was myopic.

I decided to start my *Esquire* contract with him both because of my longtime curiosity about copyreaders—modern-day Bartlebys—and the fact that Whitman was now in charge of obituary writing. Although he was an isolated member of the reportorial staff, the only one whose published writing did not carry bylines, he nonetheless possessed considerable arbitrary power within the paper. It was primarily up to him to decide who was, and who was not, newsworthy enough to warrant an obituary.

In Whitman's world, the recently deceased were either a "somebody" or a "nobody," and if the family survivors of the latter wished to call public attention to their loss, the only way they could do it was by buying space within a newspaper's tiny-type death notice column.

One mourner who did this, because her husband had died in obscurity, was a widow named Elizabeth Melville. After he suffered a fatal heart attack at the couple's home in New York, shortly after midnight on September 28, 1891, she purchased a six-line announcement that appeared on the following day in several newspapers.

Herman Melville died yesterday at his residence, 104 East Twenty-sixth Street, this city, of heart failure, aged seventy-two. He was the author of "Typee" and "Omoo," "Mobie

Dick," and other seafaring tales, written in earlier years. He leaves a wife and two daughters, Mrs. M.B. Thomas and Miss Melville.

Melville's situation was a case in which the name died before the man, to borrow a phrase from A. E. Hausman. Melville's career had begun auspiciously when he had two bestselling novels before turning thirty: *Typee,* in 1846, and its sequel, *Omoo,* in 1847, both based on his travel adventures in Polynesia. But none among his following sixteen books—his novels, collections of poetry, or such stories as "Bartleby, the Scrivener"—drew a wide readership, and in fact during the last third of his life all his books were out of print and forgotten, including his most ambitious undertaking, *Moby-Dick*, the title of which was misspelled in several of the Melville death notices.

It would not be until the centennial of Melville's birth, in 1919, followed by the successful publication in 1924 of the novel that he left behind—*Billy Budd*—that literary scholars and readers would discover and appreciate his earlier writings and recognize him as being among the nation's leading literary figures.

Chapter 11

When I met Alden Whitman, in September of 1965, I was stunned to hear him say that I had been wise in putting him at the top of my *Esquire* list because he did not expect to live much longer. I did not reply, thinking that this fifty-two-year-old man must be kidding—he was being melodramatic or had spent so much time writing about death that the subject was consuming him.

"I'm really not well," he continued softly. "I've recently returned from eight weeks at Knickerbocker Hospital following a major heart attack, and I'm concerned that the next experience could be fatal."

He was sitting on a sofa across from me in the living room of his four-and-a-half-room apartment on the twelfth floor of an old brick building on West 116th Street. We were surrounded by shelves packed with books, and there were even more books stacked below on the floor. He shared the apartment with his third wife, Joan, sixteen years his junior. They had met in 1958 at the *Times*, where she was (and remained for another two decades) an editor in the style department.

A slender and attractive brunette, she was getting ready to leave for work as I arrived for the first of three scheduled interviews. This had been settled by phone earlier in the week, and although he had not then mentioned his health, he described himself as very busy, and therefore I agreed that each of my visits would not last much longer than an hour.

After Joan had left, he went on to say that in addition to his heart problems, he also had glaucoma. It required that he douse his eyes with drops of pilocarpine every three hours, and there was a possibility that he would go blind before he died. And this was why, not knowing how long his vision would last, he was eager to complete his obituary. He said he had already delivered parts of an early draft to his assistant on the obit desk, and that when it was completed, and the occasion called for it, it would be promptly printed in the paper.

"One of the reasons your *Esquire* assignment appeals to me," he said, "is that it gives me a chance to review my past, and in talking to you I might remember things I would have forgotten."

As I sat across from him, taking notes, I could hardly believe what I was hearing. Here I was doing what he usually did, having an antemortem interview with a candidate presumably ready for a funeral. I had heard that Alden Whitman had already written dozens of advance obituaries on noteworthy elderly people who in some cases he had traveled great distances to meet in person, and describe at close range, before it was too late—Charlie Chaplin, for example, and Vladimir Nabokov, Graham Greene, Charles Lindbergh, Francisco Franco, and the British scientist and novelist C. P. Snow, who was known to have referred to Whitman as the *Times* "ghoul."

Still, as far as I could see, and despite what Whitman had been telling me, he did not look like a dying man. He was much as I remembered him from the year before in the cafeteria—jaunty in a colorful bowtie, puffing a pipe, no signs of emaciation, weariness, or inattentiveness. He spoke in a strong and clearly modulated tone of voice, and his manner was as casual when discussing his ailments as it was when he had greeted me earlier and asked if I'd like something to drink. I thought it might be an indication of

Whitman's detached persona, a characteristic of many people in journalism.

"I'd like to show you what I've written so far," he said, reaching for a manila folder on a nearby table and handing it to me. It contained carbon copies of several typed pages. "You can keep this," he said." There might be some background material you can use."

I took the folder and saw that some of the pages were marked up. There were a few words and phrases scratched out and replaced by not-always-easy-to-read handwriting, and so for clarity's sake I began reading aloud while counting on him for any corrections or explanations. The first page began:

Alden Whitman, a member of The New York Times staff for 14 years, died today of a coronary thrombosis at the age of 52. As a reporter he wrote obituary articles on many of the world's notable personalities.

Before becoming a full-time obituary writer Mr. Whitman was a copy editor on the metropolitan and national news desks. He came to The Times in 1951 from The New York Herald Tribune, where he had been a copy editor since 1943. He had previously served for two years on the copy desk at The Buffalo Evening News.

Decades of hard work lay between the mellow years of Mr. Whitman's journalistic prime and his boyhood in Connecticut and New Albany, Nova Scotia, where he was born on Oct. 27, 1913, the son of Frank Seymour Whitman, a Canadian-born manual arts teacher and carpenter, and Mabel Bloxsom Whitman, a native of Connecticut who for many years was a public school teacher in Bridgeport.

He interrupted to explain: "I was an only child. When I was two, my parents moved from New Albany to Bridgeport to live with my maternal grandmother. She was a widow who had a rambling ten-room house. Since my parents were out working most of the day, it was my grandmother that I went running to after school for cookies or whatever. She was warm-hearted but frugal. She considered it a positive sin to buy in a store what you could make at home. She said no to store-bought bread. One of my chores as a youngster was to turn the crank in a tub of dough for the week's baking."

None of this was mentioned in the pages I held, but I sat quietly as he continued: "I was very studious and twice skipped grades. This enhanced my mother's pride and her status among other teachers, but it didn't make us any closer. My father was deferential toward her—she wore the pants in the family—but otherwise he was also in his own world. He was a teetotaler, very religious, a deacon in the Baptist church, a man who never swore. He had grown up in a farm family in Nova Scotia that had seven children, but only he survived. The other six died of various childhood diseases. He never discussed this."

Alden Whitman went on to say that in 1928 he graduated from high school near the top of his class, although he was only fifteen. Having earlier skipped two grades meant that he was less physically mature than his classmates, and therefore he shied away from competing in intramural sports, although he did serve as the coach's assistant and phoned in the game scores to the local newspaper.

"I had six years of Latin and I was the only kid in high school reading Horace and the naughty poet Catullus, but I couldn't add or subtract. Throughout my life I've had difficulty balancing my checkbook."

Still, he got into Harvard. His parents contributed what they could but he himself covered most of his expenses by waiting tables and holding other jobs when not in class or when not indulging his passion for reading at the magnificent library—and not venturing off campus as a 50-cent patron of the Boston Symphony; or not sitting in the balcony of the Colonial Theatre watching a play bound for Broadway; or not at the Tremont Temple listening to the evangelist Billy Sunday; or not tuned into the radio hearing Rudy Vallée singing one of the Depression era's hit songs, "Life Is Just a Bowl of Cherries."

"And then suddenly all went wrong," he told me. "I ran out of money. I had to take a year's break from Harvard between my junior and senior years and accept a job as an inventory clerk at the Underwood typewriter factory."

He paused momentarily. He lit his pipe and stared around the room. Then he turned to me and, lowering his voice, explained that another reason he dropped out of Harvard was that his girlfriend had become pregnant.

During the summer of his sophomore year he had begun dating a pretty woman who worked in a Bridgeport bookstore. Her name was Dorothy McNamara. She was five years older than Alden, but, like him, an only child who read a lot and was remote from her parents. Her disgruntled mother was then in the process of divorcing her husband, an Irish-born circus worker.

After Alden and Dorothy got married in 1933, and after their daughter was born, he began working for Underwood with the expectation that his parents would help him look after his young family. Alden's father, Frank, was then still busy teaching, but his mother, Mabel, had time on her hands because the local administrators of education, wanting to spread jobs to as many families as possible during the Depression, currently employed only one person per household, and thus Mabel was eliminated from the faculty.

Alden's grandmother had died a few years before, so there was extra living space available, but the fact remained that Mabel disliked Dorothy, and only with much reluctance did she even allow her new daughter-in-law and the baby to move in temporarily. Dorothy was seen as a seductress, a calculating and common person who had latched on to Mabel's brilliant son and caused him to drop out of Harvard. Mabel on one occasion carried the couple's wedding photo from the living room into her bedroom and, with a scissor, sliced off Dorothy's image and dropped it into a trash basket.

Alden, meanwhile, believed that he had no future unless he completed his education at Harvard, so he quit his Underwood position after a year and returned alone to the campus. Graduating in 1935, he began searching for a job, but the only one that appealed to him was as a reporter at the *Bridgeport Post-Telegram*. The starting salary was $10 per week.

"How can anybody live on $10 a week?" he asked me. "And yet, in those days during the Depression, publishers got away with it. They fed young reporters' egos with bylines and the highfalutin' notions that newsmen met interesting people. It usually turned out that the only interesting people newsmen met were other newsmen."

He took the job anyway, although the first thing he did was help launch the Bridgeport Newspaper Guild and demanded higher wages. As a left-wing idealist at Harvard he had championed the cause of workers during these hard times, and now, at the age of twenty-two, he saw himself as a muckraking journalist who would expose the inequities in capitalism and inspire reform. It was while in this frame of mind that he joined the Communist Party.

One early evening while devoting himself to party priorities, standing on a soapbox in Bridgeport advocating the unionization of a brass-fitting factory, he was jumped by three anti-union brawlers. After dragging him into an alley, they beat him with sticks and fists and succeeded in knocking out every one of his thirty-two teeth.

"They were filled with cavities, a blessing to be rid of them," he said blithely, with an upward thrust of his pipe in my direction. "The false teeth I have now are a great improvement." He opened his mouth and tapped them with the tip of his pipe.

During this one-hour interview, and the two that followed later in the week, Alden recalled his past with some humor but, when dealing with his personal life, much regret. Although he soon got a higher-paying job with the *Bridgeport Sunday Herald*, and was living rent-free with Dorothy and their child at his parents' place, he never seemed to have enough money to pay for the essential needs of his family. Then things got worse when the couple had a second child, a son, born in 1936.

No longer willing to further crowd the household, Mabel made it clear to Dorothy that the new child was not welcome, and as a result Dorothy soon packed her things and left with her infant son to move into the home of her divorced mother, Anne. She left behind her nearly three-year-old daughter, who would be raised thereafter by Mabel and Frank Whitman. Indeed, the little girl would grow to love them, and be loved in turn, while remaining with them as their "daughter" until she was nineteen and met a DuPont engineer she would soon marry.

"I and my father, Alden Whitman, had the same parents," she would say in later years, as the longtime wife of the engineer with whom she would have three children. However, she would never reconcile with her estranged mother, Dorothy (who would years later marry again, and again unsuccessfully), nor with her younger brother (who would become a college-educated marketing executive and marry four times).

During the summer of 1937, a few weeks after Dorothy had exiled herself from the Whitman household, and as her elusive husband seemed to be too preoccupied with his own concerns to help or care for anyone else, Alden came close to killing himself. He was supposed to be researching an article for the *Bridgeport Sunday Herald*, and he certainly knew that with jobs so scarce this was not the time to take liberties, but on impulse he decided to go for a swim nearby at Fairfield Beach.

"I'm not a good swimmer," he told me, "but it was a hot day, and I went ahead and got my bathing suit and jumped in. Not long after, as I'm splashing around, I blacked out. I went down twice, and almost a third time. What I most remember is that it seemed like a pleasant way to die . . . you gulp in water and you lose consciousness very painlessly. Yes, my last thought was how pleasant it was . . . And the next thing I knew, I was in St. Vincent's Medical Center in Bridgeport."

He told me he had no idea how he got to St. Vincent's, nor who rescued him. Nor did he try hard to find out. He told no one about the incident—not his parents, not anyone at the newspaper, and certainly not his wife, whom he was trying to avoid because she was pursuing him for child support. It was difficult for her to find him, however. He rarely visited his parents and daughter, his residential address was unknown, and, when he was not working for the newspaper, he was sequestered somewhere reading a book. And it was in the Bridgeport Public Library during this period that he met the woman who would cheer him up and become his second wife.

Chapter 12

She was a Smith College graduate employed in the main reading room, and her name was Helen Kaposey. She was personable, comely, and perfectly proportioned insofar as the 5'7 1/2" inch Alden Whitman was concerned, being at least three inches shorter. Helen would soon leave her library job for New York to begin working in the letters department of *Time* magazine. She was the granddaughter of Hungarian immigrants who had been house servants in Bridgeport for the prominent Wheeler family, inheritors of the Wheeler & Wilson sewing-machine assets, and it was through this connection that she had received the funds for her college education. It was also at Smith that she became politicized and decided to join the Communist Party.

Beginning in the fall of 1938, whenever he could, Alden would drive down to New York in his secondhand Chevrolet coupe to visit Helen Kaposey, and she in turn introduced him to her circle of her friends, among them a few Communists, and some of these friends made efforts to get him job interviews. No newspaper or magazine in New York City would hire him because of his limited experience in big-city journalism, but when a public-relations firm offered him a position, he accepted immediately.

Gradually at first, and then more deliberately, he cut his ties to his hometown, his parents, his children, and his now-divorced wife, Dorothy, and started life anew in New York City at the age of twenty-four.

Later in 1939, at the New York Society for Ethical Culture on West 64th Street, Alden and Helen got married, then rented an apartment in Sunnyside, Queens. After work they often remained in the city to attend concerts and plays, or dine with other young couples at small restaurants, mainly in Yorkville or Greenwich Village. While they were still social activists with party credentials and concerns for the proletariat, Helen was also a frequent shopper at Peck & Peck, while Alden, in the mode of some faculty members he remembered from Harvard, began wearing bowties.

Due to cutbacks at the public-relations company that had initially hired him, Alden considered himself lucky to find short-term work with another PR firm as well as a few enterprises that Senate investigators in later years would identify as Communist front organizations. One that Whitman worked for called itself the North American Committee to Aid the Spanish Democracy. This group supported the Loyalist cause against General Francisco Franco's fascist forces during the Spanish Civil War, and part of Whitman's job was to speak at fundraising meetings sponsored by Loyalist sympathizers.

In terms of employment, the closest he got to journalism during this time was when he was hired as a desk editor at the New York office of TASS, the Soviet news service. One of his tasks was to eliminate needless words, commas, and personalized phrases from English-language newspaper and magazine articles prior to their being translated for Russian readers.

In 1940, after one year of marriage, Alden learned that there was a job available on the copydesk at the *Buffalo Evening News*. While eager to join a prominent metropolitan American newspaper, he knew, if hired, that he would be going to Buffalo alone, as Helen intended to remain at *Time* magazine. Still, when the newspaper made him an offer, Helen did not discourage him from accepting it, and that is when he booked a

$16-a-week room at the Ford Hotel in Buffalo and began what would be a more than two-year stay at the *Buffalo Evening News.*

During this period the couple communicated almost daily, and he also drove down to see Helen every few weeks; but this situation became less satisfactory the longer it lasted. Fortunately it changed in January of 1943, with word that the *New York Herald Tribune* had responded positively to Alden's letter of application and offered him a copydesk job at a salary higher than he thought he would ever receive. It was $70 a week.

Brimming with an unprecedented sense of prosperity, he moved with Helen into a relatively expensive $100-a-month apartment near the Hudson River at 104th Street. He also exchanged his old Chevy for a Model A Ford in better condition, and on weekends he and Helen would sometimes go on picnics outside the city. Whatever leisure time the couple had together was for the most part on weekends, since Alden's duty hours with the *Herald Tribune* were from five o'clock in the afternoon to one in the morning, and Helen worked at *Time* from nine in the morning to five.

Their schedule bothered Helen more than it did Alden because he was enthralled with his position and the late-night social life attached to it: mingling with sophisticated, older, and more experienced newsmen at Bleeck's bar on West 40th Street ("a stein's throw away from the newspaper's back door"); being active in the newspaper union's grievance committee along with other party members; and, more important, though barely twenty-nine, becoming accepted as one of the most reliable and knowledgeable rim men on the paper. All those years since childhood of being an omnivorous and compulsive reader, all those countless books he absorbed on history, politics, literature, and sundry other subjects, had created within him the makings of a pedagogue and imbued his vast frame of reference and intellect into the daily process of editing the *Herald Tribune*.

With the birth of a daughter in 1944, and then a son in 1947, Helen became a stay-at-home mother and, in order to enlarge the family income, Alden began moonlighting at other newspapers when not at the *Tribune*. On weekends and other occasions he shifted back and forth between the copydesks of the *New York Post*, the *New York World-Telegram*, and the Newark *Star-Ledger*.

Once in a while Helen would hire an off-duty nurse from nearby St. Luke's Hospital to babysit while she and Alden went to a concert or met friends for dinner; but these occasions were insufficient to overcome her nighttime loneliness, as he was often working in various places till dawn, and sometimes not coming home at all. She felt more isolated now than she had during the years Alden had worked in Buffalo. Then at least she had been connected to the energy of Manhattan, being busy at *Time*, occasionally having lunch with friends near the office, and going to Peck & Peck now and then to buy a new dress or a hat.

"In retrospect, I guess it was a mistake that Helen quit her job to devote herself entirely to the children, because that's when we began drifting apart," he told me, adding that even after he stopped moonlighting, and got a large pay raise when hired by the *Times* in 1951, there was no refuting the fact "that we had fallen out of love." He paused, then repeated: "Nobody's fault, we had just fallen out of love."

The couple nevertheless remained married through most of the 1950s and, for the children's sake, relocated to more spacious living quarters and good public schools about twenty miles north, in the village of Hastings-on-Hudson, a half-hour commute for Alden. But their situation worsened when Alden's political background was exposed and he was subpoenaed to testify in Washington, where the Senate was beginning a headline-making investigation regarding the infiltration of Communists into the ranks of the American press.

In the obituary he had handed me, he referred to this crisis briefly:

> In hearings in 1956 before the Senate Internal Security Sub-committee, he acknowledged having been a member of the Communist Party from 1935 to 1948, but refused to identify other members of the party. His refusal resulted in a contempt citation, and a Federal court convicted him of contempt of Congress in 1957 . . .
>
> After twice being convicted of contempt of Congress, Mr. Whitman obtained a new trial; the case was then dismissed at the request of the Justice Department.

What was not explained in the last paragraph, however, was that nearly ten years had elapsed before the Justice Department finally cleared him in 1965, and that during this extended period he had constantly been called and recalled to testify, with his name printed frequently in the *Times* and his photograph on display in *Time* magazine's "press" section—to the embarrassment of his school-age children and his estranged wife, who had left the party approximately when he did. With his personal life a wreck, and his job in jeopardy, Alden Whitman described himself during these years as feeling "like Jean Valjean at the penal oars."

But it was the belief among the top bosses at the *Times* that the Senate investigators were not primarily interested in humiliating such newsmen as Whitman but wanted, rather, to smear the paper itself—an opinion that the publisher, Arthur Hays Sulzberger, expressed in a statement released as the inquiry began in 1956. He said that the probe, headed by Mississippi senator James O. Eastland, was targeting the *Times* because its editorial policies clashed with those of Eastland and most of his colleagues—namely, the paper's condemnation of segregation in southern schools, its denunciation of McCarthyism, its opposition to the discriminatory provisions of the McCarran-Walter Immigration and Nationality Act of 1952, its exposure of various abusive methods by various congressional committees, and because it insisted that the true spirit of American democracy demanded a scrupulous respect for the rights of even the lowest individual.

Fortifying this viewpoint was the fact that of the thirty-five subpoenas issued by the subcommittee, twenty-six were to former or present *Times* employees. When I reviewed this list—I had returned from the army to the *Times* a month before—I was saddened to see that it included a desk editor in the Sunday department, Seymour Peck, who had greatly encouraged me during my copyboy days and was instrumental in the publication of my first magazine piece, based on my interview with the silent-screen star Nita Naldi.

But while the *New York Times* reaffirmed its liberal editorial policy and recognized its adversarial relationship with Eastland's committee, it was not thrilled in having on its staff such individuals as Alden Whitman, Seymour Peck, and others who were charged with contempt of Congress. In a public statement, Sulzberger identified himself as a "prejudiced witness for the capital system" who did not want a single Communist on his payroll, and he insisted that all employees who had been called by the subcommittee should cooperate.

Sulzberger went on to explain: "Like any other citizen, a newspaper man has the undoubted right to assert his constitutional privilege not to incriminate himself. But invocation of the Fifth Amendment places upon him a heavy burden of proof of his fitness to continue to hold a place of trust on the news or editorial staff of this newspaper. Nowhere is it written that a person claiming protection against self-incrimination should be continued in these sensitive departments where trust and confidence are the tool of a good workman."

Sulzberger had already fired a few *Times* workers who had pleaded the Fifth, prompting protests from members of the American Civil Liberties Union and like-minded editorialists on his own paper. But neither Whitman nor Peck were seeking protection on those grounds; instead, as American citizens, they believed that they had the right not to be coerced into becoming informers. They had admitted to being party members for more than a decade and then dropping out years before joining the *Times*. Beyond that, however, they had nothing to say, although Whitman said so rather fulsomely.

Wearing a bowtie, and with his pipe and tobacco pouch tucked into his breast pocket, he took the stand in the marble-columned Senate chamber and stubbornly rejected the demands of the counsel, J. G. Sourwine, to be more forthcoming. "I have, as I think I have said before, an extremely active New England conscience," he told Mr. Sourwine, "and I cannot answer these questions and maintain my self-respect."

While this attitude did not save him from the scorn of the Senate, neither did he nor Seymour Peck ultimately spend any time in jail; and they, together with most of their ex-Communist *Times* staffers—except for those few who had earlier sought Fifth Amendment protection—retained their jobs on the paper. Whitman, Peck, and the rest also received individual letters from Sulzberger clarifying the situation.

"As you are already aware," he wrote, "the *Times* would have preferred that you answer all such questions frankly . . . We have, however, carefully reviewed the facts with relationship to your one-time membership in the Communist Party, and we are prepared to accept your statement that you have now severed all connections to it. This note, therefore, is to advise you that your association with the *Times* will continue."

Alden Whitman's personal life also took a positive turn when he began dating a woman in the *Times* style department named Joan McCracken. A graduate of Oberlin College, and the daughter of a Congregationalist minister, she had come to the paper in 1955 after working for the World Council of Churches in Geneva, Switzerland. The couple met during the spring of 1958. Alden was then forty-four and separated from Helen; Joan, never married, was twenty-eight.

One afternoon Joan had come down to the third-floor newsroom from her office on the ninth floor carrying an inky page proof to be approved by the city editor. Alden, editing copy at the national desk, looked up to notice this petite brunette standing not far away in a paisley dress.

After learning her name, he began sending anonymous notes in brown envelopes up to her through the house mail, the first of which read: "You look ravishing in paisley," and he signed it: "The American Paisley Association." Later he identified himself, and they dined at the Teheran Restaurant on West 44th Street, where they enjoyed one another's company immensely until being interrupted by the maître d', who told them he had to close the place.

In my interview with Joan for the *Esquire* article—it was over lunch at Sardi's after my third visit with Alden—I quoted her telling me that she had been immediately fascinated by his marvelous magpie mind, cluttered with all sorts of useless information. She mentioned that he could recite the list of popes backward and forward; knew the names of every king's mistress and his date of reign; knew that the Treaty of Westphalia was signed in 1648, that Niagara Falls is 167 feet high, and that snakes do not blink; that cats attach themselves to places, not people, and dogs to people, not places; he was a regular subscriber to the *New Statesman*, *Le Nouvel Observateur*, and to nearly every journal in the out-of-town newsstand in Times Square; he read two books a day; and he had seen Bogart in *Casablanca* three dozen times.

After their first date, Joan knew she had to see him again, notwithstanding the fact that she was a minister's daughter and he was an atheist; nor did she condemn his political past, nor his so-called "larkish" younger years that had led to two unhappy marriages and four children to whom he had largely been an absentee father.

In fact, after Joan had married Alden in November of 1960, one of her missions was to reach out to his children and help him achieve, however belatedly, some form of reconciliation—and this was done. Indeed, after his second wife, Helen, suffered a fatal heart attack in 1961, leaving behind a fourteen-year-old son and a daughter in college, Joan promptly and capably assumed the role of substitute mother. She and Alden shared their apartment for a few years with his son (who would later attend Harvard and become a physician); and, in addition to getting his daughter summertime jobs in the *Times* morgue, they both visited her regularly at college and attended her graduation. She would eventually become a librarian.

In early 1964, Alden marked his twenty-fifth year as a copyreader. He was now fifty-one, and, as he himself conceded, "Time was passing me by, and I wanted to ride for a while on a merrier carousel than the *New York Times* national desk." The opportunity arrived later in the year, when, following the retirement of an elderly ex–foreign correspondent who had long specialized in writing obituaries, Alden was named to replace him, and he thus began his new career as "a happy oarsmen on the Styx."

His first task was to update and rewrite if necessary a lengthy advance obituary on Winston Churchill that had been sitting idly for some period in the *Times* morgue; but with reports that the British wartime leader was in rapidly declining health, Alden's assignment immediately became urgent. After working for several long days rearranging the material, he managed to get it ready for publication two weeks before Churchill's death in London, in January of 1965. It was twenty thousand words long and took up sixteen pages in the *Times*.

The first obituary that Alden wrote from the beginning dealt with the poet T. S. Eliot, who also died in London in January of 1965. Alden had met Eliot a few times when the latter was poet-in-residence at Harvard, and the six-thousand-word tribute to the poet began: "This is the way the world ends / This is the way the world ends / This is the way the world ends / Not with a bang but a whimper." It went on to describe Eliot as a most unlikely poetic figure, lacking "flamboyance or oddity in dress or manner, and there was nothing of the romantic about him. He carried no auras, cast no arresting eye and wore his heart, as nearly as could be observed, in its proper anatomical place."

From his start as chief obituary writer, Alden Whitman expanded the scope of the assignment beyond the practices of his predecessors. The older *Times* staffers had produced advance obituaries largely based on information obtained from news clippings stored in the morgue; or, if the subject was a very prominent individual, there might be magazine profiles or even biographies and autobiographies upon which to draw.

In addition to all this, however, Alden convinced the top editors to allow him to travel around the nation and abroad in order to conduct face-to-face interviews that provided closely observed details: For example, after meeting with Pablo Picasso at the artist's studio in Paris, he wrote that Picasso "was a short, squat man with broad, muscular shoulders and arms. He was most proud of his small hands and feet and of his hairy chest. In old age his body was firm and compact; and his cannonball head, which was almost bald, gleamed like bronze."

After compiling a list of people he hoped to interview, Alden would write them flattering letters explaining that the *Times* wished to "update its files" on the lives of such distinguished individuals as themselves, seeking their "biographical insights and reflections," and therefore a request was being made for a brief personal visit. While there was no mention of "advance obituary" or "death" in these letters, nor was it explained that such interviews were slated for posthumous publication, the letter's purpose was still fairly obvious to most recipients; and, indeed, after being granted an interview to meet in Missouri with Harry Truman, the former president greeted Alden with: "I know why you're here, and I want to help you all I can."

While there were some who turned down the interview request without explanation—for example, the writer and literary critic Edmund Wilson, the French minister of culture André Malraux, and Viscount Bernard Law Montgomery, the British World War II general—Alden Whitman himself often refused to interview many people who were not "sufficiently notable." Who did, and who did not, meet the "notability" standard was largely his decision. The editors and reporters in the news department devoted their days to the coverage of the living, while it was his prerogative to deal as he wished with the dead and the almost dead.

He also made it clear—in a statement published in the monthly trade news magazine *Editor & Publisher*—that he was not receptive to any solicitations from public-relations firms or from other influence peddlers, who might have clients desiring an antemortem interview with him. "This is strictly a business where we call you, don't call us," he said, adding, "The *Times* will place its own value on an obit, and I refuse to talk with anyone who calls up to suggest that so-and-so, still living, would make an interesting obit, and I can have an interview . . . I simply refuse to speak with anybody trying to guarantee immortality before he dies."

In completing my own interview with Alden Whitman for *Esquire*, one of my final questions concerned his own termination, especially since during our time together he had emphasized his failing health.

"But what will happen to you, then, after you die, Mr. Whitman?" I asked.

"I have no soul that is going anywhere," he said. "It is simply a matter of bodily extinction."

"If you had died during your heart attack, what, in your opinion, would have been the first thing your wife would have done?"

"She would first have seen to it that my body was disposed of in the way I wanted," he said. "To be cremated without fuss or fanfare."

"And then what?"

"Then, after she'd gotten to that, she would have turned her attention to the children."

"And then?"

"Then, I guess, she would have broken down and had a good cry."

"Are you sure?"

Whitman paused.

"Yes, I would assume so," he said finally, puffing on his pipe. "This is the formal outlet for grief under such circumstances."

Chapter 13

Three months after I had finished interviewing him, my article about Alden Whitman appeared in the February 1966 issue of *Esquire*. The magazine's editor, Harold Hayes, liked it and published it under the title "Mr. Bad News," with the subtitle "Death, as it must to all men, comes to Alden Whitman every day. It's a living."

I began the piece by re-creating a scene that Joan had described during our lunch:

"Winston Churchill gave you your heart attack," the wife of the obituary writer said, but the obituary writer, a short and rather shy man, wearing horn-rimmed glasses and smoking a pipe, shook his head and replied, very softly, "No, it was not Winston Churchill."

"Then T. S. Eliot gave you your heart attack," she quickly added, lightly, for they were at a small dinner party in New York and the others seemed amused.

"No, the obituary writer said, again softly, "it was not T. S. Eliot."

If he was at all irritated by his wife's line of questioning, her assertion that writing lengthy obituaries for The New York Times under deadline pressure might be speeding him to his own grave, he did not show it, did not raise his voice; but then he rarely does.

The piece drew a favorable reaction from not only the magazine's subscribers but from some top editors at the *Times,* and they soon reversed the paper's anonymity rule for obit writing and began attaching Whitman's byline to his work. And as he continued to produce his well-written and informative memorials, he became a mini celebrity within the journalism profession and subsequently took a bow in front of millions of viewers while discussing his job with Johnny Carson on NBC's *The Tonight Show.*

He not only continued to write obituaries for the next ten years, but he also contributed book reviews and conducted interviews for the paper over lunch with many well-known novelists and poets, usually showing up wearing a cape. He also had his photograph taken by Jill Krementz, who specialized in shooting literary figures and was the wife of the writer Kurt Vonnegut.

But in 1976, after another heart attack and almost total blindness, he was forced to leave the *Times.* Others would inherit his position, of course, although none would be so singularly identified with it. With his retirement, Joan quit her job in the style department and the two of them moved to Southampton, Long Island, where she hired students from Long Island University to read books and newspapers daily to her husband. She meanwhile worked as a freelance book editor, co-authored a few books on cooking, and helped to edit the big bestselling books written by the *Times* food critic, Craig Claiborne.

When Mr. Claiborne marked his seventieth birthday in Monte Carlo in 1990, Joan flew over to join the party, accompanied by her seventy-six-year-old husband in a wheelchair. Providing added assistance during the journey was Alden's forty-three-year-old bachelor son, Dr. Daniel S. Whitman.

In addition to his vision problems, Alden was barely able to speak, but he appeared to understand everything said to him.

The day after their arrival, the three of them attended a cocktail party on an outside terrace of the Hotel de Paris, where all the guests were staying. Alden sat in his wheelchair and Joan brought several guests over to be introduced, and he greeted each with a smile of recognition. Then later he began to sneeze loudly and repeatedly, and his head slumped forward. Joan and his son immediately wheeled him back to their hotel room and put him in bed. He remained alive but unconscious through the evening.

The next day it was decided that his son would remain with him, and Joan would attend the birthday dinner being held at a location beyond the hotel. But as she was waiting in the lobby with the other guests for their transportation, Alden let out a sigh in bed and then died immediately of a cerebral hemorrhage. His son was able to reach Joan before she left for the party, and then the two of them contacted the hotel manager, who notified the police. Alden's body was later moved to a funeral home where, in accord with his earlier instructions, the cremation was performed.

Joan and Dr. Whitman then flew to Paris with Alden's ashes and sprinkled them around his favorite spot in the city, the Luxembourg Gardens. The next morning the *Times* published a twenty-three-paragraph obituary accompanied by his picture and the headline "Alden Whitman Is Dead at 76; Made an Art of Times Obituaries."

There was little in the obituary that resembled what he had shared with me when I was interviewing him for *Esquire*. Apparently his version was rewritten and updated by other staff members; and, in any case, the *Times* story carried no byline. It began:

Alden Whitman, a retired reporter for The New York Times who pioneered the use of interviews of notable people to personalize and energize their obituaries, died yesterday . . .

Mr. Whitman put out two book-length collections of his writings, in edited form, "The Obituary Book," published in 1971 by Stein & Day, and "Come to Judgment," issued in 1980 by Viking Books. In an introduction to "Come to Judgment," he offered this criterion for an exemplary obituary:

"A lively expression of personality and character as well as a conscientious exposition of the main facts of a person's life. A good obit has all the characteristics of a well-focused snapshot, the fuller the length the better. If the snapshot is clear, the viewer gets a quick fix on the subject, his attainments, his shortcomings and his times."

His widow, Joan, who was fifty-nine when he died, never re-married. She continued to live in Southampton, Long Island, until her own death of emphysema, in 2016, at the age of eighty-six. In her obituary, in the *Southampton Press*, it was mentioned that she was a cultural leader in the community, a board member at the local library, the manager of its popular book sale, and served on the steering committee of the John Steinbeck Project. It also mentioned that she enjoyed playing duplicate bridge at tournaments in the nearby hamlet of Water Mill.

She did not have an obituary printed in the *New York Times*.

PART II

In Sinatra's Shadow

Chapter 14

Honoring my earlier understanding with Harold Hayes, after he published my Whitman story, I would pursue his idea on Frank Sinatra. Hayes suggested that the story would not only be fun but easy to do. Sinatra's representatives and the magazine had already reached an agreement. *Esquire* would devote its cover exclusively to the article while indicating it would not be a "hatchet job," and the singer promised to make every effort to be available to the interviewer despite his very busy schedule during the winter of 1965.

On Monday, November 8, Sinatra was to appear at the Warner Bros. Studios in Burbank, outside Los Angeles, to record several songs for an NBC-TV special called "Frank Sinatra: A Man and His Music," an hour-long program in color that would be broadcast during the evening of November 24. He was also finishing the final scenes of the movie *Assault on a Queen*, after which he would star in two others. He had already appeared in more than forty films, beginning in 1944. Until then he had been known principally as a skinny crooner whose soothing voice and romantic manner on the radio and on stage appealed primarily to teenaged girls known as "bobby-soxers."

Within a little more than a month, on December 12, Sinatra's family and friends would mark his fiftieth birthday with a celebration at the Beverly Wilshire hotel in Los Angeles. Hayes arranged for me to stay in the same hotel, but I would not be there long enough to attend the party, to which I most likely would not have been invited. I would arrive, however, in time for my November 5 meeting with Sinatra's publicity director, who would provide my itinerary—which was to include witnessing the NBC recording session—and then Hayes expected me back in New York within a week.

Harold Hayes was known for his tight management and high expectations. Born in Elkin, North Carolina, he was the forty-year-old son of a Baptist minister, and during the Korean War he had served as an officer in the Marine Corps. Although at *Esquire* he wore Brooks attire and possessed an almost sommelier's knowledge of fine wine, he nonetheless came across as a tall and rangy, bright-eyed dark-haired country boy who downplayed his keen intelligence and awareness, and yet he accentuated his looming presence by walking around the office with metal tips clamped to the soles of his shoes.

In providing me with first-class airfare to Los Angeles, he was not only signaling the high priority he attached to the Sinatra assignment but also expressing confidence that what I later wrote would increase newsstand sales and thus justify his generosity toward me. During the last five years, beginning in 1960—using some of my vacation time and weekends off at the *Times*—I had written more than a dozen pieces for *Esquire*, some requiring air travel, but never before had Hayes voluntarily provided first-class accommodations.

In doing so now he seemed to be saying that my stature had risen in his estimation and I had fewer excuses for disappointing him. He said that once I returned from Los Angeles, he hoped that I would deliver the Sinatra piece in final form within a week or ten days. I did not argue, especially after he said that I could then proceed with what I really wanted to do for *Esquire*, which was to provide a profile on Harry Truman's son-in-law, Clifton Daniel, managing editor of the *New York Times*.

I left New York on an afternoon TWA flight to Los Angeles on Wednesday, November 3, arriving well ahead of my scheduled meeting with Sinatra's press agent on Friday morning. This would be my third trip to Los Angeles for *Esquire*. The first was a success, the second a disaster.

The first was in early February of 1962 when, after spending a few days in New York interviewing the former heavyweight champion Joe Louis, I accompanied him back to Los Angeles, where he was living with his third wife, Martha, a prominent and prideful African American defense attorney in that city. Whenever her courtroom associates or friends would ask "How in the hell did you meet Joe Louis?" she would quickly reply: "How in the hell did Joe Louis meet me?"

The ex-champ was then forty-eight, and, although I was aware of some of his memorable comments made during his prime—when asked in 1941 how he could catch up with such a fleet-footed and elusive contender as Billy Conn, Louis replied, "He can run, but he can't hide"; and when questioned about fighting for virtually nothing as a private in World War II, Louis answered, "I'm not fighting for nothing, I'm fighting for my country"—I was nevertheless surprised during our talks by his absurd sense of humor.

For example, as we boarded the flight to Los Angeles, I decided to upgrade my coach ticket to first class in order to sit next to him, while at the same time I wondered aloud how the airlines could justify such a big difference in price. "First-class seats are up in front of the plane," Joe Louis replied dryly, "and they get you to L.A. faster."

My article, titled "Joe Louis: The King as a Middle-Aged Man," appeared in the June 1962 issue. Hayes liked it and reimbursed me for the cost of the upgrade.

But later that same year, I was sent out coach-class to interview the movie star Natalie Wood, who was then at the peak of her long career, having begun as a child actress. In 1961 she had earned a best-actress Oscar nomination for *Splendor in the Grass*, followed by the hit musical *West Side Story*, and then in 1962 came her acclaimed performance in *Gypsy*. Between these, and her involvement with two forthcoming films, her press representative set aside three one-hour interviews for me. But Natalie Wood failed to show up for any of them; and since I was due to return to my job at the *Times*, I quit the assignment and flew back to New York, contented that at least my expenses over a three-day period were covered by *Esquire* — and contented, too, that Natalie Wood had inadvertently been responsible for my meeting a married couple in Beverly Hills that would become long-lasting friends.

They were attractive and personable, Jack and Sally Hanson, and they owned and operated a popular sportswear boutique for women called Jax, located on the corner of Bedford Drive and Wilshire Boulevard, two blocks from the Beverly Wilshire hotel, where I was not then staying. Hayes had booked me into a cheaper hotel on a nearby side street. The reason I went to Jax was to meet Natalie Wood, whose agent had initially invited me there for an introduction prior to our proceeding to our first interview over lunch. Ms. Wood was a regular customer at Jax. After she stood me up, I was taken to lunch by Jack and Sally Hanson, and I continued to see them not only in Los Angeles but later in Manhattan, where they had a Jax store on East 57th Street, between Third and Lexington Avenues.

In fact, there were then at least half a dozen Jax stores around the nation, including locations in Chicago, San Francisco, Palm Beach, Southampton, and three in Southern California. The forty-four-year-old Jack Hanson, a tall and ruddy onetime professional baseball player, and his thirty-two-year-old second wife, Sally, a slender and stylish honey blonde in a ponytail, were millionaires who drove around town in Rolls-Royce convertibles—his was painted white, hers was powder blue— and they lived in a fifteen-room white-columned, neo-southern house that resembled Tara, the plantation manor in *Gone with the Wind*. Located on North Beverly Drive, a few blocks from their flagship store, it stood behind a wide lawn fronted with a gigantic magnolia tree and flanked by a dozen pine trees each more than sixty feet high.

Jack had bought the property in 1958, a year after marrying Sally, from the estate of the producer Hal Roach, who had gotten rich decades earlier with his Our Gang series, the comedies of Harold Lloyd, and more than a hundred films starring Laurel and Hardy. An avid tennis player, Roach had a court in the rear that was overlooked by a white triple-arched portico; and in later years Jack Hanson, who also loved tennis, would play singles and doubles there on weekends with such friends as Paul Newman, Robert Duvall, the photographer Gordon Parks, the designer Oleg Cassini, the veteran tennis pro Pancho Segura, and the footballer-turned-actor Jim Brown.

Hanson's own ambitions as a professional athlete were cut short when he entered the service in 1942. Before that, in 1940, after starring at Hollywood High School and the University of Southern California, he had signed a baseball contract with the Chicago Cubs organization and was assigned to a minor league franchise in the Pacific Coast League. On the team bus, some of his teammates were amused, if not perplexed, by his practice of sitting with a sketchbook in hand, drawing pictures of women wearing sports outfits. While not discussing it with his fellow players, he had often thought that if he failed to make enough money playing ball, there might be a place for him in the world of fashion.

In 1945, after three years in the Army Air Force—during which he had befriended Sergeant Joe DiMaggio at the base in Santa Ana, California—he decided to quit baseball and invest his savings, plus a loan, in opening the first Jax store, south of Los Angeles on Balboa Island. In partnership with his first wife, Nina, with whom he had a son in 1946, they sold shorts, sportswear, and beach attire.

But he and Nina soon proved to be incompatible as co-owners. They had wed in 1939, during Jack's senior year at USC, and now as their marriage approached its eighth year, and with a child at home to be cared for, Nina ceased appearing at the store regularly and she was also increasingly unhappy at home. Making things no easier was her disapproval of how her husband was promoting the business. Unable to afford advertising, he had hired several young beach beauties to stand in the store's front windows for a few hours each day striking alluring poses while wearing Jax merchandise. This stimulated traffic and sales but accelerated the termination of his union with Nina, especially after Jack had begun socializing after hours with some of his window models. The couple divorced in 1948.

A year later, Jack met Sally. She was then eighteen and, like Jack, a graduate of Hollywood High School. When she first walked into the store on Balboa Island, it was not to apply as a window model, which Jack would have welcomed—she was a perfect size 10 and quite stunning—but as an aspiring fashion designer.

She had been born in Erie, Pennsylvania, and arrived in Los Angeles as a four-year-old in 1935 with her divorced mother who, like many mothers at that time and in that city, fantasized that her young daughter was the next Shirley Temple. As an eight-year-old, Sally did get to play a munchkin in the 1939 film *The Wizard of Oz*. In 1940, she was one of the unborn children that Shirley Temple imagines in the fairy-tale film *The Blue Bird*. Sally made a brief appearance as well in *Lassie Come Home*, the 1943 movie starring ten-year-old Elizabeth Taylor and fourteen-year-old Roddy McDowall.

But more than appearing before cameras, Sally enjoyed being off stage with the wardrobe mistresses, and from them she learned a lot about stitching, fitting, and styling.

As a twelve-year-old, using her mother's sewing machine, she began making all her own clothes. When she first walked into Jack Hanson's shop, she discussed the possibility of introducing a unique item that he had never contemplated stocking—pants tailored exclusively for women.

Up to that time, except for factory-working females during the war years, few women wore pants in public. If they did, the cut of the garment was similar to the men's: wide-legged trousers with pleats, side pockets, cuffs, and fly fronts, although for women the zipper was sometimes on the side. In any case, it was still a masculine look defying extensive social acceptance, notwithstanding the fact that such adventuresome actresses as Marlene Dietrich had often appeared in prewar films dressed ostensibly as a man in trousers and jackets, usually together with a bowler or beret and a cigarette in hand.

As a fashion statement, however, Jack Hanson dismissed it as "Parisian lesbian," but what Sally had in mind appealed to him immediately. She suggested creating hip-hugging women's pants in which the zipper would be stitched into the back seam, thus accentuating and flattering the curvature of the rear; and there would be the elimination of pockets, further slenderizing the garment; and while the legs would follow a slim and elongated line, the fit would not be skintight. The pants would also be silk-lined so as to avoid showing wrinkles around the backs of the knees.

Sally made samples and returned to Jack's store wearing a pair; then, after she had outfitted Jack's young women to model them in the windows, there was such a boom in sales that it was difficult to keep them in stock. Sally soon became the chief designer not only of Jax pants but also shirts, pants suits, and other clothing; and, after opening the Beverly Hills store in 1952, the brand quickly caught on with movie actresses, one of the first being Marilyn Monroe, although at the time she was not yet a star.

She had received good notices in 1950 for her small part in *The Asphalt Jungle*, although her name was not on the film's poster; and when Sally first met her and sold her a pair of pants priced at $50, Monroe was driving a battered 1937 Chevy. But a year later, in 1953, with leading roles in *Niagara* and *Gentlemen Prefer Blondes*—and on the way to marrying Joe DiMaggio in 1954—Marilyn Monroe was spending lavishly at Jax, as would in time also Aubrey Hepburn, Natalie Wood, and Elizabeth Taylor, the latter once ordering $3,000 worth of merchandise in a single day.

In addition to enlarging their number of stores, Jack and Sally Hanson in 1962 bought a piece of property near the Beverly Wilshire Hotel, at 326 North Rodeo Drive, and there they built a private club called the Daisy. It had a limited membership of four hundred, nearly all of them well-known figures in entertainment, fashion, and sports.

During the afternoons the members met for lunch within the sidewalk patio, and in the evenings, resonant with piped-in music, they sat at dozens of tables within a large dimly lit room in which the ceiling was lined with crystal chandeliers bearing low-wattage, teardrop-shaped bulbs. Beyond the bar was a billiard room with two tables and several padded stools placed along the walls for the convenience of spectators watching, and sometimes placing bets on, the club's hustlers competing at eight-ball.

I had visited the Daisy once in 1964, as the Hansons' guest, and after I called them from New York a year later to say that I was on a new assignment for *Esquire* and would be arriving in town on the evening of November 3, they invited me to join them for dinner on the following night at their table.

It would prove to be a fortuitous time for me to be at the Daisy. Standing in a dark corner of the bar that night, holding a drink in one hand and a cigarette in the other, and flanked by two well-coiffed and besuited blondes, would be none other than Frank Sinatra.

Chapter 15

On the Trans World Airlines flight into Los Angeles I had read in a newspaper column that Sinatra was unhappy with the CBS broadcaster Walter Cronkite and was in fact threatening to sue the network because, in a forthcoming documentary to be broadcast in less than two weeks, Cronkite suggested that Sinatra was on friendly terms with members of organized crime.

Until then I had been unaware of the CBS documentary, and I wondered why, if Harold Hayes knew about it, he had not mentioned it. Hayes had led me to believe that *Esquire* had been promised cooperation, but after reading the item I wondered how open Sinatra might now be with journalists — and this was why, after noticing him at the bar, I resisted the impulse to get up from the Hansons' table and make my way across the crowded room to introduce myself.

Contributing to my caution was an earlier conversation I had had on the plane with a red-haired flight attendant named Betty Guy, who told me that Sinatra often traveled on Trans World Airlines and that, in her opinion, he was "Jekyll and Hyde" — sometimes very friendly toward her and his fellow passengers, while at other times, unpredictably, he could be ill-tempered, sullen, and mostly silent during the long flight between New York and Los Angeles. He was usually accompanied by a few men, she said, assuming they were his bodyguards or management assistants; but he ignored them as well as he sat alone at a window seat, alternating between drinking bourbon and sleeping, giving her the impression that he was perhaps the loneliest person on board.

As I sat at the Hansons' big table with half a dozen other guests, participating in the general conversation while keeping an eye focused on Sinatra at the bar, Sally, sitting next to me, said: "He often comes here, and usually brings Mia." She was referring to Mia Farrow, the twenty-year-old actress whom Sinatra had been dating all year, but she was not in sight tonight. Sally did not know the names of the two blondes who sat at the bar, both in their middle thirties, but she was acquainted with a couple of Sinatra's male friends who stood nearby, both wearing suits and ties.

One was Brad Dexter, a big broad-shouldered character actor in his late forties who had appeared in several films and television shows but was currently best known in Hollywood for having saved Sinatra from drowning a year before in Hawaii. Sinatra had then been directing and starring in *None but the Brave*, a World War II film involving the Japanese, and in it Dexter played a cigar-chomping sergeant. But during a break in the action, while Sinatra and the producer's wife were taking a swim, they were swept out to sea by the outgoing tide and might have died were it not for the efforts of Dexter, who swam a few hundred yards to the rescue, being assisted by two surfers. After this, a grateful Sinatra hired Dexter as an executive within the Sinatra Enterprises operation and the two men became intimate friends.

The other man standing near Sinatra at the Daisy was sixty-year-old Leo Durocher, whose longtime association with Sinatra went back to the mid-1940s, when Durocher was the loud-mouthed manager of the Brooklyn Dodgers and popularly known as "Leo the Lip." In his earlier years, beginning in the mid-1920s, he had been an infielder with the Yankees during the Babe Ruth era; but no matter where Durocher was employed during his decades in baseball, both as a player and manager with a number of teams, he was distinguished for his combativeness and determination to win at all cost. The quotation that best characterized him, one that he himself co-opted though probably apocryphal, was "Nice Guys Finish Last."

Wanting to get a closer look at Sinatra and his friends, I excused myself from the Hansons' table and made my way across the room, cutting through dozens of couples wiggling to folk rock from the stereo, and took a position in the shadows a few yards away from the bar. Sinatra's back was to me, but even if he turned around or caught my reflection in the bar's mirror, there was no reason I should be recognized. I had never met him before.

The only other time I'd seen him was at some distance earlier in the year at Jilly's saloon on West 52nd Street in New York, where he sat at a big private table in the rear surrounded by close friends—Sammy Davis Jr. being one of them—and his daughters, Nancy and Tina. Earlier in the evening Sinatra had delivered a concert to a standing ovation in Forest Hills, Queens, and at Jilly's he seemed to be in a very celebratory mood. There was lots of laughter, drinking, and embracing at the table.

But now at the Daisy it was very different. Sinatra stood silently sipping bourbon, and except for occasionally flicking his gold lighter under the extended cigarette of one of his female companions, he otherwise ignored them. He also said nothing to Durocher or Dexter standing nearby. I was reminded of how the TWA attendant, Betty Guy, had described Sinatra to me earlier: a lonely looking individual sitting at the window seat sipping bourbon, avoiding everybody around him—so different from the friendly and vivacious figure that she had seen on other TWA flights. "Jekyll and Hyde."

But to me on this occasion he seemed for the most part to be anxious and impetuous. I say this because when the phone rang at the bar and the bartender was slow in answering it, being several steps away putting drinks on a waiter's tray, Sinatra suddenly rose on tiptoes and reached out to grab hold of the white Bakelite push-button land line resting on a towel on the far side of the bar. Holding the mouthpiece to his lips, Sinatra then curtly said, "Hello." Without identifying himself, he listened for a second to the person on the other end, and then, after laying the phone down heavily on the bar, yelled in the direction of the bartender: "George, it's for you."

George, a stocky bespectacled man in his midforties, immediately stopped what he was doing and came running toward the phone, wiping his hands on a towel before picking it up. He then nodded in the direction of Sinatra, saying, "Thanks, Frank, sorry to bother you," before greeting his caller. Sinatra had meanwhile turned away to resume sipping his bourbon while the two blondes conversed and smoked, and Dexter and Durocher leaned against the corner of the bar, drinks in hand, watching the young couples jumping around the dance floor.

Then, some minutes later, the phone rang again, and again Sinatra picked it up before the barman could get to it—this time he was bent low filling an ice bucket—and after Sinatra said, "George, it's for you," the barman not only again apologized but he might well have felt demeaned in failing to keep pace with his impatient and self-appointed secretary.

I stood watching and wondering why Sinatra was doing this. Why was he answering the barman's phone? Maybe he was just a control freak, I thought, one predisposed to take charge, to command the phone, to preside over the entire club. Or maybe Sinatra, having such a delicately tuned musical ear, was hypersensitive to the grating sound of this meddling instrument; while a convenience to the bartender, it was a nuisance to such individuals as Sinatra, especially during evenings when he was not feeling well.

Or maybe he was answering the phone as a favor to George, whom he perhaps saw as an overburdened bartender with a dependent wife or girlfriend at home calling to say that she was lonely and needed him and wanted to know how late he would be working. How would such a woman react if she knew that the first voice she had just heard on the telephone belonged to the most famous lonely man in America?

Or it was possible that Sinatra was so eager to pick up the bar phone because he hoped that the call would be from Mia Farrow trying to reach him, needing him!

As I was pondering, the Daisy's disc jockey suddenly switched from rock music to "In the Wee Small Hours of the Morning," a beautiful ballad that Sinatra had recorded ten years earlier, in 1955, when he was miserably married to the movie star Ava Gardner, whose independent spirit and aloofness both frustrated him and enhanced her desirability—and the song's lyrics probably reflected the sense of longing that he had then felt:

"In the wee small hours of the morning / while the whole wide world is fast asleep / you lie awake and think about the girl . . ."

As the music swept through the room, and as the dance floor was now jammed with slow-moving couples holding one another very close, and as the two blondes sitting at the bar now turned around to watch the dancers and shift their own bodies to the soft rhythm of Nelson Riddle's orchestra that accompanied Sinatra's mellifluous voice, I kept my eye on the man himself, expecting that he would soon change his posture, would turn around and join the moment and pay respectful attention to the Capital Records classic that he had completed ten years earlier.

But he did not move. There seemed to be no connection between his recorded voice and his physical presence, except that he now personified the image of himself featured on the "Wee Small Hours" album—a melancholy man, dapper, wearing a fedora, cigarette in hand, standing alone on the corner of a shadowy street late at night near a lamp post.

I had thoughts buzzing in my head that I wanted to write down before I forgot them, so I left the bar area and headed toward the men's room. Whenever I want to make notes in private, preferring not to call attention to myself as a reporter, which too often alters the relationship between the observer and the observed, I remove myself to such places as a bathroom, often behind the closed door of a toilet stall; and instead of writing on flimsy pieces of overlapping paper, or on a pocket-sized pad—the latter typically bound by circular wiring that frequently gets caught on the inner lining of my jacket—I write on the white surface of a piece of shirt folderboard that comes with my laundry.

Once a dress shirt is washed and ironed, the laundry worker either places it on a hanger or folds it around a 14 x 8 inch section of cardboard that the customer usually throws away after putting on the shirt. But I always save these cardboard sections and stack them in a pile near my desk at home; before going out for an interview, I take a scissor and cut a folderboard sideways into five pieces, after which I trim and round off all the edges. I thus create a firm and handy little pack of 7 x 3 inch writing surfaces that easily slip in and out of my jacket pocket; on certain occasions, I might even tuck a single slice inside the cuff of my shirt and surreptitiously scribble a few words on the cardboard's edge when I think there is little risk of being observed.

I would never dare make notes in a crowded room, especially in the proximity of Sinatra's pals and protectors, and even in the privacy of the bathroom I do not linger long with my writing. All I do on these strips of cardboard is jot down in abbreviated form a reminder of what I'd seen, felt, and thought while watching Sinatra—ergo:

FS brooding at bar
FS mood music lures dancers
FS voice airy aphrodisiac?
FS lyrics >multitudes love-making in parked cars,
     penthouses, rented rooms, etc.
FS being stood up tonight by Mia?

During the time I was away, Sinatra and his pals, Durocher and Dexter, had left the blondes at the bar with the singer's bodyguard, Ed Pucci, a 250-pound ex-lineman who had played pro ball with Washington, and made their way into the pool room. There they joined about fifty or sixty young people who were standing or sitting on stools watching the eight-ball competition in progress at the two tables.

When I had settled myself inconspicuously within a crowd near the door, I noticed that Sinatra, drink in hand, was sitting with his back against the wall on the other side of the room. He was wearing a well-cut, three-piece Oxford gray suit with a pocket square, and the jacket had red silk lining. Sitting with his legs crossed, he displayed highly buffed burgundy shoes of British design that seemed to be shined even on the bottom of the soles. I also noticed that on at least two occasions he removed a white handkerchief from his hip pocket and wiped his nose; I learned later that he had a cold.

Only he and his companions, Dexter and Durocher, were attired in suits and ties, while the others were more casually, though not inexpensively, dressed—cashmere sweaters, Gucci loafers, tailored jeans, and, of course, prevalent among the women members of the club, Jax pants. Although everyone seemed to be comfortable in Sinatra's presence, having seen him there often in the past and being used to having famous people as fellow members, they still kept a respectful distance, being mindful of his volatile nature.

Leo Durocher, meanwhile, had gotten hold of a cue stick and had insinuated himself into a game at the near table. He quickly demonstrated why he had often been described in newspapers as a pool shark, one who'd grown up playing the game and had greatly augmented his income while hustling teammates during his years as a baseball player. As he skillfully slammed the billiard balls back and forth across the green felt surface, Sinatra and Dexter took turns clapping and shouting out words of encouragement; but then Sinatra abruptly shifted his attention toward a short young man who stood behind Durocher wearing a green shaggy-dog Shetland sweater, brown corduroy slacks, a tan suede jacket, and game warden boots.

In time I would learn that this sharp-featured, 5'5" individual with blondish hair and squared eyeglasses was a prolific thirty-year-old writer of science fiction stories and screenplays named Harlan Ellison. But what most impressed Sinatra about Ellison were his boots.

"Hey," Sinatra asked in a loud voice, sniffling a bit from his cold, "those Italian boots?"

"No," Ellison replied, turning and staring at Sinatra. The room suddenly went quiet. Durocher, who had been poised behind his cue stick and was bent low, just froze in that position for a second.

"Spanish boots?" Sinatra asked.

"No!" said Ellison.

"English boots?"

"Look, I don't know, man," Ellison said impatiently, frowning and turning toward Durocher, perhaps seeking his intercession. Durocher did not move. Sinatra then stepped away from the stool and walked with a slow, arrogant swagger toward Ellison, the hard tap of Sinatra's shoes the only sound in the room. Looking directly at Ellison with a slightly raised eyebrow and a tricky little smile, Sinatra asked: "You expecting a storm?"

Ellison moved a step to the side and said, "Look, is there any reason why you're talking to me?"

"I don't like the way you're dressed," Sinatra said.

"Hate to shake you up," Ellison said, "but I dress to suit myself."

Now there was some rumbling in the room, and somebody said, "C'mon, Harlan, let's get out of here." Leo Durocher made his pool shot and said, "Yeah, c'mon."

But Ellison stood his ground.

Sinatra asked, "What do you do?"

"I'm a plumber," Ellison said.

"No, no, he's not," another young man quickly called out from across the table, "He wrote *The Oscar*."

"Oh, yeah," Sinatra said, "well I've seen it, and it's a piece of shit."

"That's strange," Ellison said, "because they haven't even released it yet."

"Well, I've seen it," Sinatra repeated, "and it's a piece of shit."

Now Brad Dexter, very anxious, and very big opposite the tiny figure of Ellison, said, "C'mon, kid, I don't want you in this room."

"Hey," Sinatra interrupted Dexter, "can't you see I'm talking to this guy?"

Dexter was confused. Then his whole attitude changed. His voice went soft and he said to Ellison, almost with a plea, "Why do you persist in tormenting me?"

The whole scene was becoming ridiculous, and it seemed that Sinatra was only half serious, perhaps just reacting out of sheer boredom or inner despair; at any rate, after a few more exchanges, Harlan Ellison and a buddy of his left the room, and I soon followed them, my interest in Sinatra temporarily put aside. I felt I had to speak to Ellison, and if I did not catch up with him now, I might have a difficult time tracking him down later.

Tapping him on the shoulder and apologizing for my intrusion, I introduced myself and asked if he would talk to me for a few minutes outside the club.

"Sorry, I have to go somewhere now," Ellison said. "Call me tomorrow." He gave me his number and I quickly wrote it down on a slice of cardboard: BR9-1952.

After Ellison had left the club and I had rejoined the Hansons' table, I noticed that Sinatra, along with Dexter and Durocher, had returned to the women and the bodyguard at the bar, but I was satisfied that on this particular evening I had seen enough. I now wanted to hurry back to my hotel, and to my Olivetti portable traveling mate, and do what I always do before going to bed while on assignment: take some typing paper and write a page or two or more describing what I had so far observed that day, the people I had seen and my impressions of them, getting it all down while still fresh in my memory.

I began by typing the day's date at the top of the lead page ["Thursday, Nov. 4, 1965"]; where I was doing the typing ["in my room #451 at the Beverly-Wilshire Hotel"]; and, after referring to my cardboard jottings: FS brooding at bar . . . FS "Wee Small hrs" . . . FS voice airy aphrodisiac? . . . FS>Harlan Ellison. I then began expanding the material and creating scenes as if I were a short-story writer, while at the same time reminding myself that I was a reporter striving for accuracy.

Although I did not take notes in the pool room, I felt confident as I typed that I was faithfully reproducing the dialogue I had heard earlier involving Sinatra and Ellison. This is not to suggest that I have "total recall"—that would be Truman Capote's claim while researching *In Cold Blood*—but during my decades of listening to people sans tape-recorder I think I have cultivated a fairly high degree of retentiveness.

Still, I planned to go over everything with Harlan Ellison when I later met with him, not only to confirm and perhaps enlarge upon what I remembered but also to ask Ellison what he himself was feeling as he was being targeted by Sinatra. Was he surprised by the encounter? Did he think that Sinatra might throw a punch at him? Or throw a drink at him?

What was in Ellison's head the whole time? As a reporter I am always interested in describing what my subjects are thinking as well as what they are doing and saying. And I am also interested in what I myself am thinking while I'm devoting my attention to other people. For example, what was on my mind as I observed Sinatra in his contrasting moods at the Daisy? On this evening I had most recently seen him behaving aggressively in the pool room, while earlier at the bar he had been a quiet and isolated figure. He did not even react to the playing of "In the Wee Small Hours of the Morning," although this romantic music promptly drove dozens of couples to the dance floor; and as I stood watching while they held one another very close, I was thinking that Sinatra's voice was an airy aphrodisiac—the very words I would write on cardboard in the men's room—and I had visions of these young couples later leaving the Daisy and making love in their beds at home, or in rented rooms, or in any of a dozen other places—all sorts of places, including in parked cars, while Sinatra's music was playing on the radio and the batteries were burning low.

I not only imagined such a scene, and got a first draft of it on paper, but many weeks later, when I submitted my article in final form to Harold Hayes, it had obviously been guided by what I had typed on my Olivetti on the night of November 4 in the Beverly Wilshire hotel, albeit in a more polished and fully realized form:

"In the Wee Small Hours of the Morning" . . . like so many of his classics, a song that evokes loneliness and sensuality, and when blended with the dim light and the alcohol and nicotine and late night needs, it becomes a kind of airy aphrodisiac. Undoubtedly the words from this song, and others like it, had put millions in the mood, it was music to make love by, and doubtless much love had been made by it all over America at night in cars, while the batteries burned down, in cottages by the lake, on beaches during balmy summer evenings, in secluded parks and exclusive penthouses and furnished rooms, in cabin cruisers and cabs and cabanas—in all places where Sinatra's songs could be heard were these words that warmed women, wooed and won them, snipped the final thread of inhibition and gratified the male egos of ungrateful lovers; two generations of men had been the beneficiaries of such ballads, for which they were eternally in his debt, for which they may eternally hate him. Nevertheless here he was, the man himself, in the early hours of the morning in Beverly Hills, out of range.

Chapter 16

On Friday morning, November 5, I walked from my hotel to the nearby office of Sinatra's publicist, Jim Mahoney, an affable, broad-shouldered, sandy-haired man of thirty-seven who greeted me while wearing a custom-tailored nut-brown suit, a tan silk tie, and a striped shirt with his initials J. M. monogrammed on the breast pocket.

His initials in gold were also on his leather briefcase, which was lying flat on his desk, next to a thick stack of unopened mail. After waving me to a seat opposite him, he carelessly pushed aside the mail, allowing some pieces to fall to the floor. "Bills, bills," he said, in a bemused manner. "No money, just bills, bills . . ." He left the fallen envelopes on the floor.

Then his secretary walked in to say that Kay Gardella of the *New York Daily News* was on the line. After apologizing to me for the interruption, he grabbed the phone and leaned back in his leather chair, listening for a moment, and then in a loud voice said: "That's right, Kay, I'm telling you that CBS played Frank dirty. They lied to him, Kay, they made a gentleman's agreement to not ask questions about Frank's private life and then Cronkite went right ahead: 'Frank, tell me about those associations.' That question, Kay—out. That question should never have been asked."

As their conversation continued, I glanced around the room and noticed an autographed photo of President Kennedy hanging on the wall, a few photos of Sinatra standing next to

Mahoney at public events, and one of Mahoney posing with his wife and their five children. On the shelves were a number of Mahoney's golf trophies, and also on display was a mounted wood photocopy of the $240,000 ransom note that Sinatra received in 1963 from the kidnappers of his nineteen-year-old son, Frank Jr., who was then launching his musical career at Harrah's Club Lodge in Lake Tahoe. It was Mahoney who delivered the cash that freed Frank Jr. The FBI soon caught and imprisoned the criminals, and nearly all the ransom money was recovered.

After Mahoney had hung up on Kay Gardella, his secretary again came in to say that a certain gentleman was on the line.

"Does he know that I'm here?" Mahoney asked.

"No," she said.

"Well, tell him I'm not here."

Then, turning to me, he said, "I'm really sorry to burden you with what's going on, but Frank isn't feeling well and I'm afraid your talking to him will have to be put off for a while."

"For how long?" I asked.

"I'm not sure," he said. "Frank is nursing a cold, and he just left earlier today to spend the weekend at his place in Palm Springs, where he expects to recover in time to record some songs this Monday at the NBC taping in Burbank. But there's another matter that's bothering him and his attorney, Mickey Rudin, and this concerns you."

"Me?"

"They're really upset about being betrayed by Cronkite and his coming CBS interview, and they would like you to sign an agreement allowing Rudin to review your article before it's published."

"Jim, you know I can't do that," I said quickly. "I couldn't do it at the *Times*, and I can't at *Esquire*, or any other place that I know of."

"Unfortunately, this is all out of my hands," Mahoney said. "But Frank and Mickey Rudin need some assurance or else we can't proceed with this interview."

"I can assure them that I won't associate Sinatra with the Mafia in my piece," I said, "but that's as far as I can go."

"That might not be far enough," Mahoney said.

"Harold Hayes will hate hearing this," I said, adding that I had flown in with the understanding that *Esquire* and Sinatra's people had reached an agreement, and furthermore I was not expected to remain in Los Angeles for much longer than a week. "Now I have to call Hayes and tell him the deal is off, and, as I already said, I'll bet he'll be furious."

"Again, I'm sorry," Mahoney said. "Maybe we can find a way to pick up your expense and fly you back ourselves."

"I doubt that Hayes would agree," I said, although I was not so sure. Maybe he would agree and cancel the Sinatra assignment, and consequently free me to do what I preferred doing— interviewing the *Times* managing editor, Clifton Daniel. In any case, it was Harold Hayes's decision to make, and so as I stood to leave Mahoney's office I told him that I'd go back to my hotel and try to reach Hayes, and I would let Mahoney know the results.

"No, wait," Mahoney said, "I might have a better idea. Let's not call Harold Hayes until we know how Frank feels this Monday, after he does the NBC rehearsal in Burbank. I was planning to take you with me to the recording session. You'll be able to watch him sing, but not to try to interview him then. You must give me a chance to see if I can smooth things out. Is that agreeable?"

After I agreed, he said he would pick me up in front of my hotel at 10:00 a.m. sharp on Monday—and he was there promptly as promised, sitting behind the wheel of his Mercedes convertible. During the half-hour drive to Burbank, in response to my questions, he told me about himself.

He was born about five miles south of Beverly Hills in Culver City, which was well known as the site of Metro-Goldwyn-Mayer studios. His father, a house painter, was often hired to work on the residences of MGM movie stars, and one such individual was Clark Gable, who occupied a nine-room ranch house on a twenty-acre property in Encino, in the San Fernando Valley.

As a teenager, Jim Mahoney sometimes accompanied his father to jobs, and that is how he met Clark Gable, who soon took a liking to him and arranged for him to work as an assistant to MGM's head of publicity, Howard Strickling. One day in 1953, Strickling assigned Mahoney to drive the MGM star Ava Gardner, then married to Sinatra, to the airport for her flight to Africa to be featured with Clark Gable and Grace Kelly in *Mogambo*.

When Mahoney arrived at Ava Gardner's home in Nichols Canyon, in the Hollywood Hills, she was not quite ready, so she told him to come in and make himself a drink. As he entered the living room and headed to the bar, he was interrupted by a male voice demanding: "Who the fuck are you?" Frank Sinatra was sitting on a stuffed chair in a shaded corner of the living room, obviously in a foul mood.

"I'm from Strickling's office," Mahoney said, "and I'm supposed to take Mrs. Sinatra to the airport."

Sinatra's attitude softened and he stood up, saying, "That's fine, kid. What are you drinking?"

But moments later, as Ava Gardner came down with her luggage and said goodbye to her husband, Mahoney noticed tears in Sinatra's eyes. Mahoney later heard that she was determined to get away from Sinatra, that she had recently aborted their child, and that Sinatra was so depressed that he had on at least one occasion attempted suicide. In addition to personal problems, he had financial ones prompted by his declining stature in the entertainment business. He had already tested for what would become his Oscar-winning role in *From Here to Eternity*, but at this point he did not know that he had won the part.

Years later, after Sinatra's triumphant career had been fully restored, Mahoney met him a second time on the MGM lot, where Sinatra was starring in *Kings Go Forth*. Mahoney was helping with the promotion, and one day Sinatra asked: "When are you going to get out of this hokey business?"

"When something better comes along," Mahoney replied.

"Something just did," said Sinatra. He offered him a big raise and a position as the singer's exclusive publicist. That was in 1958, and since then, said Mahoney, "I've been with him through the good years, the lean years, and the in-between years."

While Mahoney drove into the parking lot of the sprawling sixty-acre Warner Bros Studios in Burbank, which consisted of dozens of soundstages resembling airplane hangars, I noticed several people unloading musical instruments from their cars and entering the side door of one particularly busy building. I was also aware of a very familiar male figure stepping out of a limousine wearing an orange sweater, a snap-brimmed fedora, and carrying under one arm a briefcase and a raincoat on this cloudy and unseasonably cool California day.

"Jim," I called out, "isn't that Frank Sinatra!"

Mahoney stopped his car and squinted through his windshield in the direction of the individual I was pointing to.

"No," he said. "That's not Frank. That's his double, Johnny Delgado."

I was surprised to hear that Sinatra had a double, but I said nothing, knowing instinctively that whatever I was thinking was best kept secret from Mahoney. He had warned me not to approach Sinatra, but he'd said nothing about the double. Johnny Delgado was the type of subsidiary character who always appealed to me as a writer. The same might be said of many others who worked for, or who were socially connected with, Frank Sinatra—a list that included his publicist Mahoney, his lawyer Rudin, his bodyguard Pucci, and dozens more, including some of his special household servants and countless backstage characters and hangers-on.

In any case, were I not beholden to Harold Hayes and the fulfillment of my assignment, I would have much preferred profiling the double than the real thing; and in my mind I had already assembled many questions for Delgado. How did he ever get this job? What were its pleasures, perks, and pitfalls? Knowing that Sinatra was currently working on *Assault on a Queen*, a film being shot along the Pacific coastline, I guessed that Delgado was sent out to appear in the water scenes while Sinatra stayed dry on the beach, but what was Delgado doing here today at the recording session? Could he carry a tune? Was he once an aspiring singer or an actor? If so, what were his experiences? Did he have a personal relationship with Sinatra?

If I pursued him, would he talk to me? Or would he avoid me, fearing he'd lose his job? I would know the answer only if I could get to him, but before I could do that I would have to somehow circumvent Jim Mahoney.

Chapter 17

I stayed close to Mahoney as we entered the vast and clamorous television studio where hundreds of people were gathered in conversation around the elevated platform on which some seated musicians were warming up; and overlooking the bandstand was the glass-enclosed control booth in which the director and his assistants were testing their cameras and sound equipment in the hope that Frank Sinatra would battle through his cold today and offer a worthy performance.

After passing the bandstand, we continued walking until we reached the rehearsal room in the far corner of the studio. Mahoney paused to speak to some people who stood outside the door, introducing me to none of them. Three of them were well-dressed men in dark suits approaching middle age, and there was also a gray-haired woman wearing a floral print dress who carried a small suitcase. I later learned her name was Helen Turpin, and that her full-time job was quietly following Sinatra around wherever he performed while bearing a suitcase filled with his hair pieces. As his toupee toter, she earned $400 a week.

Inside the rehearsal room, accompanied by a pianist, Sinatra was testing his voice. Since the door was partly opened, we could hear him frequently interrupt his singing to complain about something, and twice he even pounded his fists on the piano, while the accompanist pleaded with him, softly but repeatedly: "Try not to upset yourself, Frank."

Those standing outside said nothing, but I guessed that they, like Mahoney, were closely associated with the singer and must have been shocked and concerned by what was going on. Mahoney might also have been displeased with himself for allowing me to be present when Sinatra was so clearly out of control.

"Come on," Mahoney then said, taking me by the arm and leading me in the direction of a man in the near distance who was waving at him. "There's someone I want to talk to."

Soon he introduced me to Andy Williams, the recording artist of such hits as "Moon River" and the host of a weekly variety show on NBC. As the two men held a long and friendly conversation, I paid little attention because I was more interested in watching the stage lights on the bandstand being tested on Johnny Delgado, positioned behind a standing microphone. Then we were joined by a gregarious young brunette who was Andy Williams's wife, Claudine Longet, a French-born actress and dancer.

How she first met Andy Williams five years before had been widely reported in the press. She was then a Folies Bergere dancer at a Las Vegas casino, and one afternoon, when she was stalled on the roadside with car trouble, he drove by and stopped to assist her. He was then thirty-two and she was eighteen. They began dating and were married a year later. He had earlier had a longtime love affair with a woman twice his age—Kay Thompson, a singer and vocal coach who had helped launch his career. She later wrote the Eloise children's books. Following Andy Williams's marriage to Claudine, Kay Thompson relocated to Rome.

After Claudine had joined her husband's meeting with Mahoney, she did most of the talking, pressing Mahoney to escort them to Sinatra. "He's busy and not feeling great," Mahoney said.

But she insisted: "Frank adores Andy, and we'll both cheer him up."

"He's rehearsing now, and I can't interrupt him," Mahoney said.

To which she replied: "We'll wait outside for him. Please, I need to talk to him. It will make him feel better."

Finally, Mahoney relented. "All right, let's go over and see what's going on. But I can't promise anything." Before leaving with the two of them, Mahoney turned to me and said, "Wait for me here, okay? I won't be long."

I remained in the middle of the crowded room, surrounded by masses of people I had never seen before. Mahoney had earlier mentioned that lots of beer salesmen and their families would be here—Budweiser was the NBC show's sponsor—and also many secretaries and other employees from various offices within the Warner Bros. property. Finally I spotted someone whom I remembered seeing at the Daisy—Ed Pucci, the ex-NFL lineman who was Sinatra's bodyguard. He was headed in the direction of the rehearsal room, and, after catching up with him, I introduced myself as an *Esquire* writer profiling his boss.

"*Esquire*!" Pucci repeated cheerfully. "That's my favorite magazine. I read it all the time. I really like the 'Dining Out' column. I'm a part owner of a terrific restaurant out here, and maybe you'd like to eat there with me some night, and maybe get me a write-up in 'Dining Out'?

"I'd love to join you," I told him, "and I'll be glad to alert the column editor to your restaurant." I quickly jotted down Pucci's phone number on the slice of cardboard I lifted out of my jacket, and we set a date to meet for dinner later in the week. It was my hope, of course, that Pucci would not mention this to Mahoney.

After Pucci had gone, and Mahoney had not yet returned, I noticed that Delgado and the lighting crew were taking a break near the steps of the bandstand, so I hurried over and found him quite cordial and receptive. I got his phone number and his promise of an interview as soon as his schedule allowed. He did explain that as a young aspiring actor in 1953 he had auditioned for a part in *From Here to Eternity*, but the casting director, impressed by his resemblance to Sinatra, hired him as the singer's double.

Since then Delgado had been regularly employed as a stand-in when Sinatra was on stage or making a film in the United States or overseas. Sometimes when Delgado was off duty in foreign cities, and strolling through the streets or sitting in cafes, people mistook him for Sinatra and approached him for autographs and pictures—which, after clarification, he politely declined. Now and then, however, there were young women who pursued him romantically. In such situations, he admitted to me with a raised eyebrow and wink, he was not always so resistant.

I backed away from him as I saw Mahoney headed my way with the Williams couple. Claudine seemed subdued, and she remained silent when I asked if she had seen Sinatra. Mahoney answered for her: "Frank was busy, but I'm glad to say he's feeling better. He'll be ready soon to begin."

Five minutes later, accompanied by much cheering and hand-clapping, I noticed Pucci pushing through the crowd with Sinatra walking behind him. They were headed toward the bandstand. Sinatra was wearing a fedora and black horn-rimmed glasses, and he was carrying what I assumed was sheet music. He also had on brown slacks and shoes and a high-necked orange pullover sweater.

Orange was his favorite color. I learned this from Sinatra's much-publicized haberdasher, Richard Carroll, whose Beverly Hills store I had visited during the weekend. Mr. Carroll, a prematurely gray-haired man in his early forties who opened his place in 1949 and was appareled and accessorized as stylishly as the mannequins that surrounded him, told me that Sinatra bought luxurious orange Scottish cashmere sweaters not only for himself but for many of his friends and such employees as his pilot, who always wore an orange sweater when flying Sinatra around in the singer's Lear jet—which, incidentally, had orange carpeting, orange leather side paneling, and an orange stripe painted across its fuselage.

Through the years Richard Carroll's tape measure has explored every inch of Sinatra's body—his waist is 32", his hips 39", his trouser inseam 30", the length of his jacket 29¼", his hat size 7¼", his shoe size 8. Although at 5'7" he is an inch taller than was Napoleon Bonaparte, Carroll knew that this brought little satisfaction to Sinatra, and so all his shoes were layered with lifts that elevated him close to 5'9".

Carroll also knew, in consultation with Sinatra's clothing valet Dominic Di Bona, exactly what the singer would be wearing on the three occasions he would have a wardrobe change while singing eighteen songs during the forthcoming hour-long NBC special on November 24. The show would begin with Sinatra filmed in full stride crossing the length of the studio. Then, after tossing his hat into a corner, he would ascend a white platform and, with members of the orchestra playing in the shadows behind him, he would take hold of a microphone and begin singing "I've Got You under My Skin."

For this song, and the five that followed, he would be wearing a Carroll-designed beige tweed jacket with an orange vest, brown trousers, brown shoes, a brown print silk tie, and a white dress shirt with tiny circular pearl cuff links. Also sprouting from his jacket would be an orange pocket square. For his seventh song, "It Was a Very Good Year," Sinatra would change into a three-piece dark gray suit with a pin-collar shirt, a gray silk tie, and a pocket square of reddish orange hue.

His final wardrobe change would occur when he donned a tuxedo for his fifteenth song, "Come Fly with Me." The black jacket was designed with raised shoulders and satin-faced lapels, and under a vest Sinatra would wear a white shirt with a wing-tipped collar, a black bowtie, and studded buttons. His trousers were tailored with a built-in cummerbund, and, again, his jacket was embellished with a tomato-red pocket square.

Carroll had already made the singer forty tuxedos, but since formal wear was so ubiquitous to Sinatra's presence as a performer, it was necessary to deliver seven new tuxedos every year. Carroll said that it took his tailors about four weeks to make each one, and that two were in the process of being made at all times.

After Ed Pucci had opened a path through the crowd surrounding the bandstand, he stepped aside as Sinatra climbed onto the small white platform on which was a microphone, a music stand, and a white leather cushioned stool; the stool was flanked by white plastic trees with branches bearing dozens of artificial orange-colored marigolds. Removing his glasses and tucking them into the breast pocket of his sweater—all of his sweaters came with pockets for his glasses—he turned around and looked up toward the rows of seated musicians; most of them now tooting their horns and testing their strings while positioned about ten yards behind Sinatra and several feet above him.

Sinatra smiled and pointed up toward a trombone player who stood to take his photograph and then, looking around, asked aloud: "Where's Nelse?"

Nelson Riddle, the bandleader and arranger—a hefty, dark-haired, modest and mellow man in his forties who had been Sinatra's musical collaborator for more than a decade—quickly appeared from the left side of the platform and said: "Ready to go, Frank." Five minutes later, with Riddle behind the podium and his baton in motion, and with his forty-three-piece orchestra in vibrant response, the voice of Frank Sinatra, accompanied by his fingers snapping behind the microphone, reverberated through the sound system:

"I've got you under my skin / I've got you, deep in the heart of me /So deep in my heart that you're really a part of me . . ."

He stopped singing before finishing a third of the song because this was merely an orchestra-accompanied warm-up, not intended for taping, and also because he was interrupted by the show's director, Dwight Hemion, calling down from the control booth.

"Voice sounds great, Frank, but would you mind coming up here for a moment to take a look? We might have too much hand movement."

Hemion was a soft-spoken, sandy-haired gent in his early thirties, moving around soundlessly in sneakers while wearing a suit and tie. In the past decade he had won several Emmy Awards for directing musical variety shows, most recently one starring Barbra Streisand.

As Sinatra, followed by Nelson Riddle, went up to review the monitors with Hemion, there was a ten-minute pause in the proceedings. Since Sinatra was apparently healthy enough to perform, there were expressions of joy and relief coming from his friends and associates gathered in a circle near the bandstand. In addition to Mahoney and Andy Williams and his wife, Claudine, the group now included Brad Dexter, Leo Durocher, my new best friend, Ed Pucci, and several other people I had not seen before. With Mahoney busy talking to Dexter, I quietly asked Pucci who they were, and he identified them as Mo Ostin, an executive with Sinatra's Reprise record company; Layne Britton, Sinatra's makeup artist; Al Silvani, a boxing trainer and ex-stuntman who appeared in many of

Sinatra's movies; and John Lillie, Sinatra's golfing partner and insurance broker.

Standing not far away I noticed the toupee lady, Helen Turpin. I briefly slipped away to introduce myself to Ms. Turpin and was pleased to get her phone number and her willingness to later schedule an interview.

Meanwhile, Frank Sinatra had returned to the platform and was standing near the music stand in conversation with Hemion, Riddle, the composer Gordon Jenkins, and a few lighting technicians. They were discussing how Sinatra should be positioned after he had finished singing the second number, "Without a Song," and then faced the television camera to read the opening lines from the script, which began: "Did you ever stop to think what the world would be like without a song? . . . It would be a pretty dreary place . . . Gives you something to think about, doesn't it?"

After reading the line once, Sinatra coughed. "Excuse me," he said, adding, "Boy, I need a drink."

"Take it slow, Frank," Hemion said encouragingly, and, then from behind him and the other men on the platform, a brunette woman suddenly slipped through and placed an arm around Sinatra's shoulders, then whispered something into his ear. Sinatra did not seem to mind her presence, but from in front of me I heard Jim Mahoney yelling and pointing to the platform: "What the hell is Claudine doing up there?"

Furious and red-faced, Mahoney turned toward the man standing beside him, Andy Williams, to whom he had previously been so solicitous, and repeated the question. Shrugging and apologizing, Williams rushed up to the platform and took his wife by the hand, then escorted her down the steps and toward the rear of the studio, far away from Mahoney.

"Did you ever stop to think what the world would be like without a song?" Sinatra repeated, this time without coughing, and then, with the orchestra accompanying him, he managed to flawlessly get through parts of the show's third number, "Don't Worry About Me," after which he directed his attention to Dwight Hemion, now returned to the control booth, and asked: "Why don't we tape this mother?"

Hemion paid no attention; so Sinatra repeated: "Why don't we tape this mother?"

Immediately, the production stage manager, standing below the platform and wearing a headset, repeated Sinatra's words up to Hemion exactly: "Why don't we tape this mother?"

Sinatra was becoming very impatient. He had been standing under the hot lights for twenty minutes, had already invested his energy in three songs, and still the NBC crew was not ready to roll. There were no less than thirty NBC employees under Hemion, plus twenty stagehands, and they frequently bumped into one another as they ran around adjusting camera angles, moving scenery, realigning the orchestra's seating, and debating how spread out Sinatra's shadows should be when the singer was perambulating on stage with a microphone in hand. Johnny Delgado was sometimes summoned to stand in Sinatra's spot and create shadows on the stage that would be filmed and later be represented as Sinatra's.

One of the contraptions in the studio that required testing and retesting was a leaf blower that, when Sinatra was to begin singing the fourth verse of "It Was a Very Good Year"—"By now the days are short / I'm in the autumn of the year . . ."— this elevated machine was to release a fluttering cascade of orange-colored leaves that were supposed to twirl slowly around in the air for a while before falling and spreading out to all parts of the floor around the microphone. But regrettably the blower frequently malfunctioned and the leaves remained blocked in the container. As Sinatra stood watching the unreliable apparatus, he shook his head in annoyance and remarked, "It's like waiting for your kid to be born."

In his long career as a troubadour and movie star, Sinatra was notoriously known for his confrontations with directors and particularly his wrath when he thought that his work pace was being delayed due to their lack of preparation or their excessive fastidiousness. He believed that a well-organized film director should be able to shoot a scene in one or two takes, and not expect an actor to repeat it several times because of avoidable mishaps on the set or perhaps a director's false notions of what constituted perfectionism.

As for Dwight Hemion, a courteous and accomplished master of concert performance specials, Sinatra certainly could not blame him for over-shooting scenes, but rather the opposite. Hemion was seemingly so mired in minutiae that he was shooting no scenes at all—and Sinatra was tired of waiting. He wanted to go to the dressing room, take off his sweater, put on his jacket and tie, and return to the stage to start the show for real.

And so he again glanced up at the glass booth and called out to Hemion:

"Why don't we put on a coat and tie and tape this?"

Continuing silence from Hemion. Maybe the switch in his booth was off. Or maybe he was simply in no rush to answer, being a deliberative individual of inculcated calmness who routinely proceeded through life on his own terms and at his own tempo. And then, at last, Hemion's voice, in a relaxed and muted tone, was heard saying, "Frank, would you mind going back over . . ."

"Yes, I would mind going back," Sinatra suddenly snapped. "When we stop doing things around here the way we did them in 1950, maybe we . . ." Sinatra continued with his rant, but he got no rise from the tuned-out Hemion; so Sinatra went on shouting: "What the hell are you doing up there, Dwight? Got a party or something going on up there, Dwight?"

Sinatra remained standing alone on the stage, arms folded, waiting for a reply that never came. The inactive musicians seated behind him were undoubtedly restless as well, and perhaps that was why Nelson Riddle soon joined Sinatra on stage, put a hand on his shoulder, and engaged him in quiet conversation for a few minutes.

Riddle then returned to the bandstand and signaled for his orchestra to begin playing the fifth number listed on the program: "Nancy (With the Laughing Face)". This was one of the signature tunes in Sinatra's vast repertoire; it was written more than twenty years before by Jimmy Van Heusen and Phil Silvers, and was associated with the birth of the singer's first-born and presumably favorite child, Nancy: "If I don't see her each day / I miss her / Gee what a thrill / Each time I kiss her / Believe me I've got a case / On Nancy with the laughin' face . . ."

Soon Sinatra himself was accompanying the orchestra, and because of his peerless phrasing and distinct enunciation, his audience could clearly hear every word that the lyricists had written. The writer Pete Hamill once suggested that multitudes of newcomers to America familiarized themselves with English by listening to Sinatra sing.

"She takes the winter and makes it summer / Summer could take some lessons from her / Picture a tomboy in lace / That's Nancy with the laughin' face . . ."

Sinatra completed this song satisfactorily, but when Nelson Riddle led him through parts of the sixth song—"My Kind of Town"—his voice emitted raspy notes and twice cracked completely. The orchestra suddenly stopped as Sinatra bent over and sneezed. Getting through "Nancy" was probably all that he had in his voice on this day, and so, after removing a handkerchief from his hip pocket and blowing his nose, he left the stage and headed up to the control room to tell Hemion that the rehearsal was over. It would have to be rescheduled.

As a result, everything that happened today would be scrapped, except for the bill of perhaps two hundred thousand dollars or more that would nevertheless have to be paid to cover the day's expenses—such items as the rental fee for the studio, the assemblage of the forty-three-piece orchestra, the salary of the stagehands, the security guards, the NBC crew and its director.

Before saying goodbye to Sinatra, Dwight Hemion sat with him briefly in front of the screen, watching him trying to get through "My Kind of Town" while being betrayed by his voice. "This should've been stopped before this," Sinatra said, his words heard through the sound system. "We shouldn't have gone on this long." Hemion did not disagree.

Regarding the image of himself on the screen, Sinatra said: "That's a man with a cold."

Chapter 18

While driving me back to my hotel, Mahoney told me that Sinatra had gone to his desert home in Palm Springs to recover and that meanwhile my interview with him was on hold.

"For how long?" I asked.

"I won't know until I speak to Frank," Mahoney said, repeating that the Sinatra organization would arrange to have my expenses covered if I wanted to quit the assignment and return to New York.

"Jim, you know I can't make that decision," I said, adding: "When I get back to my room, I'll contact Harold Hayes and let you know what he says."

But even before I called him, I assumed that Hayes had too much pride as an editor to consider such a proposal, and moreover, knowing how keen he was on getting a Sinatra article into print, I felt obliged to accommodate him. Years before, when I was still employed as a reporter at the *Times*, I peremptorily canceled an *Esquire* freelance assignment in Los Angeles due to Natalie Wood's tardiness, but my situation now was different. Now I was a thirty-three-year-old writer with a one-year contract that made me answerable exclusively to Harold Hayes. Also, my wife and I recently had our first child, and *Esquire* was our main source of income. And finally, I felt both loyalty and gratitude toward Hayes for allowing me to write more freely and at greater length than would have been possible for me at the *Times*.

After I had called him from my hotel and recounted what Mahoney had told me, Hayes responded as I thought he would by rejecting Mahoney's offer as ridiculous. He also disregarded my suggestion that we reduce *Esquire*'s expenses by transferring me from the Beverly Wilshire to a cheaper hotel.

"Stay where you are," he said, "and keep doing what you're doing. Keep talking to whoever talks to you out there."

Among the people I hoped to talk to, without Mahoney's awareness of course, was Nancy Sinatra Jr., whose home phone number I obtained from Sally Hanson, who knew Nancy as a member of the Daisy.

Another individual whom I believed might influence Frank Sinatra to my benefit was the heavyweight fighter Floyd Patterson, a longtime friend of mine whom Sinatra also liked. He was betting on him to defeat Muhammad Ali in two weeks in their heavyweight title fight in Las Vegas, on November 22. Sinatra not only planned to attend the event, Mahoney told me, but he was sending to the Patterson camp in advance a fifty-five-year-old functionary, Al Silvani, who had once been a renowned boxing trainer and presently had a strategy that could presumably help Patterson defeat Ali.

Sinatra had long been an avid boxing fan, with many ex-fighters and their attendants on his gift list and payroll. Sinatra's Sicilian-born, blue-eyed father, Marty, before becoming a fireman and bar owner in New Jersey, had been a bantamweight boxer with eighty professional fights, until he broke both wrists and was forced to retire.

Sinatra himself took boxing lessons early in his singing career from Henry "Hank" Sanicola, a song plugger and one-time fighter who eventually became Sinatra's first manager. In

1942, when Sinatra started performing at the Paramount Theatre in Times Square, Sanicola rented space in the building in order to spar with Sinatra and teach him the fundamentals of self-defense. Sanicola was a powerful, barrel-chested man of two hundred pounds, and, wanting to avoid facial injury to the singer, he insisted that while jabbing they limit contact to one another's shoulders and resist hitting above the neck.

But one day while sparring, and perhaps unable to resist the temptation to intimidate the larger man, Sinatra rammed his fist against Sanicola's jaw. More surprised than physically hurt, Sanicola instinctively retaliated with a punch to the belly that sent Sinatra sprawling to the floor. Sinatra remained there momentarily, saying nothing. And then he slowly climbed to his feet and, with a half-hearted smile, apologized to Sanicola.

When Mahoney told me that Sinatra would be going to the Patterson-Ali fight, I neglected to tell him that I also planned to be there, having attended more than a dozen of Patterson's fights since he first won the heavyweight title in 1956, at the age of twenty-one.

During that year and the years that followed, I wrote more than thirty pieces about him in the *Times*, plus a profile in *Esquire*—articles that dealt with his challenges in the ring as well as those within his private life.

I reported on his upbringing as an impoverished Black youth in Brooklyn, a truant and petty thief who at ten was sent to the Wiltwyck School for Boys—a reform school in upstate New York that truly reformed him. There he was trained to accept discipline and personal responsibility, and as a fourteen-year-old who received boxing lessons in a gym, he finally experienced within the ropes a place where he did not feel inferior.

At seventeen he won a gold medal as a middleweight in the 1952 Olympics in Helsinki, after which he turned pro, gained weight, and signed on with an ascetic, Bronx-born manager named Cus D'Amato, who wore dark suits and a bowler and once contemplated the priesthood despite being known in the neighborhood as a street fighter undeterred by a permanent eye injury. D'Amato not only served as Patterson's matchmaker but also his patriarch until 1962, when Patterson—who had just turned twenty-seven and had regained his heavyweight title from Ingemar Johansson—defied D'Amato by signing a contract to fight Sonny Liston, a much larger and more powerful brawler with a disproportionally long reach.

The event was set for September 25 at Comiskey Park in Chicago, and a few days before the fight I visited Patterson's camp in suburban Elgin, Illinois, about forty miles northwest of the Loop, bringing with me a novelist friend, James Baldwin. I had met Baldwin two years before at an *Esquire* party celebrating the monthly magazine's issue of July 1960, a special issue to which we both contributed and was devoted entirely to people and places within New York City.

After that, I often had Baldwin to dinner at my home with my wife, close friends, and sometimes a few colleagues from the *Times*—pleasant occasions for the most part, except for one evening when Baldwin got into an argument with the paper's political correspondent, Tom Wicker, whose expressed white liberal sympathies and suggestions Baldwin dismissed and ridiculed with such ardor that Wicker's wife, Niva, soon left the dinner table in tears, beseeching, "How can you talk to Tom that way?"

In Chicago, before the Patterson-Liston fight, I was surprised to see Baldwin in the elevator of my hotel; and, after he'd explained that he was in town to describe the event for *Nugget* magazine, I convinced him to drive with me to Patterson's camp, stopping along the way to buy a couple of Baldwin's books that I wanted him to inscribe to the fighter.

Following an hour-long ride, during which Baldwin said he'd ceased caring much about boxing ever since the debt-ridden thirty-seven-year-old Joe Louis was knocked out by the twenty-eight-year-old Rocky Marciano in 1951, I parked my rental car on a muddy lot in the woods on a hill near a two-story white clapboard house with green shutters and a goat in the front yard tied to a stake.

This was where Patterson was staying, and behind it were smaller houses of similar design occupied by his sparring partners, a trainer, and a second trainer who doubled as a cook. Patterson was just waking up from a midafternoon nap when we arrived, and here was how Baldwin remembered the occasion and later described it in *Nugget* magazine:

> He greeted Gay, and took sharp, covert notice of me, seeming to decide that if I were with Gay, I was probably all right. We followed him into the gym . . . watched him jump rope, which he must do according to some music in his head, very beautiful and gleaming and far away, like a boy saint helplessly dancing and seen through the steaming windows of a storefront church.
>
> We followed him into the house when the workout was over, and sat in the kitchen and drank tea; he drank chocolate. Gay knew that I was somewhat tense as to how to make contact with Patterson—my own feeling was that he had a tough enough row to hoe, and that everybody should just leave him alone; how would I like it if I was forced to answer inane questions every day concerning the progress of my works?—and told Patterson about some of the things I'd written. But Patterson hadn't heard of me, or read anything of mine.
>
> Gay's explanation, though, caused him to look directly at me, and he said, "I've seen you someplace before. I don't know where, but I know I've seen you.". . . .

Gay suggested that he had seen me on TV. I had hoped that the contact would have turned out to be more personal, like a mutual friend or some activity connected with the Wiltwyck School, but Floyd now remembered the subject of a TV debate he had seen—the race problem, of course—and his face lit up. "I *knew* I'd seen you someplace!" he said, triumphantly, and looked at me for a moment with the same brotherly pride I felt—and feel—for him.

The two of them continued to get along nicely during the remaining half hour of our visit, and near the end I reached for the two bestselling Baldwin books I'd bought—*Another Country* and *Nobody Knows My Name*—and asked the author to inscribe them to the fighter. "For: Floyd Patterson," Baldwin wrote. "Because we both know whence we come, and had some idea of where we're going." In saying goodbye at the door, Patterson not only thanked Baldwin for the books but for expressing the hope that he would emerge the winner in the fight with Sonny Liston.

But on the following day, as Baldwin and I and dozens of others among the working press visited Liston's camp in Aurora, Illinois, about twenty miles south of Patterson's site in Elgin, we were impressed by Liston's superiority in size over Patterson. The 215-pound, 6'1" Liston outweighed the 6' Patterson by more than 20 pounds in addition to possessing an arm reach advantage of 13 inches. After sitting near ringside at Liston's camp watching him pulverize his sparring partners as if they were punching bags, Baldwin and I conceded that Floyd Patterson was probably overmatched.

Indeed, the outcome at Comiskey Park in Chicago turned out to be even more one-sided than we had imagined. Liston knocked Patterson out within a little more than two minutes of the first round, thus becoming the heavyweight champion.

And in their rematch ten months later, in Las Vegas, Patterson did no better; Liston again knocked him out in the first round.

It would seem that Patterson's career was now over and that Liston would be dominant in the heavyweight division for a prolonged period—except in February of 1964, in Miami Beach, Liston, a 7-1 favorite, lost his crown after the sixth round to the faster and surprisingly stronger 6'3" Muhammad Ali; and furthermore Liston failed to regain the title in Lewiston, Maine, in May of 1965, when Ali demolished him in the first round.

Because of this, and perhaps for political reasons as well, Floyd Patterson was able to sign a contract in 1965 challenging Muhammad Ali for the world title in Las Vegas on November 22. Patterson was fortunate in being a contender at a time when the heaviest hitters in the sport were unpopular with most boxing fans. Liston was burdened by his earlier criminal record—two years in jail for larceny and armed robbery—while Ali was openly associated with the Black Muslims and often publicized as unpatriotic, especially after refusing the draft during the war in Vietnam. When compared with these two, Patterson retained a certain box-office appeal by default.

In addition to his moral advantage and the tendency of many people to root for the underdog, Patterson was singled out by writer Norman Mailer as "the first of the black fighters to be considered, then used, as a political force. He was one of the liberal elite, an Eleanor Roosevelt darling, he was political mileage for the NAACP . . . a man of the nicest, quietest, most private good manners."

While Patterson had been ineffective against Liston, and had probably been knocked down more times than any highly ranked heavyweight in history—he went down seven times in a single fight in 1959 while losing his title to Sweden's Ingemar Johansson—it was just as true that Patterson was the all-time heavyweight leader in getting up off the floor. He was climbing to his feet after Johansson had decked him for the final time in 1959, but the referee stopped the fight. In the second Liston fight in 1963, the referee stopped it as the twice-floored Patterson was trying to rise a third time.

So no matter how unqualified Patterson might have seemed to be in the upcoming title fight with Muhammad Ali, he nevertheless was advertised by the promoters as an exemplar of perseverance, a man who never quit and always tried to get up. And among the many boxing fans who still believed in him was Frank Sinatra, an individual who knew firsthand about the possibility of making a big comeback.

Chapter 19

During the time when Sinatra was trying to recover from his cold in Palm Springs, and I was having headaches dealing with Jim Mahoney in Beverly Hills, I did manage to track down Floyd Patterson at the Thunderbird Hotel in Las Vegas, and, with no coaxing on my part, he promised to put in a good word for me with Sinatra.

Although I did not have Sinatra's home number in Palm Springs, Patterson said that he could probably get it from the singer's associate Al Silvani, the ex-trainer who was due to arrive in a day or two to help in the preparation for the Ali fight. Patterson also said that Sinatra himself planned a prefight visit to Patterson's camp and therefore I should be assured that my appeal for an interview would be heard.

I was both relieved and gratified after speaking with Patterson. Having hung around the Beverly Wilshire hotel for more than a week without much hope of getting to Sinatra, I now suddenly felt a shift in the momentum. I was further encouraged that same afternoon when, while trying to contact Sinatra's daughter Nancy, her mother picked up the phone and engaged me in very friendly conversation.

"Yes, I've heard of you and the article you're doing," Nancy Sr. said after I had introduced myself. "My daughter's not here now, but she will be at six o'clock, and if you want to drive over here then you can speak for a little while to the two of us."

"I'd be honored," I said, barely suppressing my enthusiasm. She then offered directions to their residence, at 700 Nines Road in Bel Air, and reminded me to enter via the east gate.

After hanging up, I sat next to the phone in my hotel room for a few minutes, quietly celebrating my luck. I was soon to meet the first Mrs. Sinatra, the petite brunette secretary whom Frank married in 1939 when he was a singing waiter in New Jersey. She would later make all the bowties that he wore with his suits and tuxedos while performing on stage as the heart-throb of the bobby-soxers.

Despite divorcing her to marry Ava Gardner in 1951, Frank and Nancy, along with their three children, maintained a loving relationship through the years, and from my perspective as an interviewer there was no one anywhere who knew Frank longer and better than the woman I was scheduled to meet at six o'clock.

Then the phone rang in my hotel room, and the angry voice on the other end asked: "Didn't I tell you not to talk to Frank's daughter?" It was Mahoney.

"I didn't talk to her," I quickly replied. "I talked to her mother."

"But didn't I warn you not to pull any of this stuff?"

"I don't know what you're talking about," I said. "I talked to her mother, who was very nice to me, and she also invited me over there tonight at six."

"Well, you can forget it."

"What do you mean, 'forget it'?"

"I've canceled it," he said. "She won't see you."

"How dare you!" I shouted. "You're not her publicist! You're working for Frank, not his former wife. You have a hell of a nerve interfering."

"She won't see you," he repeated. "So don't even bother driving over there. The guards at the east gate won't let you in." He then hung up.

Infuriated but not knowing what to do, I sat gazing idly around the room for a while, and then up at the ceiling, wondering if my room might be bugged. How else would Mahoney have known so quickly about my conversation with Mrs. Sinatra? It certainly would not have been difficult in this town, where Sinatra had so much influence and power, for someone on his staff to bribe one of my hotel's maintenance workers to install somewhere in my quarters a tiny listening device.

From that point on I began using the pay phones in the lobby when requesting interviews or communicating with Harold Hayes. Indeed, I had already compiled a list of prospective sources that included some people who might dislike Mahoney, Sinatra, or the people around them—including some people who had perhaps once been part of Sinatra's inner circle but had then been ousted and might be willing to discuss it.

When I began at the *Times*, the staff's most famous member was the Washington-based columnist James Reston, whose recurring advice to fellow journalists was "Talk to the unhappy ones." In creating my own list of unhappy people who might talk about Sinatra, one name near the top of the list was that of Warren Cowan, the publicist whom Sinatra fired before hiring Mahoney.

In calling Cowan's office requesting an appointment—he was a partner in the firm of Rogers & Cowan—I did not initially mention Sinatra but rather introduced myself as a newly hired contract writer for *Esquire* who was interested in discussing Mr. Cowan's longtime experience in the world of entertainment.

Within a day or two I had an appointment, but when I sat in his office and alluded to his relationship with Sinatra, Cowan promptly terminated the interview. "I must tell you that while I'm indeed sorry I no longer represent Mr. Sinatra, I still consider him a very good friend that I hope to regain someday as a client. Before I say anything about him, I prefer to clear it with

him first, and since he is very busy it might take some time."
Mr. Cowan then stood up, thanked me for stopping by, and
from then on was unavailable to me.

This would be my experience as well with others on my
presumed unhappy list. I had heard that the screenwriter, play-
wright, and producer Rod Serling was infuriated with Sinatra
because the latter had tampered with Serling's script for *Assault
on a Queen*, the movie scheduled for release in 1966 starring
Sinatra and the Italian actress Virna Lisi.

"I turned in a good script, but that scrawny little bastard
pissed all over it," Serling told me over the phone, after refusing to see me in person and insisting on not being quoted
by name in my *Esquire* article. He did concede that Sinatra
was a "fine instinctive actor," if not a great one; and that while
few films starring Sinatra were masterpieces, most of them still
made money that enriched the lives of everyone from the studio heads down to the stagehands—which was partly why the
producers and directors deferred to him, allowing him to edit
scripts, shape scenes, and influence the length of a shooting
schedule.

Hollywood executives were generally afraid of him, Serling
went on, knowing that before his comeback many of these
people had cut him down and lived to regret it, and now nobody was making that mistake again. Serling concluded by
reminding me that the entertainment industry was a risky
business in which huge sums were invested in projects that
often failed. And since nobody at the top could confidently
predict what the public would accept or reject, the decision-
makers at the studios shared a collective sense of anxiety
and panic at the prospect of being blamed for a box-office
bust—in which case they might be deprived of indulging in
the luxurious lifestyle to which they had become accustomed
in and around Beverly Hills.

"They have it so good that they don't want to risk anything," said Peter Bart, a friend of mine from the *Times* newsroom who now headed the paper's Los Angeles bureau. "Everybody here is so rich—everybody but reporters and process servers have swimming pools." The privileged world to which he referred I had observed myself during this and earlier visits to Beverly Hills: the magnificent homes erected along palm-lined boulevards; the expansive lawns and private tennis courts; and the abundance of beautiful people like Sally Hanson, often stalled bumper-to-bumper on Wilshire Boulevard while seated in her Silver Cloud Rolls convertible with the top down on a sunny afternoon, who lent a touch of glamor to a traffic jam.

It seemed to me that almost everyone I saw in the Beverly Hills area, men as well as the women, were physically fit and attractive, perhaps being the offspring of people who, generations ago, from all parts of the country, had been voted "Best Looking" in their high school yearbooks and then headed to Hollywood dreaming of making it big in the film business. Although few of them would ever come close to having a successful career in front of a camera, they did pass on their physical attractiveness to their children and grandchildren. Some of these California people with whom I came in contact—waiters and waitresses, car-rental agents, haberdashers, hairstylists, counter clerks in the drugstore of my hotel—were perhaps embodied in a slender and graceful blue-eyed chambermaid who each morning came to clean my room. She told me she was taking acting lessons and enjoyed an acquaintanceship with such full-time residents of the Beverly Wilshire hotel as the actor Warren Beatty and the chairman of the William Morris Agency, Abe Lastfogel.

None of these working people whom I met ever gave me the impression that they were unhappy or unhopeful here.

Maybe, like my chambermaid, they were influenced by their acting lessons or by the ambience of unreality that surrounded them. In any case, with one notable exception, they smiled a lot and seemed to be self-assured and contented even in their servitude.

The exception was represented by the low-paid and frequently stiffed young males who worked through the day and past midnight as valet parking attendants outside some of the city's better restaurants and private clubs. These were the men holding claim tickets who stepped forward to greet, while receiving a minimum of personal acknowledgment from, the newly arrived drivers of expensive cars that in some cases cost more than the attendants earned in two or three years—Bugattis, Ferraris, Daimlers, Rolls-Royces, Bentleys. Many of these cars were custom-fitted with so-called "valet keys," which unlocked the side doors but not the trunks or glove compartments in which valuables might be stored: jewelry, cash, plastic sandwich bags stuffed with cocaine, or other possessions that the owners wished to keep out of the reach of these temporary caretakers of their cars.

Nowhere in Hollywood did the Haves and Have-Nots co-exist in such close proximity as they did along the curbs of valet stands. The concierge at my hotel and another individual who once worked as a valet manager told me that while some nighttime car parkers were students working to help pay for their tuition, the majority were malcontents who were otherwise unemployable and whose sour personalities were further aggravated by the disrespect they commonly received from the rich and privileged people who owned the cars: film moguls, or super agents, or the spoiled grown-up children of movie stars who were similar in age to the parkers but otherwise had little in common with them and not much to say to them as the car keys were transferred and the owners went off to dinner (sometimes with female companions as decorative and stylized as the hood ornaments that adorned the front end of the automobiles) while the valet drivers, before driving these classics toward a nearby garage or parking lot, took a joyride around the block and asserted themselves by adjusting the seat and mirror, revving the engine and blasting the stereo, and then (I'd like to think) sticking their head out the window and yelling aloud to everyone within hearing distance in this tinsel town of pretense and make-believe: "Why not me?"

And again, louder: "Why not me?"

Chapter 20

Having more or less recovered from his cold at his desert retreat in Palm Springs, about 120 miles east of Beverly Hills, Frank Sinatra decided that the taping for the NBC special that he had earlier canceled would be rescheduled for Wednesday, November 17, at the Warner Bros. Studio in Burbank, but I was disappointed to learn that my name would not appear on the guest list.

Jim Mahoney had so informed me two days prior to the event, in a noonday phone call to my hotel room that began:

"Well, Gay, it happened as I expected it would."

"What happened?" I asked.

"Frank said 'no dice.'"

"He said 'no dice' to what?"

"Because you wouldn't live up to the deal, he wouldn't go along with it," Mahoney said.

"There wasn't any deal, except that one you cooked up," I said, referring to his request that Sinatra's lawyer review my manuscript prior to its publication in *Esquire*.

"Well, that's the way it is," Mahoney went on.

"You mean I won't be able to follow Sinatra around, or go with you to the taping in Burbank?"

"No, you won't," he said.

There was silence for a few seconds.

"Okay, Jim," I said finally, "I'll call Harold Hayes and tell him."

"Don't make me look too bad on this," Mahoney said.

"Of course, Jim," I said.

"I mean, explain to Hayes that there was nothing I could do."

"Of course, Jim," I repeated, and hung up.

I then headed down to the lobby to call Hayes, but he was involved in a conference, so I took a seat at the drugstore's counter to order lunch and consider my options. First, I decided that it was pointless to further associate with Mahoney. Since he had nixed my meeting with Mrs. Sinatra, I suspected that he had been involved in canceling other interviews with people who had initially agreed to see me, then offered various excuses to avoid me—among them was Sinatra's double, Johnny Delgado; the toupee lady, Helen Turpin; Sinatra's sidekick, Leo Durocher; the actor Richard Conte, who had appeared in a few of Sinatra's films but said he might be available if I wanted to write about him; and Sinatra's valet de chambre and resident cook, George Jacobs, a handsome and raffish thirty-eight-year-old African American ex-sailor who later worked as a process server in Los Angeles, then as a Rolls-driving chauffeur for the Hollywood talent agent Irving Paul "Swifty" Lazar.

Still, I knew that my predicament was not entirely attributable to Mahoney. He was merely following the orders of Sinatra's attorney, Mickey Rudin, and no doubt the singer himself. I could also understand why my presence now would make these people so uncomfortable and uncooperative. Sinatra was a prideful artist who functioned best when he was entirely in control, and having a prying reporter on the scene was hardly desirable when he was clearly not in control—when he was uncertain about the full use of his voice; when he was presumably being targeted as a Mafia crony on a CBS show to be aired this upcoming Tuesday; when he was starring in *Assault on a Queen*, a film about which he had misgivings; when he was now required to rise above his ailments, doubts, and distractions and guarantee a knockout performance in Burbank this Wednesday at the taping of the NBC special "Frank Sinatra: A Man and His Music."

Under such stressful and demanding circumstances, how many other achieving and artistic individuals would make themselves available to reporters? Would Ella Fitzgerald? Would Elvis Presley? Pavarotti? Picasso? Such people, in my opinion, would be no more available than Sinatra. I also recalled James Baldwin's comment after we had attended some of the promoter-arranged Patterson-Liston daily press conferences prior to their fight in Chicago: How would I like it if I were forced to answer inane questions every day concerning the progress of my work?

Indeed, Mahoney and I were not adversaries, but rather men caught in the middle. He had to answer to Sinatra, and I to answer to Harold Hayes, a tough ex-marine who had ordered me uphill to do battle with a recalcitrant superstar. In this situation I likened myself to Herman Melville's subordinate scrivener, whose "I would prefer not to" pleadings were overwhelmed by the determination of my boss at *Esquire* to have it his way—to push me to capitalize on Sinatra's fame and satisfy magazine readers with a cover story that would send newsstand sales soaring.

Not for the first time did I remind myself that I was no longer the freewheeling, independent-minded young bachelor reporter I had once been, but now a married man with family obligations that demanded I make the best of my situation. Fortunately, while seated at the drugstore counter, I met two strangers at a booth nearby who offered to help me.

I had overheard them talking about Sinatra and their past experiences working with him. One was a casting director, Mike McLean, and the other was an actor, James Brolin.

Both were in their midtwenties and shared an apartment in Los Angeles, and, after I walked over to introduce myself, they invited me to sit with them and join their conversation. Brolin was particularly illuminating because the year before in Europe he had spent several weeks around Sinatra while the latter was starring in the World War II adventure film *Von Ryan's Express*.

Sinatra portrayed Colonel Joseph Ryan, a U.S. P-38 pilot who is shot down in Nazi-occupied Italy, ends up in a POW camp with several Allied soldiers—Brolin played Private Ames—and then conceives their escape. The film was directed by Mark Robson, but, according to Brolin, Sinatra was frequently infuriated by the slow pace of the filming and once showed his displeasure by grabbing a machine gun and firing a whole round of blanks in the air. On another occasion, after the progress had again been stalled due to what Sinatra interpreted as excessive pondering by the director, the singer left the movie set, which was located in the outskirts of Rome, hopped into his helicopter, and landed on the rooftop of the RCA building in that city to record a few songs in the studio.

It was never boring being around Sinatra, Brolin continued, adding that he agreed that directors tended to take more time than necessary to shoot scenes and cared little when actors were expected to be on the set at six in the morning and then stand around for hours waiting for the cameras to roll. In movies featuring Sinatra, the cast arrived for work not much earlier than noon at his insistence, and after work he frequently took them out to dinner, followed by late-night parties.

When the film work on *Von Ryan's Express* shifted northward from the Rome area to Cortina d'Ampezzo in the Italian Alps, and the production company took over part of the Cristallo Hotel—where the tennis courts' nets and supportive poles were removed in order to create an unobstructed landing space for Sinatra's helicopter—he hosted a birthday celebration for a cast member one night that got out of hand. People drank excessively, spritzed one another with bursts of champagne, tossed creampuffs around the room, bumped into lamps and knocked over vases, creating such damage that Sinatra on the following day, in order to make amends for their fun and frolic, slipped the hotel manager a thick roll of hundred-dollar bills, amounting to about $1,500 in cash. Brolin quoted Sinatra as saying, "It was worth it."

But despite such nocturnal escapades, Brolin emphasized that everyone worked together smoothly on the film day after day, and, thanks to Sinatra's influence, the shooting schedule was reduced from eight weeks to five. When *Von Ryan's Express* was released in June of 1965, it was a box-office triumph, earning more than $17 million on a budget of $5.76 million.

Before I left the drugstore, James Brolin recommended that I look up a few other actors and agents who had been involved with the film—among them the publicist, Martin Fink, and a thirty-four-year-old character actor of Armenian-Canadian ancestry named Richard Bakalyan, who had been cast as a corporal in *Von Ryan's Express* and had earlier appeared in two other films with Sinatra, playing a gangster in the comedy *Robin and the 7 Hoods* and a rugged marine vet in *None but the Brave*.

I reached Bakalyan first, and he agreed to meet me for breakfast on the following day at the drugstore. On this particular evening, I was scheduled to dine at the restaurant owned by the bodyguard Ed Pucci, the only individual within Sinatra's circle who was friendly to me—no doubt because he was hoping that I could get *Esquire*'s "Dining Out" columnist to plug his restaurant, which was located in Encino, in the San Fernando Valley region, about fifteen miles from Beverly Hills.

Greeting me at the door with an exuberant 250-pound bear hug, Pucci proceeded to escort me around a large and crowded dining room, with a booming piano player in the back and an unctuous maître d'hotel in the front named Fred Farouk, whom Pucci introduced as "King Farouk." The first thing Farouk told me was that his favorite magazine was *Esquire*. After I had remarked on the beautiful jeweled wristwatch he was wearing, he said that it was a present from Pucci. When I turned to Pucci and asked why he had presented Farouk with such an impressive gift, he responded: "Because he minds his own business."

As we sat down to dinner, we were joined by another guest whom Pucci had invited to sit next to me—a perky and heavily perfumed brunette in a red cocktail dress who, before the first course, had slipped me her phone number and volunteered to show me around town whenever I had free time. I had no proof, of course, but it occurred to me that she might have been part of Pucci's ploy to put me in a compromising position for his benefit—or Sinatra's benefit. Prudently, I never called her, although I did later relay Pucci's desire for publicity to the editor of *Esquire*'s food column. The editor was not interested.

The next morning, Richard Bakalyan, an intense, rough-hewn, dark-haired individual with a resemblance to fellow actors John Garfield and Peter Falk, arrived for breakfast at the drugstore and, perhaps because of his falling-out with Sinatra earlier this year, was quite candid.

He said that he first got to know Sinatra in 1963 during the shooting of *None but the Brave*, a World War II film in which sixteen Japanese soldiers stranded on a Pacific island are eventually joined by nineteen Americans who survive the crash of their transport plane after it was shot down by a Japanese pilot.

Sinatra not only directed the film but also starred as a conscience-stricken medic who decides to treat a gravely wounded, doomed-to-die Japanese officer; and while Bakalyan had only a small role as a corporal, he nevertheless closely observed the film-making progress every day and once was brash enough to offer advice to Sinatra. It seemed to Bakalyan that a scene shot in Hawaii did not match well enough with a connecting scene shot at the Warner Bros. Studio in Los Angeles; and, in the presence of other actors during a break in the action, he pointed this out to Sinatra.

"Frank went cold with anger," Bakalyan recalled, "and he nastily asked me: 'What are you, a fucking cutter?' Then he looked at the other people standing around, including the executive producer Howard Koch, and said sarcastically: 'Fucking actors are cutters now.'

"Nobody said anything, but I could see they were scared, especially Koch, who was always intimidated by Sinatra. I just threw up my hands and walked away, and from then Sinatra snubbed me. Then a couple of days later, Sinatra came over and said: 'I want to talk to you before you leave today,' and I thought: 'Oh shit, I'm either going to be fired or get cut out of the film.' I remember it was a Friday afternoon, and when Sinatra is on a film he always gives a party at the end of the work week, on Fridays, not only for the actors but the entire technical crew. He orders in food and all kinds of drinks and usually is a gracious host. So as the party is beginning, I walk over and say, 'You want to see me, Frank?' and he says, 'Yeah, get a drink and come back.' And when I do he says, 'I want you to get in touch with your agent and say you're not going to work as an actor anymore.' 'What?' I say, and he says: 'You're going to become my assistant.'"

Bakalyan did not know whether or not his forthrightness had belatedly gained Sinatra's respect. "Frank never says 'I'm wrong,' or 'I'm sorry,'" Bakalyan explained, "but he shows it in other ways." For Bakalyan, it was shown in his sudden change of status on the set, the deference exhibited by the cast and technical crew, and by his gradual admission into Sinatra's circle of friends and associates, which included Brad Dexter,

Leo Durocher, the valet George Jacobs, Mahoney, Pucci, and others.

Sinatra also made it clear that after the completion of *None but the Brave* and two subsequent movies—*Von Ryan's Express* and *Assault on a Queen*—Bakalyan would assume full-time duties as his assistant in the following year's film *Marriage on the Rocks*, a comedy starring Sinatra along with Deborah Kerr and Dean Martin; but meanwhile Bakalyan was to familiarize himself with Sinatra's way of working by accompanying him to Italy for *Von Ryan's Express* and, in addition to playing Corporal Giannini, he was encouraged to share with Sinatra any suggestions about the film's progress.

Prior to a preproduction flight to Italy for *Von Ryan's Express*, Bakalyan joined Sinatra's retinue for a weekend's visit to New York, staying in the singer's penthouse apartment near the East River in the 70s. He also had access to the always-crowded table in the back room of the West 52nd Street saloon owned by Sinatra's itinerant bosom buddy Jilly Rizzo, where he met the singer's East Coast publicist, Henry Geni, and Jilly's azure-haired wife, Honey, who, within this circle, was sometimes referred to affectionately as the "Blue Jew."

Later in Rome, Bakalyan stayed with Sinatra and others at a villa outside the city, but on certain nights they would come to eat and drink at one of the sidewalk cafes along the Via Veneto, being inevitably swarmed by the paparazzi. And since Ed Pucci worked only in California, Bakalyan felt inclined at times to assume the role of Sinatra's bodyguard, not only protecting him from the paparazzi but also aggressive women who wanted pictures taken with their arms around him.

Sinatra especially liked having Bakalyan close to him in Rome as he sought extra privacy during visits from his ex-wife whom he still loved—Ava Gardner, then working in southern Italy under the direction of John Huston in *The Bible*. One day a photographer in Rome approached Bakalyan and said he would pay $15,000 if Sinatra would pose with Ava Gardner. Bakalyan relayed the message, and Sinatra made a counteroffer of $30,000 to break one of the photographer's legs.

Once the scenes of *Von Ryan's Express* in Italy were finished, Sinatra sponsored a celebratory cruise through the Mediterranean on a 210-foot rented yacht on which he hosted not only members of the cast but some Hollywood friends vacationing in Europe.

Sinatra then sailed to Monaco to visit Grace Kelly, followed by a flight to Spain (with Bakalyan on board) to relax for a few days in Madrid. While there, after Bakalyan learned that his girlfriend in Los Angeles was slightly ill, Sinatra made the production company's telephone available so that Bakalyan could remain in regular contact with her; and after Sinatra learned that she liked owning items decorated with animals, he had a beautiful jeweled animal pin delivered to her.

At the end of 1964 Bakalyan returned to Los Angeles with Sinatra and the film crew to begin shooting some interior scenes of *Von Ryan's Express*, and during the holiday season he and his girlfriend were invited to attend Sinatra's large Christmas gathering at Chasen's restaurant.

But at the start of the new year and extending through February into March, Bakalyan gradually became aware of a cooling off in his relationship with Sinatra. He was no longer receiving frequent calls from Sinatra or anyone else in the singer's office. At first he reasoned that Sinatra was just a much busier man in California than he had been in Europe; or that Sinatra was now burdened with responsibilities remote from the film business, namely his recordings and a concert tour that took him beyond the West Coast; or perhaps there were such personal matters as his grief in February over the death of his forty-five-year-old friend Nat King Cole, due to throat cancer; or maybe Sinatra was distracted by his on-and-off relationship with the twenty-year-old Mia Farrow.

Whatever it was, Bakalyan decided that perhaps Brad Dexter might enlighten him, and, later in a phone call, Dexter did.

"We hear you've been putting Frank down," Dexter began.

Bakalyan was momentarily speechless, shocked; this was absolutely untrue.

"This is high school shit, Brad," he then responded, "and you know it."

"I don't know it," Dexter said. "I'm only telling you what I heard."

"Where'd you hear it?"

"Can't say, but word gets around." Dexter then hung up.

Bakalyan soon thought that Dexter himself might be involved, trying to poison Bakalyan's close relationship with Sinatra because Dexter was jealous or somehow felt threatened professionally.

Bakalyan next called the office of Jack Donohue, the director who was currently finishing *Assault on a Queen* while his next film, *Marriage on the Rocks*, was the one in which Bakalyan was to be Sinatra's assistant; but he learned from one of Donohue's aides that *Marriage on the Rocks* was being held up due to union problems and other issues. A day later, Bakalyan received a phone call from Sinatra's lawyer, Mickey Rudin, who asked, "Are you looking for a settlement?"

"No," Bakalyan answered, "I'm not looking for money. I'm just trying to find out what's going on. And I can't reach Frank."

"He's away," Rudin said, "but I'll let him know you're trying to reach him."

Weeks passed, and still no word from Sinatra. It was now near the end of March, and he had not seen Sinatra since the Christmas party. On March 25, he wrote a letter to Sinatra, slipping it under the door of his Los Angeles residence, which said: "If somebody is shooting me down, I'd like to know who they are." Some days later, Sinatra telephoned him from an undisclosed location overseas and said in effect: "Don't worry. Everything will be worked out. I'll deal with it when I get back to LA in a week or so."

Two weeks passed. Nothing was happening. Bakalyan was making no money, and he was eager to ask Frank directly: Am I going to be your assistant or not? Using a private telephone number that he had been reluctant to use before, being aware of Frank's irregular sleeping hours and unpredictable nature, he called several times but all went unanswered until, finally, the valet, George Jacobs, picked up one afternoon and said Frank was sleeping but would return the call. He did not. Instead, someone from director Jack Donohue's office telephoned, asking Bakalyan if he would like working under Donohue as the dialogue director on *Assault on a Queen*. This was not what Sinatra had promised him, so Bakalyan turned it down.

A day later, Brad Dexter telephoned. "You sure you don't want the dialogue director's job?"

"Stick it, Brad," Bakalyan said, slamming down the phone.

And that was the end of it. From then on—from sometime in April of 1965 to the morning I was having breakfast with him in the Beverly Wilshire drugstore on this Tuesday, November 16—Bakalyan had lost all contact with Sinatra's team and still had no idea what had caused the rupture.

Was it possible that he had inadvertently said something somewhere to someone that had been misinterpreted as a criticism of Sinatra and it had been brought to the attention of Brad Dexter? Bakalyan doubted it, but could he be entirely sure? Bakalyan also conceded to me the possibility that, after Sinatra had offered the job of assistant, and the intimate access that accompanied it, Bakalyan had perhaps taken it all for granted and been negligent in reinforcing his bond with Sinatra. No matter how busy Sinatra was, or perhaps because of it, Bakalyan should have known that he had to be very aggressive in remaining what he called "tight" with Sinatra, and thus less vulnerable to the singer's gate-keepers who had apparently exiled him.

"If you want a friendship to last with Frank Sinatra," Bakalyan conceded to me, "I guess you have to be there every minute."

Just as he was saying this, I heard my name being announced on the drugstore's loudspeaker. A call from my hotel room had been relayed to the cashier's desk, and I was invited to respond to it there. Excusing myself from Bakalyan, I left the table and took the receiver from the cashier.

I heard Mahoney's voice on the other end: "What are you doing?"

"Nothing," I said, trying to sound casual, although caught off-guard.

"What are you up to?"

"Nothing much, Jim," I went on.

"Why don't you come over?"

"I can't now," I said, "but I can come over this afternoon."

"I won't be here then. I'll only be here for an hour or so."

"Sorry, Jim, I'm all tied up now, but I'll check with you later tomorrow."

As I hung up, I quickly looked around at the crowds of people seated at the soda fountain or at the white leather booths, and I wondered: Am I being watched? Did Mahoney have a spy in here tracking my whereabouts?

After hurriedly paying the check at the cashier's counter, I returned to Bakalyan and said, "I can't explain it now, but let's get out of here." Moments later, in the lobby, without sharing my suspicions about Mahoney, I asked Bakalyan if I could meet him later in the day somewhere outside the hotel. He said that he and his girlfriend were staying home that night, but that I could join them there and watch the CBS broadcast in which Walter Cronkite would be interviewing Sinatra. I gladly accepted, and, after writing down Bakalyan's address and escorting him to a taxi, I headed toward one of the telephone booths in the lobby to contact Harold Hayes.

"Oh, don't worry," he said, after I speculated about being followed. "I already sent a special-express letter that should shake-up Mahoney. There's probably a copy already waiting for you at your hotel desk. Go get it and read it."

November 16, 1965
Mr. Jim Mahoney
120 El Camino
Beverly Hills, California

Dear Mr. Mahoney:

I am most distressed by the manner in which you have operated in processing our request for an interview with Frank Sinatra, and I really don't think I ought to let your actions go by unrecorded and without complaint . . .

I have just received confirmation from Talese that our request for time with Mr. Sinatra has been denied. And that, further, Talese is not to be allowed on the set of the film that Mr. Sinatra is preparing and that, by implication, he is not to expect cooperation in preparing a story from any person close to, or sympathetic with, Mr. Sinatra.

As I told you earlier, it was our intention—and still is—to prepare a favorable story on Mr. Sinatra. We will now proceed on this story without your cooperation, and presumably without Mr. Sinatra's, since I can only assume from what you have told Talese over the last few days that, somehow, this

*contretemps is all our making, and that you are damned sore
that we've put you in such a position with your boss, and by
extension, he's sore too.*

*Let me assure you that I'm not sore, but I do feel I've
gained some insight into the way the ball bounces at Jim
Mahoney Associates . . . Sincerely, Harold Hayes, Editor.*

— —

cc: Mr. Robert Stein, Editor, McCalls
Mr. William Emerson, Editor, Saturday Evening Post
Mr. Don Schanche, Editor, Holiday
Mr. Sey Chassler, Editor, Redbook
Mr. Frank Sinatra

My first reaction to the letter was that it was unnecessarily
harsh with regard to Jim Mahoney's agency. Instead of lim-
iting the issue to *Esquire* and Sinatra, Hayes the leatherneck
had widened the conflict by recruiting his high-level editorial
friends from other magazines to ally themselves with his cause
and perhaps create a kind of embargo that might not only negatively affect the future coverage of Frank Sinatra in five magazines but also that of many other performers that Mahoney
and his assistants also represented—a list that included Liza
Minnelli, Yul Brynner, Debbie Reynolds, Glenn Ford, Bob
Newhart, and others whose framed photographs I had seen
hanging on Mahoney's office walls during my visit.

If what Hayes had in mind was to teach Mahoney a lesson,
that was one thing; but if he wanted to cripple his entire business,
then my sympathies were with Mahoney, together with his five
dependent children and his youthful smiling wife whose photo
I had seen on his desk. On the other hand, Hayes's letter made
it very clear that he was determined to get a story on Sinatra
in *Esquire*; and although Mahoney had recently disinvited me
to the NBC taping of "Frank Sinatra: A Man and His Music,"

which was to take place in Burbank on the next afternoon, I decided I would go anyway. I felt I had to. I had to get this piece behind me. I had to get Hayes off my back. I had already been in LA for more than two weeks, had rung up huge expenses, and so far had little to show for it. Yes, I repeated to myself, on the following day I had to get into my midsized Avis rental car, drive to Burbank, crash the party, and see how far I could get.

Chapter 21

During the forty-minute drive toward the Burbank studio, although I was never tempted to turn back, I did experience some anxiety about how I would be greeted. What would Mahoney do when he saw me there? Would the bodyguard Pucci still be friendly? Suppose I found myself face-to-face with Sinatra: What would I say to him?

At the same time, I thought I was being overly dramatic. Ever since arriving in Los Angeles I had perhaps acquired an exaggerated sense of reality because everything about Sinatra tended to be exaggerated—his power, his sexual appeal, his loneliness, his extravagance, his generosity, his vengeance, his quasi-membership in the Mafia.

I had been thinking about this during the previous evening when I was with Richard Bakalyan and his girlfriend Dolores, watching CBS's Walter Cronkite interviewing Sinatra at the singer's home in Palm Springs: a program that had been billed as an apocalyptic event, the inquisition of a crime-connected crooner, a scandalous exposé of his private life so damaging that his lawyer, Mickey Rudin, had threatened to sue CBS in advance of the broadcast—which of course prompted news coverage that heightened the controversy and foretold higher TV ratings for the network.

But the show itself was a letdown, a mellow evening during which the avuncular Cronkite sat across from the dark-suited dapper Sinatra and asked a series of softball questions that were accompanied by several film clips showing the singer on stage, at recording sessions, and at social gatherings mingling amiably with his closest friends and members of his family. A critic at the Associated Press described the program as a "nice little pussycat of a show," while Kay Gardella of the *New York Daily News* wrote that Cronkite's tough questions "were edited down to appease the temperamental star." The *New York Times* critic Jack Gould commented that the Sinatra show "wasn't authorized but it could have been."

In other words, the program was yet another example of Sinatra hype, bombast, an extravaganza that had existed for decades, ever since the skinny bowtied ballyhooed balladeer had first appeared before organized throngs of screaming bobby-soxers at the Paramount Theatre in Times Square in the 1940s; and it was perhaps with an inflated sense of significance that I was now contemplating conflict attached to my visit to the studio in Burbank.

Was I exaggerating the relevance of my arrival there? With all that Sinatra had on his mind, would he recognize me or even notice me if I were standing in front of him? And, moreover, what right did Mahoney have in banning me from this taping? It was being produced under the auspices of NBC, not Sinatra Enterprises. If he tried to block my entrance I could readily complain to NBC's publicity department, or even to the show's director, Dwight Hemion, who, though I never mentioned it to Mahoney, was a New York friend of mine. We lived in the same neighborhood, and we met regularly at an Italian family-style restaurant on Lexington near 61st Street called Gino's, an old-fashioned first-come-first-served place that did not accept credit cards, would not hire waiters wearing earrings, and was distinguished for its tomato-red wallpaper decorated with leaping zebras dodging flying arrows.

But on second thought, despite our being co-patrons of Gino's, I knew that Hemion's meal ticket was Sinatra. Still, what could Sinatra do to me? Have Pucci push me around?

Offer someone $30,000 to break one of my legs? Start a scene with me as he did with Harlan Ellison in the pool room at the Daisy?

No, I again reminded myself as I pulled into the studio's parking lot, I was being ridiculous. It was also raining heavily and I did not have an umbrella. So after slamming the car door, I ran across the lot and soon joined dozens of people who were squeezing through the entranceway without being stopped by security guards. To my surprise, there was absolutely nobody on duty there checking names or credentials, and so I kept moving ahead with all the others, many of whom I assumed were Warner Bros. employees or Budweiser sales reps and their families, until I got to within about thirty feet of the bandstand, and there I stopped.

Ahead of me I saw a smiling Frank Sinatra standing within a circle of associates and well-wishers shaking hands, embracing, and loudly engaged in cheerful conversation about the Cronkite interview the night before.

"Oh, it was a gas," I heard Sinatra say, as I paused behind the backs of two people I recognized, Brad Dexter and Leo Durocher.

"It was the greatest, Frank," Dexter said.

"You know what Jilly said after the show?" Sinatra continued. "He sent me a wire saying: 'We Rule the World.' Golden words from a drunken saloonkeeper."

"Absolutely right, Frank," someone else said, although I wasn't sure who said it. Around us were Sinatra's valet, George Jacobs; his makeup man, Layne Britton; his toupee lady, Helen Turpin; his bandleader and arranger, Nelson Riddle; the composer Gordon Jenkins; and the singer Andy Williams, without his wife, Claudine. In the near distance, heading our way, were Pucci followed by Mahoney.

"They had so much more they could have used," Sinatra went on, still referring to the Cronkite broadcast. "Did you see Jack Gould's column in the *Times* this morning? He was right. There should have been more on the man, not so much on the music."

"I agree," Durocher said.

Then the bandleader, Nelson Riddle, took Sinatra by the arm and pulled him in the direction of the stage, saying, "Frank, we're about ready." But before he left, Sinatra reached out to shake a few more hands and, noticing me behind Dexter, extended a hand in my direction. I had no idea whether or not he knew who I was, but I reached out to him and said: "I also liked the CBS show last night, Mr. Sinatra. Congratulations." He smiled and repeated: "They could have gotten more about the man."

"Well, that's why I'm here," I quickly interjected. "I've been trying to get to you, but so far no luck."

He looked at me directly and pleasantly, and, as Riddle pulled him away, he said almost apologetically: "I've been so busy." And then he added, very softly—so softly that I might have heard what I wanted to hear rather than what he said or intended: "Maybe something can be worked out."

After he left, I stood there momentarily in silence and yet aware that Pucci and Mahoney were near me and had witnessed my brief exchange with their boss; and I could sense, at least in the case of Mahoney, who shook my hand, that my status had risen. Mahoney, who days before had been so disobliging, was now very cordial.

"I'll call you tomorrow," he said, "and we can talk." Perhaps he had received Hayes's letter. But it did not matter.

"Of course," I said. "We'll talk tomorrow."

Then he waved, turned, and walked away, followed by the amicable Pucci, whom I had not yet told that *Esquire*'s "Dining Out" editor had decided against publicizing his restaurant. As the two of them ambled off to rejoin their clique currently gathered in front of the bandstand, I remained where I was, pondering my situation.

Was I now free to remain in this studio, surrounded by a few hundred people, waiting for the taping to begin? Was I at least temporarily liberated from my minder, Mahoney? A few days prior he had quoted Sinatra as saying "no dice" to my being here, and yet here I was, and nobody was threatening to eject me.

And so, though at first keeping my distance from Sinatra's circle of intimates, I spent the next two hours wandering more or less at will, and the NBC taping that I observed that afternoon was entirely different from the one I had witnessed here more than a week before. Sinatra's voice was now fully recovered from his cold, and, from the first song through the seventeen that followed, his beautiful baritone flawlessly intoned every word in such a way that the listener believed that whatever the lyricist wrote had emerged from the heart and soul of Sinatra's wide-ranging and deeply experienced life.

Even when his singing was interrupted by a musician's mistake or by a technical mishap, he remained gracious and imperturbable. As he was getting through "When We Were Young" a camera on wheels knocked over a white plastic tree that stood near the microphone. Sinatra stopped singing and casually turned around to face the orchestra.

"Hold it," he said. "We've had a slight accident." As the petrified cameraman apologized, Sinatra only shrugged. "Not to worry," he said. "We can start over."

If this collision had occurred during the first taping, when an ailing Sinatra was off key, the cameraman's clumsiness would have been dealt with in a less forgiving manner, I believe. But on this day—with Sinatra's voice in splendid form, and with him no longer concerned about what Cronkite's interview might do to his career—the prevailing atmosphere in the studio was blitheful, sanguine, and entirely devoid of the tension that had existed here nine days earlier—for example, between Sinatra and Dwight Hemion.

After Sinatra had on this occasion satisfactorily rehearsed "The Girl Next Door" and Hemion wanted to film it, he called down from the booth: "Okay, Frank, should we try one?"

Sinatra replied cheerfully: "I'm with you, Dwight." Having sung six songs wonderfully, and about to start the seventh, Sinatra glanced up at Hemion and asked: "How about something warm after this? How about some toddy for the body?"

As the orchestra cheered in the background, Hemion responded: "You got it, Frank." And so after the seventh song there was a forty-minute refreshment break during which the caterers served light snacks and drinks on the tables placed outside Sinatra's dressing room.

As I slowly joined the gathering, I heard Sinatra talking to Durocher and others about the forthcoming fight in Las Vegas between Floyd Patterson and Muhammad Ali. Although the latter in 1964 had disavowed his "slave name" (Cassius Clay) in favor of the one chosen for him by his spiritual leader, Elijah Muhammad, Sinatra and his friends, and even some members of the press and Floyd Patterson as well, were still slow in accepting the Muslim name.

"Floyd's got the equipment," I heard Sinatra say.

"Yeah, but Clay's got the reach," replied Durocher.

"But I'll tell you," Sinatra went on, "if Clay does against Floyd what he did against Liston—moving back, lowering his hands, and leaving his head open—Floyd will hit him sixty times. Floyd has the fastest hands . . ."

"Hope you're right, Frank," said Brad Dexter.

Then somebody in the rear called to Dexter, saying that the comedian George Jessel, who had previously appeared with Sinatra at a club date, was trying to reach the singer.

"Oh, don't worry about Jessel," Dexter said. "He wears a toupee . . ."

"And so does some Italian singer I know," the other person answered, someone I could not identify. But Sinatra only laughed, then he lifted a bottle of bourbon, poured a shot into a plastic cup, and gulped it down. "Toddy for the body," he repeated. His dulcet voice was sometimes referred to within his circle as "bourbon baritone."

After he had changed clothes for another set of songs, Sinatra returned to the platform and the program continued smoothly and swiftly. If at times he had to stop, it again did not seem to irritate him, as when, after missing a beat while singing— "When I was twenty-one, it was a very good year . . ."—he offhandedly said to the composer Gordon Jenkins, "We got some sand in there, let's start over." At the conclusion of his final song—"Put Your Dreams Away (For Another Day)"—he spun around from behind the microphone, pointed to Gordon Jenkins, and exclaimed, "Beautiful, Gordie." Then he invited his cronies up to the control room to see a replay of the program on the monitor.

Between twenty and thirty people gradually made their way up the steps to assemble behind where Hemion and his staff sat, to be joined quickly by Sinatra. Since no one objected, and since I felt invisible, I joined the procession and soon found myself squeezed into the third row of standees behind one of the show's writers, Sheldon Keller.

Across the way, standing in the second row right behind Sinatra and Hemion and concentrating on the monitor, were Durocher, Mahoney, Andy Williams, and Brad Dexter, who was always the first to applaud after each completed song. "Great, Frank, just great," Dexter kept saying. After hearing about a dozen songs, he said in a loud voice: "Frank, this is going to be the greatest show I've ever seen."

Sinatra then turned around and said, lightly, "Shut up, Brad."

This did not discourage Dexter, however, nor did Sinatra really seem to mind the continuous flow of adulation from his followers. He himself was clearly pleased and impressed, and near the end of the show, resplendent in his tuxedo, he leaned closer to Hemion and said: "If people still like music, I think this show will do."

After the final song, "Put Your Dreams Away," everyone returned to the tables outside Sinatra's dressing room to resume the party. Mahoney then approached Sinatra holding a small piece of paper, explaining that the CBS producer Don Hewitt wanted to reach him.

"Isn't Hewitt the guy who caused this whole mess-up?" Sinatra asked, having heard that Hewitt had been pushing Cronkite to add Mafia questions to the program.

"Yes, he's the guy," Mahoney said. "How should I answer him?"

Sinatra replied: "Can you send a fist through the mail?"

Chapter 22

In Mahoney's office on the following day, where I was greeted in the same friendly fashion as I had been in Burbank, he asked if I was interested in accompanying him to the Patterson-Ali fight, adding that he could also arrange a prefight interview for me with the veteran boxing trainer in Patterson's corner, Al Silvani, who had long been on Sinatra's payroll doing odd jobs and most recently served as a production assistant on the singer's film-in-progress, *Assault on a Queen*.

I was more than surprised by Mahoney's offer because, suspecting that the phone in my hotel room was tapped, I deduced that he knew of my private calls to Patterson (who had already set aside a ticket for me); and now perhaps Mahoney was trying to enlist me as a traveling companion so that he could keep an eye on me in Las Vegas to make sure that I did not aggressively pursue Sinatra as I might if I were on my own.

Still, I saw no reason to refuse Mahoney because being with him probably meant that I would at least be on the fringe of Sinatra's circle. And so, as suggested, we flew together to Las Vegas on Monday morning, November 22, and, after taking a taxi to the Sands Hotel and Casino, where we would be staying, we were met in the lobby by the casino's boss, a genial giant named Jack Entratter, a dark-haired, smartly dressed fifty-year-old who stood 6'4" and weighed 250 pounds and who in the 1940s had already gained popularity as a well-mannered back-slapping bouncer at the Stork Club in New York.

Mahoney had told me on the plane that Jack Entratter and Sinatra had been friends since the early 1950s, which was when Entratter had shifted from his position as manager of the Copacabana nightclub in New York to helping to introduce the Sands Hotel and Casino in Las Vegas. Having already become acquainted with many leading entertainers during his time at the Copacabana, and using his diplomatic skills to draw backing from investors, including some investors with gangland connections, Entratter soon established the Sands as the city's most luxurious casino, made millions for himself, and stood alone in featuring such top-flight entertainers as Sinatra and the latter's Rat Pack companions, like Dean Martin, Joey Bishop, and Sammy Davis Jr.

Two of these would be performing with Sinatra tonight on stage at the Sands after the fight, Mahoney had said, adding that Entratter would get me a ticket to the show, which he promptly did. Entratter proved to be even more accommodating than Mahoney had described. After checking us into our suites, confirming our luncheon reservation in the dining room with the trainer Al Silvani, and taking us to his office to get our fight tickets, Entratter then sat talking with me alone for about ten minutes while Mahoney was elsewhere, I assume checking in with Sinatra, who had arrived the night before in his private plane. When in Las Vegas, Sinatra always stayed at the Sands.

"Frank and I are about the same age, and I'm also wealthy and successful," Entratter began. "I own houses here and there, and I could afford a Learjet if I wanted one. Since my dear wife's passing four years ago, I am alone and free to do as I wish. And I wish I could live like Frank Sinatra. But I can't."

He paused, then repeated, "I wish I could. But I can't, because I really don't know how to live. I'm like a lot of fifty-year-old guys who in our early days knew excitement and adventure. But then, in spite of doing well, our lives have evened out and gone

flat. In my case, it's probably because I'm inwardly conservative."
He explained that he was religious, having served in Las Vegas
as the congregational president of Temple Beth Sholom, and he
also said that he did not gamble, smoke, or drink. He admitted
to having a girlfriend, Lari Laine, but did not mention that she
had been a cover girl on such magazines as *Playboy*.

"Lari is a lovely person," he said, "but I do not think I could
ever marry her. Somehow it would be against the teachings I've
given to my two daughters. I don't know. I'm caught up. I
feel trapped. But when I'm in Frank's company, everything
suddenly changes. He is exciting to be around. He lives every
moment. He refuses to grow old. He has great talent, yes, but
also knows how to have fun. That's how it is with so many of
us who hang around Frank. He sets an example of how to live
and have fun. It's infectious. He lives our lives for us."

Mahoney then returned to Entratter's office, and, after saying our farewells, we headed toward the dining room through
the gambling area, where only Sinatra's recorded music echoed
through the sound system. Along the way we passed a writer
friend who waved at me from one of the slot machines.

"Isn't that Norman Mailer?" Mahoney asked, pausing to
get a longer look.

"That's him," I said. "Mailer's a fight buff. I see him at all
the big fights."

"Is he rich?"

"I don't know how rich he is," I said. "He's a bestselling
writer, so I assume he does okay."

"Well, why does he wear such sloppy shoes that are practi-
cally falling off his feet? Why doesn't he dress better?" Mahoney
was, as usual, neatly attired, wearing an expensive pair of buck-
led leather slip-on shoes, a white striped shirt with a maroon
tie, and a cashmere blazer sprouting an orange paisley pocket

square. I believe all were purchased at Sinatra's favorite men's shop in Beverly Hills, Carroll & Co.

"You want to send Mailer to Frank Sinatra's haberdasher?" I asked, forcing a smile. "That would be ridiculous. Mailer isn't into wearing fine clothes like you and Mr. Sinatra."

Mahoney said nothing as we got closer to the dining area, but I was thinking that, clothes aside, Mailer and Sinatra actually had much in common. Both had enormous egos, both were prodigiously productive, both had achieved fame and success at an early age, and both spent the rest of their lives trying to retain it.

Norman Mailer's celebrated first novel, *The Naked and the Dead*, was published in 1948 when he was only twenty-five, and, like Sinatra, Mailer also had an early interest in directing and acting in films and engaging in politics and social activism. He and Sinatra were drinking men, prizefight aficionados who had also taken boxing lessons, and both were known for having physical encounters with confrontational men while at the same time craving the presence of admiring women. The forty-two-year-old Norman Mailer, whose current wife was an actress named Beverly Bentley, had so far been married four times.

In the dining room, after Mahoney had introduced me to Al Silvani, I shook hands, sat down, and wished him the best of luck in helping Patterson tonight. Silvani had been enlisted by Sinatra to serve in Patterson's corner after the latter's longtime trainer, Dan Florio, had died a month earlier.

"I think Patterson can win," said Silvani, a broad-shouldered, muscular, gray-haired man in his midfifties. Silvani, among others, had given Sinatra boxing lessons in the early 1940s and since then had divided his time between training top-ranked professional fighters—among them Jake LaMotta, Henry Armstrong, Carmen Basilio, and Rocky Graziano—and assisting Sinatra in film production and playing bit parts in movies.

"If I didn't think Patterson had a good chance of beating Clay," Silvani continued, "I would not have left the Bahamas, where Johnny Delgado and I were doing some water scenes for *Assault on a Queen*, and come all the way over here to Vegas just to pick somebody off the floor. I traveled nearly three thousand miles to get here, and so I repeat: I came because I think Patterson can win."

He then removed from his jacket pocket a white index card on which were notes printed in pencil, and, after handing it to me, he said: "Here, read this. Here's my advice telling Patterson what, and what not, to do in the fight tonight."

On the card were four succinctly expressed statements, and as I read them aloud to Silvani and Mahoney, seated across from me, Silvani listened while nodding with his eyes closed.

1. Always hands up. Weave body side to side. Follow Clay, but if he dances backward, don't run after him.

2. Never wing punches from distance. Get in close. Forget his head. Direct right cross / left hook to Clay's body.

3. Never hold in a clinch. Rip short right uppercuts. Follow with elbow aiming at his chin. Be mean. No pals.

4. By weaving side to side you avoid Clay's left jabs. Don't talk to him. He'll talk to you, but don't answer. At weigh-in, and the referee's instructions before the bell, ignore Clay. Just look directly at his chest.

I returned the card to Silvani with thanks while believing that nothing written on it would save Patterson from defeat, much as I wished otherwise. Whether one referred to him as "Cassius Clay" or "Muhammad Ali," Patterson's opponent was a bigger, taller, harder-hitting, and more talented heavy-weight, who had twice destroyed Liston, who had twice destroyed Patterson, and there was no way I could imagine Patterson ending up a winner tonight. Still, Al Silvani was a very experienced and respected individual in the boxing world, so I kept my thoughts to myself, even while wondering if Silvani might have been touting Patterson highly because Sinatra had taken a liking to the fighter and was betting on him.

I also felt somewhat awkward about having this luncheon with Silvani, which I had not sought; it had been Mahoney's idea—probably an attempt on his part to show Hayes that he was cooperating with me. Mahoney had never acknowledged receiving Hayes's condemning letter of a week before, but I was inclined to believe that he had both read it and felt threatened by it, and therefore he was now, for the first time, getting me to meet someone who was close to Frank Sinatra. Mahoney would not, or could not, get me a one-on-one interview with the great man himself, but he was nevertheless hoping that trading downward might produce positive results with Hayes. Knowing Hayes as I did, I thought it unlikely.

Hours later, close to fight time, I met Mahoney in the Sands lobby and we shared a ride to the Las Vegas Convention Center one mile away. In the car Mahoney was quite talkative, but I paid little attention. I was very worried that my longtime friend Floyd Patterson—who was thirty years old, had undergone nearly fifty professional fights, and had been knocked down several times since the early 1950s—would become seriously injured tonight while facing the ferocious and fleet-footed twenty-three-year-old Muhammad Ali in the prime of his career.

At a news conference earlier in the day, which I had watched on television just before leaving my hotel room, I noticed that Patterson had ignored Silvani's instructions by getting testy with Ali at the weigh-in, persistently calling him "Cassius

Clay" and promising to reclaim the heavyweight title from the "Black Muslim" and "return the crown to America," the inference being that the Louisville-born Ali was a foreigner because of his spiritual affiliation with the Nation of Islam and that it was Patterson's "patriotic duty" to overcome him. Ali responded by calling Patterson an "Uncle Tom" and predicting that once the bout began Patterson would be running around the ring like a "scared rabbit."

Sadly for Patterson's supporters, this is pretty much what happened. Before losing by a technical knockout in the twelfth round, the six-foot, 196-pound Patterson seemed to be absolutely helpless against a foe who outweighed him by nearly fifteen pounds, was three inches taller, and had an eight-inch reach advantage that penetrated Patterson's defenses at will; at the same time, Ali was too elusive to ever allow Patterson to get close enough to score a significant retaliatory blow.

Mahoney and I were not sitting together. I sat two rows behind him while he was in the second row with some of Sinatra's crowd, overlooking the front row where Sinatra sat at ringside flanked by Jilly Rizzo and Dean Martin, accompanied by Joey Bishop, Jack Entratter, and the latter's girlfriend, Lari Laine.

In the fourth row with me were a number of magazine writers and authors who were devotees of prizefighting. In addition to Norman Mailer, there was the novelist Budd Schulberg, who also wrote the Oscar-winning screenplay for *On the Waterfront*; and George Plimpton, the tall and patrician Harvard-educated editor of the *Paris Review* who was also an amateur sportsman known for competing with professional athletes and then writing wittily about his experiences.

In one of his books—*Out of My League*, published in 1961—Plimpton described pitching batting practice to Major League stars in an exhibition game. On an earlier occasion, in 1959, at Stillman's Gymnasium on 54th Street and Eighth Avenue in Manhattan, he sparred a few rounds against the African American light heavyweight champion Archie Moore, who was gentlemanly enough to limit Plimpton's punishment to breaking part of the cartilage in his nose, causing it to bleed. This led the trumpeter Miles Davis to ask afterward, "Archie, is that black blood or white blood on your gloves?" to which one of Plimpton's friends replied, "Sir, *that* is blue blood."

Throughout the Patterson-Ali fight, which went on longer than most of the writers had expected but whose outcome was never in doubt, it was generally agreed that Ali could have easily knocked out Patterson in an early round but instead preferred to toy with him, shaming and peppering his ears with insults— "Come on, America!"—and frustrating him by dancing menacingly and merrily around the ring while putting on a show that the boxing reporter for the *New York Times* compared to watching someone "pulling the wings off a butterfly."

In the eleventh round, with Patterson fatigued from unleashing several wild long-distance punches that ignored Silvani's instructions, he injured his back and could no longer maintain his position properly. Between rounds, Silvani tried lifting him from behind in an attempt to untangle the muscle knots, but he did not succeed. Later in the twelfth round, with Patterson hardly able to defend himself at all, the referee stopped the fight and declared Ali the winner by technical knockout.

As the triumphant Ali boasted aloud into the microphone of the ring announcer, and as Patterson's handlers wiped his battered brow and lifted a robe around his shoulders, I watched the solemn figure of Frank Sinatra leaving ringside and walking slowly toward the exit, being trailed by his friends. I guessed that they were headed back to the Sands, where Sinatra was soon scheduled to appear on stage with Joey Bishop and Dean Martin.

Mahoney was also with them, but I did not follow because I preferred attending the postfight news conference in Patterson's dressing room, joining members of the working press and others such as myself who were regular guests of the promoter's publicist. Standing in the back of the room next to Plimpton and Patterson's pilot, Ted Hanson, who would fly the fighter back to New York that night, I listened for several minutes while the reporters up front were questioning Patterson about his back problems.

"No excuse for losing this fight," Patterson responded, seated on a training table with a towel around his head. He admitted that his opponent (still called "Clay") was clearly the better boxer and was in a class by himself among the world's professional heavyweights.

With a doctor on one side of him, and his manager, Cus D'Amato, and Al Silvani on the other, Patterson continued to answer questions patiently, but he spoke so softly at times that it was difficult for me to hear him. Near the end of interview, however, I thought I heard my name being called aloud. I paid no attention. Then I heard it again, this time more clearly.

"Is Gay Talese here?" It was the voice of Floyd Patterson.

The reporters up front all turned around and stared, and then Plimpton, after regarding me quizzically, nudged me on the shoulder and said: "He's talking to you."

I straightened up, raised my right arm, and called loudly, "I'm back here, Floyd."

"Did you ever have a chance to get to Frank Sinatra?" he asked.

I was too surprised to answer, so he repeated: "Did you ever have a chance to get to Frank Sinatra?"

It was such an absurd and unexpected question coming from this uncommon prizefighter who had within the hour been humiliated in full view of a worldwide TV audience, his career in boxing perhaps ended, and *yet* here he was remembering a request I'd recently made for his help on my annoying magazine assignment!

How could one explain Floyd Patterson? How did his mind work? Maybe the famous Durocher quote applied here: "Nice Guys Finish Last"—surely within the brutal world of boxing. I had written more than thirty articles about Patterson through the years, but I remained mystified.

Nevertheless he was still looking at me, waiting for a reply. So I gave it to him.

"Thank you very much, Floyd, and, yes, I did get to Frank Sinatra," I lied.

Chapter 23

Usually at a distance, although sometimes close enough to eavesdrop, I followed Frank Sinatra at midnight after the fight into the dawn of the next day.

I began as part of the audience in the Sands's lounge watching his routine with Dean Martin and Joey Bishop, and then I took a taxi to pursue him and his friends to the Sahara, where, for more than an hour, they sat at a crowded table in the club room drinking and bantering, while at the same time Sinatra was being roasted in friendly fashion on stage by his pal the comedian Don Rickles. Finally, at close to four in the morning, he left the Sahara and headed back to the Sands with his retinue in tow, some of them carrying their glasses of whiskey with them, sipping along the sidewalk and in the cars, all of them dwelling casually and cheerfully in their chosen time zones.

Sinatra was apparently hungry, and so at the Sands he headed toward the dining room and sat at a large table in the corner that had been reserved for him and his guests. In front of the table, for added privacy, was a white wooden trellis that I saw as my line of demarcation, a spot beyond which I should not trespass; and so I sat alone at a small table close by, surrounded by dozens of other dining gamblers and tourists, and adjoining the casino floor that was vibrant with spinning roulette wheels and clamorous crapshooters.

With my beer and hamburger in front of me, and while reviewing the notes I had scribbled earlier on my trimmed slices of shirtboard, I noticed that Jim Mahoney was greeting me with a wave from Sinatra's table. I waved back with a smile, guessing correctly that our exchange was not meant as an invitation to join him and the others. They included Dean Martin, Joey Bishop, and Jilly Rizzo; Jack Entratter with his girlfriend, Lari Laine; Leo Durocher with a date named Betty; Harold Gibbons, a high-ranking official with the Teamsters union; and a few more I could not identify.

Actually, I did not mind sitting alone. At least I was being permitted to follow Sinatra and his people around Las Vegas, as I had done the previous week at the NBC taping in Burbank. And while there had been no clear concession on the part of Sinatra or his representatives, we seemed to have reached a kind of detente: As long as I did not bother Sinatra, Sinatra would not bother me. I remembered being told by the actor Richard Bakalyan, whom Sinatra had initially ridiculed and then cultivated: "Frank never says 'I'm wrong' or 'I'm sorry,' but he shows it in other ways." Maybe this explained why I was presently allowed to walk in the shadow of the man who had earlier tried to banish me with his pronouncement: "No dice." Or maybe Hayes's threatening letter was now a factor in my favor. I would never know.

Except for the few words exchanged with Sinatra a week before at the NBC taping, after I had complimented him on his CBS interview with Cronkite, we had not spoken. He also said not a word to me during our time in Las Vegas, nor did he even look at me directly; and yet, again, he appeared not to mind my presence in the crowd that regularly encircled him, such as when he briefly left the dining room to play blackjack and I was able to observe and overhear his exchange with the dealer.

In the notes later typed in my room at the Sands before going to bed at sometime after five—I was now living Sinatra hours—here is what I wrote:

. . . resting his shot glass on the blackjack table, facing the dealer, Sinatra stood a bit back from the table, not leaning against it. He reached under his tuxedo jacket into his trouser pocket and came up with a thick but clean wad of bills. Gently he peeled off a $100 bill and placed it on the green-felt table. The dealer dealt him two cards. Sinatra called for a third card, overbid, lost the hundred.

Without a change of expression, Sinatra put down a second $100 bill. He lost that. Then he put down a third and lost that. Then he placed two $100 bills on the table and lost those. Finally, putting his sixth $100 bill on the table, and losing it, Sinatra moved away from the table, nodding to the man, and announcing, 'Good dealer.'

The crowd that had gathered around him now opened up to let him through. But a woman stepped in front of him, handing him a piece of paper to autograph. He signed it and then he said, 'Thank you.'

Continuing, I also described Sinatra and his people having dinner:

The table was about the same size as the one reserved for Sinatra whenever he is at Jilly's in New York; and the people seated around this table in Las Vegas were many of the same people who are often seen with Sinatra at Jilly's or at a restaurant in California, or in Italy, or in New Jersey, or wherever Sinatra happens to be. When Sinatra sits to dine, his trusted friends are close; and no matter where he is, no matter how elegant the place may be, there is something of the neighborhood showing because Sinatra, no matter how far he has come, is still something of the boy from the neighborhood—only now he can take his neighborhood with him.

A few days after returning to Los Angeles I drove to the Paramount movie set and, while standing on the sidelines behind several stagehands and extras in the cast, I watched Frank Sinatra and his Italian co-star Virna Lisi, working together on *Assault on a Queen.* Sinatra was playing a deep-sea diver hired by some nefarious adventurers engaged in a failed attempt to hijack the *Queen Mary* during a transatlantic crossing. In the scene I saw, Sinatra and Ms. Lisi were adrift in a pool of thrashing water, struggling to climb into a flimsy float—a maneuver that the director, Jack Donohue, had to reshoot a few times because Ms. Lisi seemed to have difficulty remembering her lines or pronouncing them properly.

Ordinarily, Sinatra might have shown signs of irritation due to the delays, but on this occasion he was uncharacteristically patient and did all he could to comfort Ms. Lisi.

In fact, he was lighthearted and charming to everyone on the set throughout the afternoon, no doubt still basking in the afterglow of the rave reviews received earlier in the day from his performance in "Frank Sinatra: A Man and His Music," the hour-long special that NBC had broadcast the night before. Only after the director seemed to be unduly deliberative about inviting Sinatra and Ms. Lisi out of the water did the singer mildly complain to Donohue and the camera crew: "Let's move it, fellows. It's cold in this water, and I've just gotten over a cold."

An hour later, having changed into dry clothes, Sinatra was standing outside his dressing room accepting congratulations for the NBC show from some of his friends, a group that included the actor Richard Conte, who portrayed a nautical mechanic in *Assault on a Queen*; and the comedian Steve Rossi, who, with his partner, Marty Allen, formed the Allen & Rossi comedy team, which was currently very popular on television and in nightclubs.

At one point, since I was standing behind Rossi, I drew Sinatra's attention, and so I stepped forward to convey my own admiration for the NBC show. Sinatra smiled and conceded that the program had been excellent, adding, "I'm not that easily pleased." I then expressed the hope that we might have some private time together before I returned to New York. I had already spent three weeks in Los Angeles.

"Oh, I've been so busy," Sinatra said. Then, before turning toward his dressing room, he paused to suggest, "Maybe something can be arranged after I get back from Palm Springs on Monday." Monday was only four days away, but I had doubts that a private one-on-one meeting with Frank Sinatra would ever happen. He had offered the same excuse about being busy during our brief exchange earlier in Burbank. I also recalled a comment made to me during a recent chat with a Warner Bros. photographer named Dave Sutton:

"In order to get to Sinatra the way you want, you have to be a friend. And if you're going to be his friend, you'll find you can't write about him."

After returning to my hotel from the Paramount movie lot, I updated Harold Hayes in a note I mailed on the following day:

Friday, November 26, 1965:

Dear Harold:

Yesterday I saw Frank Sinatra very briefly. He did not have time to talk—he never seems to have time . . . but perhaps we're making progress . . . I may not get the piece we'd hoped for—the Real Frank Sinatra—but perhaps, by not getting it, and by getting rejected constantly and by seeing his flunkies protecting his flanks, we will be getting close to the truth about the man.

When Frank Sinatra returned to Los Angeles on Monday afternoon to complete his final scenes for *Assault on a Queen*, I joined a hundred others on the sidelines of the Paramount studio, a gathering that included Jim Mahoney, Brad Dexter, Ed Pucci, Mickey Rudin, Al Silvani, the singer's daughter Nancy, plus such celebrated fans of Sinatra as the 6'6" Don Drysdale, the star pitcher for the Los Angeles Dodgers, and one of the nation's leading professional golfers, Francis "Bo" Wininger.

Wininger had told me that although Sinatra did not spend much time on the course, he was capable of scoring in the low 80s, while Nancy Sinatra added that her father shied away from golf "because playing it took too long." I had become personally acquainted with Nancy during our lunch a few days earlier, on Friday, being surprised and pleased that she accepted my invitation and even more surprised and pleased that Mahoney had not canceled it in advance, as he had done previously.

Mahoney also did not interfere with a meeting I arranged a day later with Brad Dexter, who invited me to join him at Sinatra Enterprises, where he served as the vice president, and, since his boss was out of town, Dexter took the liberty of occupying Sinatra's large office—a glass-partitioned space of modern design festooned with bamboo palms and fig trees and dominated by a large tapered wooden desk shaped like the wings of an airplane. Behind it was a black leather chair with an orange-colored cushion into which Dexter made himself comfortable for the duration of our interview.

As I sat across from him, he lamented that whatever fame he possessed was largely attributable to his having saved Sinatra's life after the latter had partaken in a leisurely swim and got caught in a riptide in Hawaii. Sinatra had gone there in

1964 to direct and star in *None but the Brave*, a World War II movie in which Dexter played a tenacious marine sergeant. All modesty aside, he cited it as one among dozens of outstanding roles he performed during his twenty-year career as a talented if unheralded actor.

Indeed, shortly after we began talking, he suggested that if my planned article about Frank Sinatra did not work out, I might consider doing an *Esquire* profile on him.

Chapter 24

In my meetings with the twenty-five-year-old Nancy Sinatra, she proved to be as forthcoming as her father was evasive. Not only did she answer all my questions but she added information that I had not requested, such as how she felt about her father's affair with the actress Mia Farrow, who was five years younger than herself.

"Mia and I have been guests at the same time in my father's house in Palm Springs, and we get along very well," Nancy said during our Friday lunch at the Paramount cafeteria. "My father has his private life, and I have mine, but he knows he can be himself with me. He knows that we can double date and it doesn't upset me. He has no reason to feel guilty. He is not married. He's a single man, and yet a good family man."

Although he divorced her mother for Ava Gardner in 1951 after more than ten years of marriage, he never left his family, Nancy pointed out; he created a loving and lifelong bond with his three children as well as a respectful and caring relationship with their mother, who never changed the locks after he left, nor did she limit visitation rights in an attempt to regulate his prerogatives as a parent.

When Ava Gardner divorced her father in 1957—Nancy was then seventeen—she hoped that her parents might remarry. Her father, however, explained that her mother "could not live his life anymore," but this did not diminish their continuing closeness as a couple, which was exemplified by the fact that her mother was overseeing Frank Sinatra's forthcoming fiftieth birthday party at the Beverly Wilshire hotel.

Nancy said that she grew up "searching for a bit of her father in every eligible young man she met" but conceded it was difficult because he was a "perfectionist" with a strong personality, as well as being sensitive, intuitive, and introspective.

"He can completely take over a party, or he can be very quiet and listen and watch—and the entire mood of the party will change according to his behavior," she said, adding: "In most ways he's just like everybody else, but people don't see it that way. They think that when they're home watching television he's out swinging somewhere. They forget that he likes to sit home and watch television too. I remember once being with him for two weeks and he didn't have a woman the whole time. He also has qualities that most women would admire in any man, no matter what his last name might be—the way he dresses, that he always smells good, that he's always on time, that he is very attentive, orderly, and remembers everything. Mention a book you'd like to read, and it is in the mail the next day. When you're his guest in Palm Springs, you don't have to bring a thing. Everything is there for you. There are clothes you can wear, the bathrooms are stocked with every drugstore item you can imagine, and, before you head back home, your car is washed and filled with gas."

She paused and continued: "He is fastidious and wants to know everything. When he does a television show, he knows what's involved—the commercials, the lighting, the sound, the camera angles and blocking. He could probably do everything himself. Same with airplanes—he knows them inside and out. When he buys a car, it is not like other people buy a car. He knows everything about it. If he is going to tend bar, he knows about every kind of drink you can think of. He doesn't do anything half assed. He has a helicopter, and he doesn't have a license, but he knows how to fly a helicopter."

In addition to our long lunch at the Paramount cafeteria, Nancy Sinatra met with me briefly on two other occasions during the weekend, and on Monday she invited me to the United Western Studios in Hollywood to hear her sing a folk-rock song that would soon sell more than a million records and soar to the top of the Billboard Hot 100 chart. Written and produced by Lee Hazlewood, it was called "These Boots Are Made for Walkin'."

This would prove to be the high point of her career, the first time that she was a star soloist instead of singing, acting, or otherwise appearing with her father or Elvis Presley or some other famous performer, or being a supporting actress in several movies. I could sense her satisfaction as we left the recording studio, and I also felt that she was fast becoming accustomed to being on her own in the aftermath of her recent divorce from the singer-actor Tommy Sands. She was now living alone in a new home in Beverly Hills that was furnished and decorated entirely to her own taste, and perhaps the fact that she was fully cooperating with me—doing what her father and so many of his followers had resisted doing—testified to her budding spirit of independence.

I wondered, but did not ask, if her father knew that she was spending time with me. I assumed that he did, being so aware and conscientious, but maybe she herself decided (with her father and Mahoney later concurring) that it was a good idea for her to cooperate with *Esquire*'s writer in the hope of appeasing to some degree the magazine's disgruntled editor, Harold Hayes. Or maybe she was making herself available to me because, like Brad Dexter, she believed that she might herself be the candidate for a full-length profile in *Esquire*.

But none of this really mattered to me because, after nearly a month of stress and disappointment while in Los Angeles, I was finally enjoying my work and was pleased not only to have attended Nancy Sinatra's recording session but on the same day to accompany her, in her sporty green Ford Mustang, to the movie lot at Paramount to watch her father's final scene in *Assault on a Queen*.

There she knew nearly all the cast members and spectators on the set, introducing me to some of them, and while I was at her side I felt more credentialed and less an intruder. Perhaps this is why, after the director Jack Donohue had called a break in the action, and I noticed Frank Sinatra sitting alone in a canvas chair chatting with a cameraman, I had the confidence to take the initiative and approach him. When I had last seen him four days before, prior to his departure to Palm Springs for the weekend, he suggested that he might speak to me when he returned; and since I was tired of waiting, I thought it was now or never.

"Excuse me, Mr. Sinatra," I began, kneeling in front of him. He turned away from the cameraman and smiled as I went on: "I'm hoping that we can finally schedule an interview once you're done with this film."

"I'm sorry," he said quickly, "but I just don't have the time. When I finish here today, and a recording tonight, I'm getting on a plane and going to Mexico. I want to get away, I need to get away." He paused before continuing: "It's all been too much. It's reached a saturation point. When I was younger I was always aware of saturating the market, and now that's what happened."

"I understand," I said—and I did understand. What he was saying I myself had been saying a month before to Harold Hayes in my failed attempt to avoid this assignment. All year long there had been a nationwide overdose of publicity about

Frank Sinatra as he approached his fiftieth birthday, and now he was overwhelmed by it, and I was also. On this very day *Look* magazine was on the newsstands with yet another cover story, and from it I learned nothing that I had not already read in other magazines or newspapers or had heard during television or radio interviews.

When the director Donohue came over and interrupted us, saying that filming was about to resume, Sinatra quickly got up to shake hands, say goodbye, and walk away. I would never speak to him again. I was disappointed by the suddenness of his departure but also resigned to the fact that my quest for his attention was finally over. I had done my best to reach out to him and now there was no reason to delay my return to New York.

In my typed notes I had enough material for the *Esquire* article, nearly all of it drawn from my observations along the sidelines, or from my interviews with those who associated with Sinatra in the film or record business, or who worked for his company or him personally, or who accompanied him socially during his off-hours—in other words: friends, relatives, retainers, hangers-on, and various other relatively obscure individuals who, as I have repeatedly said, have always been my main sources for information and insights.

With very few exceptions, none of these individuals would have been considered newsworthy by an obituary editor were it not for their connections to Sinatra, and yet collectively they helped me write about him without my relating to him personally. On reflection, however, this was not entirely true because, in another context, I had been relating to him personally since my boyhood, and this is what I wish I had mentioned to him before he said goodbye.

As an Italian American who grew up in South Jersey listening to him on the radio and reading about him in the press during the 1940s, I was inspired by his life, by the way he lived it, and by the way other people responded to it. He was admired by most of my female classmates in high school as well as the matrons who patronized my mother's dress shop in my white-bread Protestant-dominated hometown of Ocean City, an island resort about twelve miles south of Atlantic City.

In the movies he romanced beautiful actresses in light comedies, co-starred in musicals along with Duke Ellington, Count Basie, and Tommy Dorsey's band, and, in an era when most Italian names in the news referred to Mafia members, he avoided gangster roles and instead presented himself as a lawful leading man, a repudiator of racism and anti-Semitism, and always an engaging performer who was generous and patriotic: dancing in a sailor suit with Gene Kelly in *Anchors Aweigh*, presenting flowers to a swooning scullery maid in *Higher and Higher*, or preaching tolerance to a gang of bigoted boys in *The House I Live In*.

In this last film he spoke about being a descendant of Italian immigrants, tracing his origins, as I did, back to the underprivileged masses of alien opportunists who, after existing for a time near the bottom of the social pecking order in America, gradually improved their lives through their own initiative, the flexibility and growth of the New World's economy, and no doubt a bit of luck.

Among the immigrants who arrived on American shores a century or more ago were people with such names as DiMaggio, Cuomo, Scalia, Iacocca, Coppola, Giamatti, DeLillo, Stella, Scorsese, De Niro, Pelosi and Germanotta (the latter being the ancestors of Lady Gaga)—but it is likely true that none of the progeny of these traveling Italians surpassed the worldwide fame and long-lasting popularity of the singing grandson of a shoemaker from Sicily named Francesco Sinatra.

Francesco Sinatra, born in 1857 in a sulphur-mining town about thirty miles southeast of Palermo where child labor was the norm, arrived alone in America in the late 1890s. After working in a pencil factory because there were then in New York too many shoemakers from Italy, he finally saved enough money to arrange for his wife and their four children to join him in 1903.

Among them was his nine-year-old son and the future father of Frank Sinatra: Antonio Martino Sinatra, who as a teenager would work as a boilermaker on the dry docks of North Jersey and then take up prizefighting under the name "Marty O'Brien," in deference to boxing's many Irish fans and promoters as well as to the fact that in those days the foreign names and customs of Italians stigmatized such newcomers as Antonio and rendered them unmarketable on the billboards of even this low-caste and barbaric sport.

The prejudice against Italians in America would continue for decades, as I myself can attest from the insults—"Dago," "Wop," "Guinea"—that I regularly received from some of the young Irish bullies who were classmates in parochial school. The wartime 1940s were a particularly troubling time for me. Not only was Italy then affiliated with Nazi Germany but two of my Italian-born father's younger brothers, my uncles Nicola and Domenico, who had chosen not to emigrate to America, were now serving as infantrymen in Mussolini's army opposing the Allied invasion of their ancestral area of Calabria, a mountainous region situated within the toe of Italy's boot-shaped peninsula, separated by a narrow strait from the eastern tip of Sicily. My uncles' military involvement would promptly prove to be a losing cause and result in their battlefield injuries and then their surrender and confinement to a British POW camp in North Africa.

On a chest of drawers in our living quarters, across from the radio where I would listen to Frank Sinatra singing on Saturday nights, were framed photos of my uncles taken earlier in the war, showing them smiling while wearing their uniforms adorned with unfamiliar epaulets; and late at night, following the news of their imprisonment, I would often overhear my father praying for their survival and well-being; and at Sunday Mass I would watch as he approached the altar to light votive candles with no doubt his captured brothers in mind.

But otherwise, while conversing with customers in his tailor shop, or having lunch across the street at the corner cafe, my father, Joseph Francesco Talese, was outspokenly pro-American; and once in a speech at the local Rotary Club he declared that were he younger he would proudly serve in the United States Army and participate in the destruction of his native country.

His remarks made the front page in our weekly *Ocean City Sentinel-Ledger*, accompanied by a photo of my smartly attired father; but though his sentiments were very well received they were not surprising because he had long been highly regarded within this flag-waving Republican community as a loyal and compatible token American, which was attributable at least in part to his tailoring talent in cutting and shaping any form to fit.

It also helped that he had been a citizen of the United States since 1928, and a resident of Ocean City since 1922, having traveled alone two years earlier at age seventeen from his Calabrian village, after the premature death of his father, to help support his widowed mother and siblings while advancing his craft as an apprentice tailor under the temporary tutelage of an older debonair cousin in Paris, Antonio Cristiani, who had first arrived there in 1911 and now operated a successful men's shop on the Rue de la Paix.

Seven months later, in the spring of 1921, my father continued his journey to America from the port of Cherbourg in northern France to Ellis Island in New York Harbor, settling first in Philadelphia—where he found work in a department store altering and measuring suits and trousers—and a year later obtained a bank loan to take over a small vacant tailor shop in Ocean City, about sixty miles southeast of Philadelphia, a popular summer resort for many of the prominent families of that city.

Many men from such families, plus the local gentry who set standards for the island's year-round population of three thousand, became in time my father's customers, being impressed with his workmanship and later as well with his slender and attractive fashion-conscious partner, my mother, who had previously sold dresses in Brooklyn's leading department store, Abraham & Straus. After meeting my father at an Italian wedding in that borough, and marrying him months later in the early summer of 1929, she and my father bought a larger building on the main street of Ocean City and expanded the tailoring enterprise to include a boutique catering to the island's leading ladies.

Like practitioners of journalism, who regularly associate with influential and noteworthy individuals, merchants of fashion who devote themselves to selling fine suits and dresses to the prominent are engaged in careers offering social-climbing possibilities. Certainly in my parents' case this applied, as evidenced by their success in first befriending their decorous clientele and eventually being invited by them to bridge parties and membership at the country club across the bay, where, removed from the dry law that reigned in Ocean City, liquor was available.

But whatever elevated status had been bestowed upon my parents by their patrons, it brought me no relief from the sons of the working-class Irish who berated me almost daily and sometimes tossed dirt at my custom-made clothing in the schoolyard during recess.

Throughout my preteen years I sensed myself as fractionized, native born but feeling foreign, a juvenile minority member in a land where Italian names were associated with fascists abroad and gangsters at home, and not even the prewar presence of the fan favorite Joe DiMaggio was much help. DiMaggio was a solitary man, an introverted self-centered superstar who communicated through his bat and did not socialize even with his Yankee teammates.

However, much had changed by the time I entered high school in 1945: The war over, the Allied armies were triumphant, Mussolini was dead, my POW uncles were released, and the fabulously famous young Frank Sinatra, thanks to his talent and his outward-reaching public persona that touched both minority groups and the mainstream, had emerged as the first fully assimilated United States citizen of Italian origin—one who also paved the way for people like me to finally feel at home in America.

I mentioned this to Nancy Sinatra during my final conversation with her in Los Angeles. She said she understood my wanting to send a farewell note to her father, and after she promised to relay it to him, I wrote:

Saturday, December 4, 1965

Dear Mr. Sinatra:

This afternoon I called to say goodbye to your lovely and gentle daughter Nancy, and in the course of our talk I expressed disappointment at not having gotten close to you in the month I spent here. If I had been allowed to share your informal company, I told Nancy, if I had been permitted to travel with you and your friends and to gain glimpses into the warmth of your inner world, there is no doubt that I would have produced a classic profile on you, one that would have fulfilled all the unfulfilled promises of the television documentaries and magazine articles of the past.

Like yourself, I want all the advantages when I work. Regrettably I had few of them this past month—there was your illness, your incredibly busy schedule, and other things that kept me a distant observer. Even so, I hope to do justice to you in this Esquire profile, to present an exciting portrait of Sinatra the Man and the effect you have on your friends, your enemies, your era.

I came as a friend. I leave as one. I took you very seriously as a living force before I met you, and now I take you even more seriously. May the very best continue to happen—I wish you the luck to match your matchless talent.

—Gay Talese

Chapter 25

I never received a reply to my Sinatra letter, nor did I ever learn from him, or Nancy, or anyone else who might know, what he later thought of my *Esquire* article, if indeed he even read it.

Published in the April 1966 issue and titled "Frank Sinatra Has a Cold," it began with when I first saw him in Los Angeles: him sitting between two blondes on a lonely night at the bar of the Daisy, smoking a cigarette, sipping bourbon, and on the verge of taunting Harlan Ellison in the pool room. It ended more tranquilly with a description of Sinatra sitting pleasantly behind the steering wheel of his Ghia coupe, driving alone on a sunny day in Beverly Hills as the traffic light is about to change:

> Frank Sinatra stopped his car. The light was red. Pedestrians passed quickly across his windshield but, as usual, one did not. It was a girl in her twenties. She remained at the curb staring at him. Through the corner of his left eye he could see her, and he knew, because it happens almost every day, that she was thinking, It looks like him, but is it?
>
> Just before the light turned green, Sinatra turned toward her, looked directly into her eyes waiting for the reaction he knew would come. It came and he smiled. She smiled and he was gone.

This street scene was related to me not only by some of the involved young women "pedestrians" whom I met during my research, but Sinatra himself corroborated it in conversations he had with such intimates as his daughter Nancy. The rest of my fourteen-thousand-word article, which covered fifty-three manuscript pages, was drawn from my observing Sinatra on the movie set, in the recording studio, during his trip to Las Vegas, and from my personal comments and complaints that I scribbled daily with a ballpoint pen on the slices of shirtboard that fit into my jacket pocket and accompanied me everywhere.

I later reviewed these working notes, eliminated what I no longer considered relevant, and, in an attempt to bring some aesthetic flair to this boring process, I used multi-colored Sharpie fine-point pens to reprint the rest of my selected material across two uncut 14 x 8 inch pieces of cardboard, producing a rather flamboyant graphic chart that served as my outline—one that presented, in summary form and with directional arrows, a scene-by-scene word picture of the entire piece along with references to some of the frustrations I experienced while researching and writing it.

One day shortly after I had finished the article but two months before it appeared in print, I was in *Esquire*'s office cooperating with the fact-checkers when someone from the promotion department, apparently charmed by the outline that I had brought along, insisted that it be photographed and later printed in the front section of the April issue, near the index and editor's page, as a gimmick calling attention to my Sinatra article that followed.

Unfortunately, the person from promotion and the fact-checkers failed to carefully read all of my tiny handwritten words that appeared in various places within the graphic chart—words in which I complained about the Sinatra assignment or referred very disrespectfully to the magazine's editor:

> I did not want to fly out here. But the magazine "Esquire" had for years wanted a cover story on Sinatra—and I was unable to talk Harold Hayes out of it. I did not fully trust him . . . and if I failed, he would not be interested in my foolish excuse about F.S.'s cold—Fuck Hayes . . .

When the article came out, and after Hayes had praised it and treated me to dinner at an expensive restaurant, I kept waiting to hear his sour response to my scribble on the chart. I also expected that he would surely fire the promotion person and fact-checkers who had carelessly allowed my rude comments to get into print. But in fact nothing happened. If Hayes had scrutinized the chart and had read what I wrote, he failed to mention it to me, and I certainly did not bring it to his attention. I was also unaware if anyone on the staff had read it, nor was there any reaction from *Esquire*'s letter-writing readers—all of which led me to conclude that either I had gotten away with what I done, or that Hayes and his underlings had decided to overlook it because no good would come from having seen it.

Still, as I noted on the chart, I did not fully trust Hayes, and it occurred to me that he was not only aware of it, but at some future time he would remind me of it and use it against me. He was known among *Esquire*'s contributing writers as one whose compliments were transitory, and doing him a favor was no guarantee of lasting gratitude.

Three years before, in 1962, after Hayes had rejected James Baldwin's article on Harlem nightlife because it was not compatible with Tom Keogh's illustrations that had already been sent to the engraving plant, and it was too late to replace them with anything else—and after Baldwin had refused to alter what he had written—Hayes telephoned me at home late on a Thursday evening desperately seeking my help.

He wanted me to take a look at the photocopies of the illustrations, which he would have hand-delivered in the morning, and then I should give thought to producing about three thousand words that would fuse with Keogh's artwork. Hayes further suggested that I register for the weekend at the Hotel Theresa in Harlem, visit the neighborhood's hot spots, interview some of the owners and patrons, and then on Monday morning deliver a printable piece in time to meet the issue's closing date later that day.

Somehow, after an almost sleepless weekend, and with some advice and contacts provided by a Black friend and fellow *New York Times* reporter, I managed to do what Hayes had requested. And after he had thanked me profusely for it—and headlined it "Harlem for Fun"—it appeared with Keogh's sketches in the September issue.

While I was not entirely pleased with the smoothness of my prose, I was comforted in knowing that, given the circumstances, I had at least met the challenge. But a few months later, after I sought a per-article pay increase, Hayes conceded that while I had made several valuable contributions to the magazine, not all of my efforts were exceptional, and he mentioned in particular "Harlem for Fun." I said nothing, but it was the last time I would ever allow him to rush my writing.

I took five weeks to write the Sinatra piece, and, while Hayes requested to see samples along the way, I showed him nothing until I had completed the entire work to my satisfaction. Fortunately he liked the result, changing not a word nor reducing its length.

Later in 1966, when I finally got to do what had always been my top priority—a profile on the *Times* managing editor, Clifton Daniel—I produced a twenty-thousand-word article that took four months to research and write, and when it appeared as the lead piece in *Esquire*'s issue of November 1966, its text and illustrations spread through 27 pages of the magazine. The article not only dealt with Daniel's management style but compared it to that of the paper's previous managing editors going back to the Civil War and beyond. It referred as well to the successes and failures of generations of reporters, copyreaders, and various other supernumeraries who had contributed to the paper's history since its founding in 1851.

The reader response to the article was enormous, surprising and impressing Hayes, who had earlier believed that the media figures I chose to explore were insufficiently famous or consequential to be of interest to *Esquire* readers. But after the Daniel piece, Hayes encouraged me to continue focusing on *Times* people. I followed with a story about the controversial foreign correspondent Harrison Salisbury; then a discontented local reporter, John Corry; and finally the frustrated bureau chief in Washington, Tom Wicker. These, plus my earlier story about the obit writer Alden Whitman, caught the attention of literary publishers and in 1967 brought me a contract offer to write a book about the *Times*. It would be completed three years later and become a national bestseller, *The Kingdom and the Power*.

After this, I ceased being a contract writer for *Esquire* and devoted myself to producing nonfiction books well stocked with unobtrusive if not kindred Bartleby personalities. Even when I centered on a Mafia leader named Joseph Bonanno, who appointed two of his henchmen to stage his fake kidnapping one night in Manhattan to help him elude rival mobsters eager to kill him and federal agents seeking to arrest him, my lead paragraph was from the viewpoint of a languid doorman who stood outside the Park Avenue apartment building where the incident took place.

Knowing that it is possible to see too much, most door-men in New York have developed an extraordinary sense of selective vision: they know what to see and what to ignore, when to be curious and when to be indolent—they are most often standing indoors, unaware, when there are accidents or arguments in front of their buildings, and they are usually in the street seeking taxicabs when burglars are escaping through the lobby. Although a doorman may disapprove of bribery and adultery, his back is invariably turned when the super-intendent is handing money to the fire inspector or when a tenant whose wife is away escorts a young woman into the elevator—which is not to accuse the doorman of hypocrisy or cowardice but merely to suggest that his instinct for un-involvement is very strong, and to speculate that doormen have perhaps learned through experience that nothing is to be gained by serving as a material witness to life's unseemly sights or to the madness of the city. This being so, it was not surprising that on the night when the reputed Mafia chief, Joseph Bonanno, was grabbed by two gunmen in front of a luxury apartment house on Park Avenue near Thirty-sixth Street, shortly after midnight on a rainy Tuesday in October, the doorman was standing in the lobby talking to the elevator man and saw nothing.

An excerpt from this book, titled *Honor Thy Father*, ap-peared in the August 1971 issue; and *Esquire* also published, in August of 1975, an excerpt from my next book, *Thy Neigh-bor's Wife*, which starts with the story of a lonely teenager in Chicago, Harold Rubin, who has a masturbatory love affair with the magazine photo of a beautiful model named Diane Webber, shown posing in the nude on a sand dune in Baja, California.

The book that followed, *Unto the Sons*, explored my obscure

Italian ancestry in Calabria, including the personal history of the two POW uncles whom I so often worried about during the wartime 1940s when I started listening to Frank Sinatra on the radio.

I spent most of the summer of 1982 in Italy interviewing these uncles, along with several other relatives whom I had never met before. In the fall I flew to Paris for the first of many conversations with my father's mentor, Antonio Cristiani, whose diary written over a forty-year period I had translated and whose retentive memory I tapped often and at length until his death in 1986, when he was in his nineties. The 661-page work was essentially the tale of two tailors, Cristiani and my father, and six excerpts from it appeared in *Esquire* before the book was published in 1992.

During these years I remained up to date on the activities of Frank Sinatra, which was easy to do because his name was constantly in the news and he was making several public appearances: In 1992, he gave 87 concerts; in 1993, 90 concerts (this was the year his buddy Jilly Rizzo died in an auto accident); in 1994, he starred at Radio City in New York and performed in Japan and the Philippines, as well as in Chicago, Atlantic City, and Las Vegas. In 1995, on his eightieth birthday, December 12, the Empire State Building glowed bright in his honor, and Bruce Springsteen praised him as the "Patron Saint of New Jersey."

In July of 1996, he and his fourth wife, Barbara Marx, celebrated their twenty-fifth wedding anniversary (his marriage to his third wife, Mia Farrow, ended in 1968 after two years), and in the middle of May in 1998, his name and photograph appeared on the front pages of newspapers and television screens around the world: At the age of eighty-two, Frank Sinatra had died of a heart attack at the Cedar-Sinai Medical Center in Los Angeles.

A large photo of him, in a tuxedo and with whiskey glass in

hand, appeared above the fold on the first page of the *New York Times*, which gave him a lengthy and very respectful obituary written by the paper's music critic, Stephen Holden. (The *Times* premier obit specialist, Alden Whitman, who died at seventy-six in 1990, was never replaced.) Incidentally, I was asked by an editor from the editorial section to contribute a piece, and while I began my commentary referring to Frank Sinatra's humble father, I did manage to end it with a tribute to the singer that I had never gotten around to expressing in person.

There was once a tattooed and florid little blue-eyed Sicilian-born prizefighter named Martin Sinatra who, wishing to enhance his employment opportunities in America at a time when there were no discernible advantages to having an Italian surname (except in the Mafia), presented himself in the ring as "Marty O'Brien."

I mean no disrespect to this man who compromised his identity in the interest of commerce, for it has historically been a very common practice, one followed by many of this nation's foreign-born whenever they have sought to masquerade within the American mainstream—or, in the specific case of Mr. Sinatra and his sobriquet, to appeal more readily to the larger number of American boxing promoters of Irish descent and to the many other Irish-Americans who in those distant days were among the nation's most ardent fight fans.

In the case of the fighter's only son, however, compromise of any kind would always be anathema, and thus he was destined to live a life that would be as turbulent as it was triumphant, a headline-making existence that, over the course of half a century, the rest of us (particularly we Americans of Italian heritage) would find inspirational because it gave us the courage, finally, to fully acknowledge and respect who we are.

Five years later, in 2003, as *Esquire* was marking its seventieth year of publication, the editors and other staff members took a vote and selected "Frank Sinatra Has a Cold" as the "Greatest Story Ever Told" in the history of the magazine. The entire piece was reprinted in a special section, and the accompanying illustrations included the "fuck you" graphic chart to which seemingly no one had ever paid close attention. Of course, none of the magazine's voting staff in 2003, mostly in their twenties and thirties, had been with the magazine when the article was first published in 1966, and indeed most of them were probably reading the piece for the first time. (Harold Hayes, who resigned from *Esquire* in 1973 following a dispute with the magazine's publisher, Arnold Gingrich, died at age sixty-two in 1989—receiving, by the way, a substantial two-column obit within the *Times,* with his picture.)

Were Harold Hayes still alive in 2003, he would probably have been the only person who knew that I was being celebrated for writing something that I did not want to write. But the tribute came at a good time because otherwise my work was not bringing me much praise or encouragement. During the last ten years—from 2003 back to 1993—I had made false starts on several projects, and when I did submit a nearly completed manuscript I was told by my book editor not to continue because my work was too arcane, or irrelevant, or, in any case, lacked sufficient commercial appeal.

For example, in 1995, after selling a short piece to the *New Yorker* on Gino's restaurant, which was celebrating its fiftieth anniversary, I wanted to expand my research and write a book that would explore the lives of kitchen workers, being inspired by what George Orwell had done in his 1933 classic "Down and Out in Paris and London." While Orwell had recounted what he had observed while working temporarily in a sweltering kitchen in a Paris hotel—associating with "fat pink cooks," "greasy dishwashers," and food-smuggling waiters—I planned to locate my story in the kitchen of a not very distinguished restaurant called Tucci, located at 206 East 63rd Street, between Second and Third Avenues.

Since I was a friend of one of the owners, I was allowed to hang out at the restaurant for as long and often as I wished, and I was even given an apron to wear in the kitchen while meals were being prepared. Sometimes I joined the maître d' at the front door, greeting and seating the guests—all in the hope of gaining inside knowledge of the operation of the restaurant and the roles that each employee played in trying to cope with the trends and capriciousness of a dining public.

Unfortunately, the staff at Tucci failed to satisfy enough customers to remain in business for very long; and in March of 1997, thirteen months after it opened, it closed and I was no longer Tucci's writer-in-residence. Putting my notes aside, I devoted myself for the rest of 1997 into 1998 pursuing two other book projects that I had long had in mind.

One was an update on the notorious old plantation town of Selma, Alabama, which had made world headlines in 1965 because of its lawmen's Bloody Sunday massacre of Dr. Martin Luther King's marchers seeking to promote voter registration in the state. I had graduated from the University of Alabama in 1953, and after having participated in the *Times* coverage of the 1965 confrontation and having also kept up with my personal contacts in Alabama with frequent visits during the next thirty years (on March 7, 1990, I wrote a front-page story for the *Times* on the twenty-fifth anniversary of Bloody Sunday), I had boxloads of material and three chapters that I hoped would gain me a book contract. But my editor, who had recently published a book dealing with civil rights issues, convinced me to forgo my Alabama project for a year or more.

The other book I was working on, but was not yet ready

to share with my editor, I called "A Non-Fiction Marriage," an intimate account of my own longtime relationship with my wife, Nan, a Doubleday editor of high standing whose authors have included Margaret Atwood, Ian McEwan, and Pat Conroy. Since our marriage in 1959, I have kept a diary of our life together, and I have cabinets filled with our correspondence and hundreds of photos showing us together. Ours is a union that quite naturally has had its ups and downs but is distinguished, I think, for being simultaneously intimate and separate.

She had her literary life with her learned colleagues and writers, and I had associations with my circle of more sporty friends, as well as an unquenchable interest in subject matter that, to put it mildly, she did not always share. When I began researching *Thy Neighbor's Wife* in the early 1970s, beginning with frequenting massage parlors and then managing two of them in Manhattan while keeping written accounts every day of my impressions and observations, Nan did not take issue with my fact-gathering methodology (since I had cleared it with her in advance). But she was very upset after *New York* magazine published an article about me cavorting in a Midtown massage parlor where nude masseuses and their customers had the option of co-mingling bare bottomed in the sauna and swimming pool ("An Evening in the Nude with Gay Talese" was the headline). After this was published, the two of us agreed to have a trial separation.

This conflict and others are fully described in my manuscript, along with reminiscences of my three-month residency at a free-love nudist paradise called Sandstone Retreat, a fifteen-acre settlement in the Santa Monica Mountains, overlooking Malibu beach. Only couples were welcomed there, and in Nan's place I was joined by my friend Sally Hanson, then in the process of divorcing her husband, Jack, while continuing with him to co-own and operate the Daisy. Sally figures prominently in my manuscript, although the main character throughout is Nan, and the big question that I as a writer must explain to readers about her is this: Why would such an intelligent, financially independent, well-connected, desirable, and lovely woman stay married for so long to me?

Putting that question aside until I felt I was ready to reveal my private papers to my editor (and share them with Nan), I flew to China in October of 1999 to explore a less complicated story: that of a twenty-five-year-old Beijing-born female soccer player named Liu Ying, who had captured my fancy months before while I watched her on network television performing in the World Cup soccer finale between the women of China and the United States, in Pasadena, California, before 90,185 spectators within the Rose Bowl (the largest turnout for any women's sporting contest in history).

Liu Ying had the dubious distinction of missing a penalty kick in overtime, thus being singularly responsible for her team's loss to the Americans—and at a time when the Chinese government was increasingly hostile toward the United States due to differences in foreign policy. It was also the year of the fiftieth anniversary of Mao's revolution, and I could only imagine what it must have been like for this young woman to return shamefully home to a prideful nation of nearly 4 billion people in the aftermath of her debacle in Pasadena.

Liu Ying had a great story to tell, I thought, and after a prolonged period of haggling with the Chinese sports ministry, I was able to gain an introduction, and for the next four months I not only interviewed her and her relatives dozens of times—via an interpreter—but also traveled with her and her teammates as they participated in warm-up matches in such places as Hong Kong, Taiwan, and the Algarve region of Portugal—all by way of tuning up for the 2000 Olympics to be held in Sydney, Australia.

I went there too and returned to China for follow-up interviews with Liu Ying in 2001 and 2002. After this I secluded myself for a couple of years in New York, organizing hundreds of pages of typed notes, and then produced a first draft of my proposed book on the trials and tribulations of Liu Ying.

But no sale. No publisher was interested. A few approving comments about the writing, yes, but the various editors I shopped it to were in agreement that there was no market for it in America. I got the same reaction later from publishers in China. The one redeeming factor is that I did manage to resurrect some of Liu Ying's hard-luck story—along with some of my material on restaurants, and Alabama, and an ill-fated and unpublished *New Yorker* assignment regarding a heavy-drinking ex-marine named John Bobbitt, who fell asleep one night and lost his penis to his angry wife's kitchen knife—into a memoir released in 2006 titled *A Writer's Life*. True to the prognosis of its prescient editor, the book attracted few readers.

At this time, however, I was already engrossed in another hopeful project—a book describing the heroic but largely unheralded contributions made by many dozens of backstage workers employed by the New York Metropolitan Opera house—namely, those who dealt with the scenery, the lighting, the rigging, the props, the costumes, plus the whispering prompter who during the singing was sequestered below the conductor's rostrum, and there were also the trainers who provided animals and birds for cameo appearances on stage during performances.

The opera's general manager, Peter Gelb, who took the job in 2006, at first graciously arranged for me to interview everyone who worked there in conjunction with operatic occasions—indeed, on some evenings I was allowed to stand hidden behind a side curtain while the singers were interacting on stage. But then, much to my surprise and disappointment, Mr. Gelb seemingly became concerned about the access I was enjoying and decided that whatever I wrote must first be submitted to him for approval.

Of course this was a deal breaker, and, since he was beyond being persuaded, I dropped the book idea and filed away my notes. My only bonus was in later writing a story about a Russian soprano named Marina Poplavskaya, whom I had met during my wanderings around the building, and this article appeared in the *New Yorker* in December of 2010.

Months later I received a note from a man named Gerald Foos who resided in Aurora, Colorado, and who for many years owned a motel there in which he'd constructed viewing vents in the ceilings of a dozen rooms that allowed him to observe his guests from his perch in the attic of the motel's pitched roof. I had actually visited this motel at his invitation back in 1980, after he had written me a letter describing what he had learned after years of invading other people's privacy; indeed, for three days and nights in the fall of 1980 I joined him in his Peeping Tom activities in the attic, and I had also read his notebook filled with his comments and observations.

However, in sharing his story with me he refused the use of his name, which is a condition I impose on whomever I write about because I want my readers to know my sources. But since he insisted that identifying himself with his lawless behavior might most likely lead to law suits and jail time, his tale remained untold by me for more than thirty years.

Then in 2010 he wrote to inform me that he was out of the motel business but still wanted to tell his story, and further, since he believed that the statute of limitations now worked in his favor, he was no longer hesitant about the use of his name. This led to years of frequent visits to his home near Denver for interviews, and my perusing his stacks of handwritten accounts of what he had seen, overheard, and learned during his career as a voyeur. After I had written a long draft of what I called "The Voyeur's Motel" and showed it to the articles editor at the *New Yorker*, I was encouraged to stay with the story—a story that I finished in final form in 2015; the *New Yorker* printed it in early April of 2016, and it came our later in book form issued by Grove Atlantic.

The publication of *The Voyeur's Motel* was almost as controversial as *Thy Neighbor's Wife* was decades earlier, which I had more or less expected considering the disreputable characters that I featured in both books; and once again the results not only disturbed readers but elicited much negative press coverage from the *Washington Post* on an issue that I deemed unfair, and as a result I stupidly allowed my ire to challenge the *Post*'s reporting and consequently earned more unflattering publicity.

But in time I grew to ignore the controversy and distract myself with another book idea that absorbed me, although this one also featured a flawed figure, and a sad one too. He was Nicholas Bartha, a divorced sixty-six-year-old doctor who worked long hours in several emergency rooms while otherwise living alone in a five-story brownstone he owned on the Upper East Side of Manhattan, and his was a story to tell that reminded me of Bartleby.

Like the Herman Melville creation, Dr. Bartha was an odd and taciturn individual who became so attached to his surroundings that he decided to kill himself and blow up his brownstone, rather than sell it or otherwise surrender it in compliance with a court-ordered eviction notice. Dr. Bartha's decision, not unlike Bartleby's own fatality due to his stubbornly clinging to his own crash pad, made headlines in New

York and elsewhere, which is how I first became informed and drawn into writing about this unhappy doctor.

But rather than explaining further, permit me to present what took me three years to research and write—a tale titled "Dr. Bartha's Brownstone," which I finished yesterday and appears on the following pages.

PART III

Dr. Bartha's Brownstone

Chapter 26

R ising within the city of New York are about one million buildings. These include skyscrapers, apartment buildings, brownstones, bungalows, department stores, shopping malls, bodegas, auto-repair shops, schools, churches, hospitals, day-care centers, and homeless shelters.

Also spread through the city's approximately 302 square miles of space are more than 19,000 vacant lots, one of which suddenly became vacant many years ago—at 34 East 62nd Street, between Madison and Park Avenues—when the unhappy owner of a brownstone at that address blew it up (with him in it) rather than sell his cherished nineteenth-century high-stoop Neo-Grecian residence in order to pay the court-ordered sum of $4 million to the woman who had divorced him three years earlier.

This man was a physician of sixty-six named Nicholas Bartha. He was a hefty, bespectacled, gray-haired six-footer of formal demeanor and a slight foreign accent. He had been born in Romania in 1940 to resourceful parents—his father Catholic, his mother half Jewish—whose home and gold-mining enterprise were confiscated first by the Nazis and later by the Soviets, prompting Dr. Bartha to vow, many decades later, after a New York judge had favored his ex-wife in the divorce case, and after a deputy sheriff had ordered him to vacate 34 East 62nd Street : "I am not going to let anybody evict me as the Communists did in Romania, in 1947." He added: "The courts in N.Y.C. are the fifth column."

In July of 2006, shortly before he set off the explosion from which he would not recover, he addressed his former wife, Cordula, in a suicide note found in his computer: "You always wanted me to sell the house and I always told you, 'I will leave this house only if I am dead.'"

"He just snapped," said his lawyer, Ira Garr, referring to Dr. Bartha's response to the sheriff's eviction notice. "It was overwhelming for him because, well, he had come to this country with nothing. For many years his parents and he had scraped together the money to buy the town house. This was his American dream, a personification of 'I'm an American, I've made it in America. I own a piece of valuable property in a valuable neighborhood. And I want to live in this place.' This home was his mistress."

He had been living alone for a few years in his fourteen-room, five-floor residence. It had arch-topped windows and an ornamental wrought-iron double door that overlooked a nine-step stone staircase that at the sidewalk level had a pair of newel posts topped by globe-shaped finials. It was the oldest building on the block, constructed in 1882. It stood between the elite golf-devotee Links Club, built in 1917, and the sixteen-story Cumberland House co-op that in 1958 had replaced a number of demolished properties, including one house that had been lived in for a while by Theodore Roosevelt when he supervised the city's police department, between 1895 and 1898.

In fact two of Roosevelt's sons, Theodore Jr. and Kermit, would become frequent visitors, between the 1920s and 1940s, of the brownstone that Dr. Bartha would own in the 1980s. Beginning in 1927, within the building's parlor floor, there existed a secret club of about two dozen prominent men that included, along with TR's sons, the banker Winthrop W. Aldrich, the philanthropist William Rhinelander Stewart, the mining expert Oliver Dwight Filley, the naturalist C. Suydam Cutting, the chief justice of the New York County Supreme Court, Frederic Kernochan, as well as others who had an interest in international affairs and, in many cases, a working experience in Allied intelligence during World War I. The leader of the group was the real-estate magnate Vincent Astor, who was very interested in espionage and, while on ocean cruises in his private yacht, had often provided the United States government with data he had collected.

Drawing upon the archival papers of Vincent Astor, Kermit Roosevelt, and a few of their friends, the history professor and author Jeffery M. Dorwart—writing in the *Quarterly Journal of the New York State Historical Association*, in 1981—described Astor's group as an "espionage ring" made up of well-born volunteers who were detached from government funding and directives and met on a monthly basis for dinner and conversation "in a nondescript apartment at 34 E. 62nd Street in New York City, complete with an unlisted telephone and mail drop."

The members referred to the site simply as "The Room," Professor Dorwart wrote, and "when members returned from their series of world travels, they reported their observations to The Room," which resembled an intelligence office, "albeit in an informal and somewhat romanticized manner."

Professor Dorwart, who taught history at the Rutgers University campus in Camden, New Jersey, wrote that although Franklin D. Roosevelt was not on The Room's roster, "he knew every member well through Groton, Harvard and New York society, business and social connections," and Dorwart pointed out that such Room regulars as Vincent Astor, Judge Kernochan, and William Rhinelander Stewart "were with Roosevelt in Miami in February 1933 when an assassin narrowly missed killing the president-elect."

Stansfield Turner, the onetime director of the Central Intelligence Agency, mentioned in his 2005 memoir, *Burn Before Reading*, that FDR had dispatched Vincent Astor and Kermit Roosevelt into the Pacific on Astor's yacht in 1938 in the hopes of discovering data about Japanese installations. "It appears that Astor had a thrilling adventure," Turner wrote, "but did not return with any ground-breaking intelligence . . . Astor, though, was a director of the Western Union Telegraph Company, which allowed him to provide FDR with the text of sensitive telegrams and cables. And he had a number of bankers in his 'Room' who allowed him to gather intelligence on transfers of funds. Roosevelt's directions to Astor are not on record, but Astor's messages to Roosevelt suggest that FDR fully approved of these questionable activities."

Dr. Bartha knew that his brownstone had once sheltered The Room, according to his close friend and colleague Dr. Paul J. Mantia. He said that Bartha had learned about it after a writer doing research had arrived one day to explain the story and then seek permission to see the parlor floor, claiming that it had historical significance.

Although the building's rental apartments from earlier times had been converted by Bartha into a single-family residence when he moved in, he nevertheless welcomed and guided his visitor through the spacious entranceway, with its high ceiling, rotunda, antique mirrors, and marble fireplace; and he soon warmed to the idea, encouraged by his guest, that they were following in the footsteps of Astor's social register spies. Later, Bartha smilingly hinted to Dr. Mantia that the space might someday serve as a museum.

The two doctors met in 1991 while working nights in the emergency room of Bronx Lebanon Hospital. At fifty-one, Bartha was fifteen years older than Paul Mantia, a slender, blue-eyed Brooklyn-born physician with glasses and an amiable and deferential manner that contrasted with Bartha's strong personality; but the latter's uncompromisingly high medical standards and ready guidance turned Mantia into his lifelong admirer, emulator, and filial presumptive. Whenever Bartha would telephone Mantia at home and his wife answered, she would call out to her husband: "Your father's on the phone!"; and Paul Mantia, who at thirteen had lost his father to a heart attack, would immediately drop whatever he was doing and take the call.

"Bartha was a great doctor," he said, explaining that physicians in emergency rooms are forced to deal with patients they do not know, patients that sometimes can barely speak due to their injuries or other illnesses; and yet somehow, through a combination of perspicacity and perseverance, Bartha could swiftly and accurately diagnose the situation and then prepare a written report upon which other doctors, perhaps those waiting in intensive care units, knew from experience that they could rely. "Whenever Dr. Bartha finished with a patient, everything was clear, everything was done, nothing was incomplete," Mantia said. "He was scrupulously thorough."

In 2001, after being friends and medical associates for ten years, Nicholas Bartha and Paul Mantia opened a private practice on the sidewalk level at 34 East 62nd Street; and from then on, during the last five years of Bartha's life, during brief but frequent conversations between patients' daytime appointments, and during equally brief late-night dinners in hospital cafeterias, Paul Mantia came to know more and more, little by little, about this serious, privately sad, but never sentimental man who was his mentor.

Chapter 27

Nicholas Bartha was born in Romania to parents of Hungarian ancestry. Although his family identified itself as Catholic, his maternal grandfather was a rabbi. As a child during World War II he remembered hiding with others in caves belonging to gold-mining families, some of them Jewish, all hoping to elude the Iron Guard's anti-Semitic, ultra-nationalist political henchmen during this period when Romania was allied with Nazi Germany.

Later, when the Nazis retreated, the Russians quickly moved into Romania to create more misery. Nicholas could recall seeing horse-drawn carriages bearing the dead bodies of those who had challenged the Communists in 1946. In the early 1950s, his father spent two years in prison on charges, never proven, that he was hoarding gold somewhere in the hills of the Carpathian Mountains not far from where he had operated his mine, before it was nationalized.

Although Nicholas managed to finish high school, he was banned from attending college as a medical student because of his father's political problems. In October of 1956, while listening to Radio Free Europe and Voice of America, he was heartened to hear of the Hungarian Revolution in Budapest; but weeks later the uprising was crushed, two hundred thousand Hungarians became refugees, and the Soviets regained their dominance.

During these years Nicholas was working in factories and operating lathe machines—cutting, sanding, grooving, and drilling with such proficiency that by 1960 he had gained enough favor to be allowed to enter medical school in the northwestern Romanian city of Cluj. But in 1963, after both parents were imprisoned for nine months, again charged with hoarding gold, Nicholas was expelled from medical school—and the frustration and despair that he then felt would remain with him forever. In fact, hours before destroying his brownstone in 2006, in the suicide note he emailed to a number of people—including his attorney, Ira Garr; his computer teacher, Alejandro Justo; his best friend, Paul Mantia; and his worst friend and ex-wife, Cordula—there were references to his feelings shaped by World War II and the Cold War years in his native Romania.

* *I hope there will be a memorial built in the memory of Eastern Europeans who were betrayed at Yalta by Pres. Roosevelt . . . [who] sent back a boat with Jewish refugees to Europe to be exterminated.*

* *The Romanians did the right thing to Nicolae Ceausescu [a reference to the 1960s Communist leader who, together with his wife, was executed by a firing squad in 1989.]*

* *I am not good material to be a slave. I rebel easily.*

He fled Romania in March of 1964. He was then twenty-four. A friendly source within the Romanian security service had told him that his arrest was imminent, saying that because his imprisoned parents were not satisfying their jailors he would soon be held hostage. On March 15, Nicholas Bartha arrived in Israel. He remained there for nine months, living and working on a kibbutz and studying Hebrew. In December he moved on to Italy after learning that his parents, recently released from jail, had relocated in Rome, assisted by a relative who was a priest at the Vatican.

After six months in Rome, Nicholas and his parents applied for a parolee visa to enter the United States, and this was granted in late June of 1965. They settled in an apartment in Rego Park, Queens, where Nicholas found work on the assembly line of the Bulova Watch Company in Queens, producing gadgets for timing devices and receiving the minimum wage of $1.98 an hour. His mother, Ethel, got a job in a beauty salon and his father, Janos, became a cook at the Plaza Hotel in Manhattan.

A year later Nicholas quit Bulova, where his advancement was stalled due to his not being a citizen, so he found work in Queens at the Astra Tool and Instrument Manufacturing Company, soon earning $5.00 an hour and saving every penny. In his personal journal he noted that he always walked to work, never bought a car, and, though tempted, never paused on his way to work to have breakfast at International House of Pancakes on Northern Boulevard.

In 1967, he obtained a Green Card and also was accepted as a medical student at the University of Rome. During the next seven years, while attending medical school, Nicholas would return each summer to live with his parents in Rego Park and resume working as a lathe machinist at Astra Tool, receiving several raises along the way.

By this time, he had become a U.S. citizen, and in the spring of 1974 he graduated from medical school. He had also been having a year-long love affair with a young woman he had met as a fellow student at the University of Rome. Her name was Cordula Hahn.

She was a petite, soft-spoken, plain but cheerful thirty-year-old brunette who had earned a PhD in German literature and later worked as an editorial assistant in an Italian publishing firm. She had lived in Italy for fourteen years, arriving there as a teenager in 1960 from the Netherlands with her parents.

The latter had been wartime Czechoslovakian refugees who had left their Nazi-occupied homeland in 1938 for the Netherlands, settling in the village of Bilthoven, an affluent community about twenty miles east of Amsterdam. Cordula was born there in 1942. Cordula's father was Catholic, her mother Jewish, and, even though she converted to Catholicism, she was forced to publicly identify with her Jewish background by wearing a star on her clothing during the years when the Germans ruled over the Netherlands.

In Italy, Cordula's academic and well-to-do parents found contentment and social acceptance—although, in 1973, they experienced and expressed disappointment in Cordula's choice of a boyfriend. For reasons never made clear to Nicholas, her parents disapproved of him, and, not one to forget a slight, he held a grudge against them thereafter.

In 2002, while testifying in the divorce trial, he mentioned the lack of warmth existing between him and his mother-in-law; and in his 2006 suicide note, he described with a condemning eye the paternal side of Cordula's family. He wrote that her father was a left-wing Bohemian German born of a fascist family, adding that *his* father "was a social climber who married the daughter of an attorney in Carlsbad."

But in spite of her parents' misgivings about Nicholas, she followed him from Rome to the United States in 1974 after he had completed medical school; and for the next three years, though still not married, she lived with him in the rent-free basement apartment of the multi-family home in Rego Park, Queens, that Nicholas and his parents, pooling their resources, had purchased seven years earlier, in 1967, for $63,000, just before he had first left for medical school. The Bartha trio had acquired the building with a $20,000 down payment and mortgage of $43,000.

In 1974, at Elmhurst General Hospital in Queens, Nicholas began serving a two-year internship, followed by a one-year residency; while Cordula, who spoke five languages, was employed in Manhattan within the cultural section of the consulate-general of the Netherlands, which had also arranged for her visa.

But in 1977 she became pregnant. Nicholas would have preferred an abortion, but she insisted on having a child—which would be a daughter, Serena, born seven months after the couple became married in a civil ceremony in Queens. They then moved from their basement dwelling into an upper-floor apartment in the Bartha building, contributing $200 a month toward the family fund for household maintenance, matching the monthly rent of the tenants they had replaced.

In December of 1978, Cordula had a second daughter, Johanna. As a result, Nicholas felt more pressure to increase his income, which he did by accepting extra hours at hospitals for extra pay. But he was less frequently at home, and when he was he got little sleep in the crowded space he now shared with the two children and his heavily burdened and unhappy wife. Cordula complained of loneliness and abandonment. In Nicholas's 2006 suicide note, his ten-page long farewell manifesto that he emailed to several people, he referred back to his first early years of regret in being married to Cordula:

> Cordula developed post partum depression and later became psychotic after she had two daughters. She refused treatment. In 1980 I was going to divorce her [but] changed my mind because of the children.

In 1980 Nicholas and his parents, again pooling their resources, bought the Manhattan brownstone at 34 East 62nd

Street for $395,000, with a cash down payment of $199,699. It was Nicholas who had encouraged their move to Manhattan.

His friend Dr. Paul Mantia remembered hearing him describe the thrill of standing in front of the fountain at Grand Army Plaza on 59th Street one afternoon, with the Plaza hotel behind him and the entrance to Central Park not far away, and him thinking: *This is where I want to live someday.*

Chapter 28

Even before the family had moved into the brownstone it was decided that Nicholas, his wife, and their two daughters would live on the upper two floors, his parents on the floor below, and the parlor floor would be used only as a spacious entranceway, a prideful *piano nobile*. On the sidewalk level of the brownstone, where in later years Nicholas and Paul Mantia would establish their private practice, Nicholas's mother, Ethel, planned a beauty salon.

Indeed, it was a business that would succeed almost immediately—serving such clients as the wife of actor Anthony Quinn, who came in to have her hair shampooed, and the television personality Barbara Walters, who had her legs waxed. But in or around 1990, a little more than a year after Ethel's salon had opened, it was shut down following complaints in the neighborhood that the street was not zoned for such a commercial enterprise.

Although Nicholas and his parents had first bought the brownstone in 1980, it actually took them more than five years to move in. This was due not only to the time-consuming remodeling and reconstruction work—new roof, new floors, new interior staircase, new bathrooms, new third-floor tile terrace and additional wall crumbling and dusty preparatory work involved in converting a century-old brownstone into a single-family dwelling [which it had been for decades until one of the owners during the postwar years had turned it into a rental building]—but the Bartha family was also forced to buy out or wait out the ensconced tenants whose leases had not yet expired or who otherwise refused to leave.

In fact, the leaseholders of the brownstone's ten apartments hired a lawyer to try to block the Bartha family's intentions to evict them. The organizer of the tenants' group was an audacious and frequent party giver in his midfifties named Joseph Conlin, who rented both apartments on the parlor floor (a total of six rooms, two kitchens, two bathrooms) for an almost bargain-priced $850 per month, and, as the president of a concert-management company, he had grown accustomed to using his vast living space for entertaining such opera star clients as Maria Callas, Carlo Bergonzi, and Renata Tebaldi.

Even though he lived part of the time in Palm Beach, Florida—where he also led an active social life, was a noted ballroom dancer, and sometimes hosted parties on a 360-foot long, four-mast sailing cruise ship called the *Sea Cloud*, which had originally been built in 1931 for Marjorie Merriweather Post, the General Foods heiress—he was determined not to be deprived of his modestly priced fancy address on Manhattan's Upper East Side without challenging the Bartha family in civil court.

Mr. Conlin's most supportive collaborator in opposing the Barthas was an attractive blue-eyed, caramel-blonde divorcée in her early thirties named Monika Barbier, who occupied the two-and-a-half-room rear apartment on the third floor for an affordable $400 a month. Like Mr. Conlin, she became attached to, and possessive of, her residency in this exclusive neighborhood, having previously shifted frequently from place to place in less desirable areas of the city.

Her apartment at 34 East 62nd Street had a sizable living room, a separate bedroom, a full-sized kitchen, and also contained fine furniture including such costly antiques as an ornate armchair, a chest of drawers, and a rolltop desk marked as being built in 1867. Ms. Barbier had purchased these pieces from a tenant who had moved out of 3R voluntarily in early 1979: Carolyn Jo Finklehoffe, the recent widow of the producer and screenwriter Fred F. Finklehoffe, who had written a number of films starring Judy Garland and Mickey Rooney.

Ms. Barbier, divorced in 1977 from a Frenchman named Jean-Marie Barbier, had been born Monika Wegener near Berlin in 1942 but spent much of her adult life in Paris before settling in New York following the marital breakup, and she was fluent in the three languages. Currently employed as the executive assistant to the president of a German educational TV network with offices in Midtown Manhattan, she had earlier worked in the city as a travel agent, a designer's assistant with a women's sportswear company, and a showroom model in the Garment Center.

She had lived alone in a cramped $200-a-month studio apartment at 307 West 29th Street that, because it was located within a noisy and dirty neighborhood, one in which she often felt unsafe at night, she believed was overpriced. And yet she also appreciated living within a section of the city that teemed daily with the energy and diversity of people walking in or out of Penn Station, or Madison Square Garden, or the popular bar at the Egyptian Gardens tavern, on 29th Street and Ninth Avenue, which featured Middle Eastern cuisine, music and belly dancing, and reminded her of her many visits to Cairo during her younger years as a Paris-based flight attendant with Trans World Airlines.

She began there in 1965, traveling to Europe, the Middle East, and the Far East. During her fifth year at TWA, while on a Boeing 707 jetliner flying from Paris to Rome, her persuasive manner helped to convince an armed hijacker to change his mind about ordering the pilot to land in Damascus, Syria,

where she believed they would be treated cruelly by the airport personnel, and fly instead to Beirut, Lebanon—where, it
later turned out, they were civilly received without any loss of
life or property to the passengers or crew.

But if she thought that charming a hijacker had better
prepared her for persuading the Bartha family to change its
mind about evicting tenants, she had greatly underestimated
the single-mindedness and fortitude of Dr. Bartha's sixty-two-
year-old mother, Ethel.

In Romania during the 1940s, before the Nazis and then the
Communists had confiscated her family's domicile and gold-
mining business, Ethel Bartha had served as the firm's accountant and resident bookkeeper; and now, in January of 1980, while
assuming similar responsibilities regarding the newly acquired
brownstone, she also took the initiative in clearing it of its tenants
in order to allow the renovation and remodeling to begin.

It required more than a year for her to achieve her goal
while being challenged all the way by the opposing lawyer
and the singular efforts of Monika Barbier—who, in addition
to her petitioning letters to Mrs. Bartha and her strategizing
with the tenants' attorney—decided to confront her lady land-
lord face-to-face, appearing one day without an appointment
at the beauty parlor where Mrs. Bartha was then temporarily
employed. It was on the ground floor of a high-rise at 209 East
56th Street. She planned to work there until she had the opportunity to open her own place within the brownstone.

When Monika Barbier arrived at the salon, Mrs. Bartha
was busy with a customer; but after the customer had gone,
and Monika stepped forward to introduce herself—the couple
had never met—Mrs. Bartha quickly turned away, and, with
arms folded, she stood rigidly still while avoiding eye contact.
For many moments this would be her posture and mindset,
remaining listless and remote.

Since the little contretemps in the center of the room was soon getting the attention of the other beauticians and their seated customers, and since Monika more or less realized that the immutable Mrs. Bartha was unlikely ever to negotiate, she eventually made her demure departure while writing that night in her journal:

"Naive as I was, I hoped I might convince her to let me stay in my apartment if I talked to her personally . . . But what I encountered was a stone-faced, unapproachable, well-groomed woman with a meticulously done hairdo."

Six months later, Monika was living in a sublet apartment on the fifth floor of a twenty-one-story building near 34th Street and Park Avenue. She had been vacated along with all her erstwhile 62nd Street co-defendants in the aftermath of a civil court ruling that entitled the Bartha family to be the brownstone's sole occupants.

Although the ruling brought considerable relief and satisfaction to the entire family, there was one member who had reservations about leaving Queens. This was the doctor's wife, Cordula. Transferring to Manhattan engendered fears that the increased real-estate taxes and higher costs of insurance and living might gradually overwhelm them. She had quit her job at the Dutch consulate in 1977 to raise the children, and though she would be rehired in 1988, it would be part-time. She was also upset that her husband refused to include her name on the brownstone's deed. He and his parents' names were listed on the original ownership document, but not hers despite their marriage. She complained of this often and brought it up decades later during the divorce trial, telling the judge that she always felt financially at risk because "if something happens to him" she might have problems because she was not a U.S. citizen. She preferred retaining her Dutch nationality, she explained, but still believed her name belonged on the deed even though her husband always said "he doesn't trust me and he's not going to die."

Always and entirely it was "his house," she continued, adding: "He was obsessed with the house. It was his only hobby."

And after the Bartha family had emptied the brownstone of its tenants, Nicholas appointed himself the general contractor so that he could oversee everything that the workers did in renovating the house, and he also placed a toolbox and lathe in the sub-basement and began making some wooden furniture. For example, he designed and constructed his daughter's beds, built a few tables, reinforced the chairs and other furniture that had been purchased in stores, stabilized the staircase in a way that rendered it soundless to footsteps, and he put up a floor-to-ceiling bookshelf in the family's living room complete with a ladder on rollers.

He chose the paint colors for the walls, decided on where all the fixtures and furniture would be placed, and made it clear that everything was to remain where he put it, and not be moved elsewhere by anyone.

He also served as the building's custodian: He cleaned the gutters, shoveled the snow, fixed whatever was wrong with the toilets, air-conditioning, and kitchen sink. His wife helped too—she watched over the workmen while her husband was on hospital duty, and she had also contributed $45,000 of her own money toward the acquisition of the brownstone in 1980. (The money had been a gift from her father.) But again, whatever contribution she made was taken for granted, she testified, repeating: It was "his house."

In order to pay for the monthly upkeep of the house, Nicholas had to earn about $9,000 a month from his medical services, which he did by hiring himself out sometimes to two or more hospitals simultaneously—a day shift at one hospital, a night shift at another, and extra hours on weekends at yet another hospital—receiving a regular weekly salary from the one while serving at other hospitals on a per diem basis, usually at the rate of between $60 and $80 an hour. His average annual income beginning in the mid-1990s was slightly more than $200,000, but it meant that he worked six or seven days a week and spent little time at home with his wife and daughters.

"He was a workaholic," said his computer teacher, Alejandro Justo. In addition, Dr. Bartha had to spend many hours each day and night on the road because the only hospitals where he could find steady employment were in emergency rooms located beyond Manhattan, at such places as the Lutheran Medical Center in Brooklyn, the Mount Vernon Hospital in Westchester County, St. Anthony's Community Hospital in Warwick, and the Mercy Community Hospital in Port Jervis. It took him one hour and ten minutes to drive from his brownstone to Warwick, and one and a half hours to reach Port Jervis.

For nearly twelve years, until he bought a new Toyota Echo in 2000, he covered hundreds of miles each week in an old red Honda hatchback with the driver's seat shoved all the way back to accommodate his girth (he weighed about 240 pounds) and with nothing to listen to on the radio because someone had stolen it shortly after he had bought the automobile. Deciding he could live without the radio, Dr. Bartha never replaced it, nor did he even cut off the dangling four-inch-long strand of sliced wiring that hung from the dashboard's empty section where the radio had been.

One afternoon, riding in the passenger seat, his friend Dr. Mantia tried to enhance the dashboard's appearance by tucking the wires back into the opening, but Nicholas interrupted him, saying, "Don't bother. Leave it like it is."

Mantia obeyed, without seeking an explanation. Maybe Nicholas wished to exhibit the fact that his car had already paid its dues to vandalism, Mantia thought, and therefore deserved a free pass from the next potential thief. Or maybe Nicholas, whom Mantia saw as an "eccentric" foreign father motivated by old-world influences, was mentally linked somehow to severed connections or stolen objects, not the least being the Bartha family home in Romania.

Still, Dr. Bartha remained the most influential figure in Paul Mantia's life. He imitated Bartha when it came to the kind of shoes he wore, the type of car he drove, and the places he patronized when buying what he needed.

Mantia remembered complaining to Bartha about his aching feet while wearing Italian loafers on the hard floors of the Bronx Lebanon emergency room. Dr. Bartha immediately recommended that he switch to soft leather rubber-soled Rockport shoes, which would indeed eliminate the pain; Bartha also told him where to purchase them at the best price at a store near Canal Street. Aware that Dr. Bartha always favored a small-sized economy car because, in addition to the mileage, he could maneuver it more easily into narrow parking spaces, Mantia bought a snub-nosed ten-foot-long Toyota Scion IQ that, if tilted all the way upward, would barely touch a standard basketball rim. Bartha told Mantia where to buy the best vegetables at the Harlem Market, where to acquire the most reliable metal roofing material at a plant in the Bronx, and where fine-quality cabinets were available at a store in Maspeth, Queens.

Bartha cultivated friendships with many hospital workers whose backgrounds were African American, Asian, and Hispanic, and he enjoyed a special kinship with a fellow physician named Rodolfo A. Nazario, who was born in Puerto Rico and earned his medical degree in the Dominican Republic.

Dr. Nazario was a short, dapper, gray-haired, sometimes cocky but never discourteous individual who was close to Bartha's age and who shared with him a skepticism of the expressed good intentions of powerful people. Dr. Nazario's father was a prominent lawyer in Puerto Rico, and he often quoted one of his father's favorite sayings: "Law and justice do not work hand in hand. Law is law. Justice is justice. Law is supposed to protect justice. But it does not."

Nazario first met Bartha in 1989 when they began working in the emergency room of Bronx Lebanon.

"Bartha was an excellent doctor who took very good care of his patients," Nazario said. "But he was also very strict. If people were doing things right, he was very nice. But if not, he was very critical. But he would tell them directly. He would never go higher and say, 'Fire this person!' No, he would say: 'This is wrong. You do not do it that way. You do it this way,' and people usually appreciated it."

When they were not limited to dining in the hospital cafeteria, Bartha, Nazario, and sometimes their younger Italian American colleague Paul Mantia, would eat outside the hospital in such places as Dominick's Italian restaurant and Patsy's Pizzeria in the Bronx; or, on the rare occasions when they were off duty together, they might meet at a Romanian restaurant in Yorkville that Bartha knew, or his favorite Uncle George's Greek Tavern in Astoria; or, at the suggestion of their computer-fixing, Buenos Aires–born pal Alejandro Justo, at an Argentinian steak house called La Fusta, in North Bergen, New Jersey, not far from where Justo lived and worked on computers.

"Dr. Bartha loved the tripe there," said Justo, a lean, brown-eyed, dark-haired man in his midthirties who left Argentina at seventeen to attend the University of Massachusetts Amherst, where he earned a degree in electrical engineering. "He was a good eater," Justo said. "He'd eat anything."

Dr. Nazario added that this included such Latin American specialties as pernil—a slow-roasted marinated pork shoulder or leg often seasoned with dried oregano, kosher salt, ground black pepper, and a couple of garlic cloves per pound of pork. Dr. Bartha was so fond of pernil that he had Nazario provide him with a recipe; and on the following Christmas Eve, when Bartha was on duty, he treated the medical staff to a pernil dinner that he had cooked earlier at home, then transferred to the hospital in containers placed in the back of his Honda.

While Nicholas Bartha enjoyed cooking and socializing at meals, he and Cordula rarely went out to restaurants together, and during the last four or five years of their marriage they dwelled quite separately within the same building. He spent most of his time in hospitals, where he concentrated his attentions on his patients and his friends on the staff. When he returned home late at night his wife was usually asleep and often irritated if he awakened her with such requests that she get out of bed and type a letter for him or perform some other chore. "I'm tired," she might explain, to which he would likely reply, "You're always tired," and he might not speak to her at breakfast on the following day—if, indeed, she had not already left the residence at seven in the morning for her job at the Dutch consulate. She had resumed full-time employment there in 1994 and often worked until seven at night. Sometimes she attended cultural events later in the evening at the consulate or elsewhere in Manhattan.

Cordula drove around town in her own car, a Ford Festiva, and she was on her way to becoming the consulate's office manager, earning more than $80,000 a year. Still, she relied on her husband's income for paying most of the bills, including the monthly living and household maintenance costs, the taxes, the insurance, the children's upbringing and education, and the one or two visits she took each year to visit her family in Europe, often accompanied by one or both of the daughters.

Her husband claimed that he had no time for vacations. He also had no time for entertainment. He had accompanied

Cordula to the movies only twice during their long marriage, and he could not remember the names or plots of either film. He never attended the theater, the opera, the ballet, a concert, or a sporting event. Once when his computer servicer, Alejandro Justo, was rebooting a medical operations system, and at the same time keeping an eye on a televised World Cup soccer match involving his beloved Argentina, Dr. Bartha sat next to him in a state of muted bewilderment whenever Alejandro would jump to his feet and roar with approval following every successful move by one of the players from Argentina.

"He just couldn't understand my enthusiasm," Justo said.

Chapter 29

Alejandro Justo was a frequent visitor to the 34 East 62nd Street brownstone, responding to Dr. Bartha's call for help whenever the home computer froze, or the printer stalled, or when there were malfunctions with any of the many mobile devices that Bartha had purchased in bargain stores, such as his BlackBerry, PalmPilot, or Startac phone.

When Dr. Paul Mantia and Bartha opened an office together on the sidewalk level of the brownstone—where they were later joined by two periodontists, who rented space in the rear—Justo arrived to install six new computers, and he was once summoned to eradicate the work of hackers who had introduced pornography into the software.

Whenever Justo could not find a parking space within the 62nd Street neighborhood, he would park illegally in front of Bartha's brownstone and wait for the doctor to send down one of his teenaged daughters, Serena or Johanna, to sit in Justo's car while he was working in the house. Justo found both daughters to be friendly and accommodating, and, on at least one occasion, he serviced their computers as well.

But he rarely felt welcome whenever Cordula was at home. If she greeted him at all, she was curt and perfunctory. Once she walked past him near the staircase without saying a word. This happened sometime in late 1996, when she and her husband were often quarreling, although Justo remembered Cordula as being quite gracious when he first met her a year or so earlier at Dr. Nazario's birthday party in Fort Lee, New Jersey. She had been introduced by none other than her husband. It might well have been the couple's final evening out together, because shortly after the party Justo and Nazario learned from Bartha that he and Cordula were no longer on speaking terms.

Both men were very understanding, since each had undergone similar difficulties in the past. Dr. Nazario's first marriage had ended in divorce. And Alejandro Justo was a historian on the subject of broken marriages. His wealthy father, an Argentine of Italian extraction who lived in Florida, had been married six times. Alejandro's mother was his father's first and fifth wife. A few years after graduating from college, Alejandro himself married a woman from Uruguay, with whom he had a daughter. This marriage ended bitterly. Even more than a decade after the breakup his daughter refused to speak to him. Justo initially sought escape from his marital misery by getting a pilot's license and flying at great distances above the clouds in his single-engine plane. Eventually he found happiness with a woman in Costa Rica who would become his second wife.

Dr. Bartha's other close friend, the onetime happily married Paul Mantia, was equally sympathetic to his colleague's marital woes but at the same time counseled him to be more patient with Cordula and not to succumb so willingly to his unproven suspicions that she had a lover in Europe and was siphoning money from their joint account and banking it in the Netherlands. One day Mantia softly chided him: "Nick, please try not to be paranoid." Nicholas Bartha replied: "If you live in a Communist country, you have to be paranoid to survive."

In the spring of 1997, believing that Romania had long risen beyond the authoritarianism of its postwar Soviet history, Bartha's mother, Ethel, at seventy-nine, decided that she must now or never try to reclaim the family's home and other property that had been stolen during the 1940s and 1950s.

Her husband, Janos, had died at eighty-three in New York in 1993, and since then Ethel had been living alone in the second-floor apartment within the brownstone.

Dr. Mantia, who had met her, remembered how hopeful she had been prior to her trip abroad; but once she arrived, he said, she encountered only bureaucratic resistance and renunciation. "She had all the documents proving that the Bartha family owned the property, but they wouldn't listen and prevented everything that she tried to do. This caused her to have a stroke during the trip, and soon she died right there in Romania. I imagine that her blood pressure went through the roof because no one would listen to her."

Prior to her death, she and her son had been listed as co-owners of the brownstone. In her will, she bequeathed half of her share to him and the other half to be divided equally between his daughters, Serena and Johanna. Cordula received a cash gift of $25,000, which she deposited, although not eagerly, in the couple's joint bank account, acceding to her husband's expressed expectations.

During these years the daughters were residing uncomfortably within their parents' frosty relationship, and the issue of how well the girls were doing (or not doing) in school and in life was crossly debated within the brownstone and later became part of the public record during the divorce trial.

Dr. Bartha always believed that his wife was coddling the girls, allowing them to do as they wished instead of meeting his demanding standards. He was appalled that Serena, who had received a superior education at the Bronx High School of Science, would later flunk out of Fordham and then enlist in a culinary school (with tattoos on both shoulders) hoping to become a chef. His younger daughter, Johanna, had gone from the Brooklyn Technical School to the Fashion Institute of Technology, with expectations of becoming a custom designer.

"I do not think that a cook and a seamstress is a very good result," he told his wife. But his daughter Serena—who testified against him in court—accused him of being verbally abusive both to her and her sister and undermining their self-confidence. "My father expected us to be the kind of people who were leaders and go-getters," she told the judge. "A lawyer or doctor or something of that nature."

When Bartha took the stand, his attorney, Ira Garr, reminded him: "Your daughter testified that you were disappointed with your daughters' academic achievements."

"I think they should have done better than I did," he replied. "I came from a village, from a political background that didn't help me on the other side. So I thought that they will go a step further than I would have done. They didn't use the opportunity . . . that's all."

His wife disagreed.

"How can you do better?" she asked Ira Garr. "My younger daughter is a fashion designer. She prepares costumes for two avant-garde performances in Brooklyn . . . Serena is excellent in her job, trying to be a chef . . . They are very artistic, fantastic children."

Although she did not testify at the trial, the sixty-year-old Ileana Cora, an elegantly dressed receptionist who ran the Bartha-Mantia office in the brownstone, had firsthand knowledge of Dr. Bartha's disruptive family life because at times it was on display in front of her and the patients in the waiting room.

Ileana Cora recalled one afternoon when Johanna, who had apparently been using one of her father's credit cards without his knowledge, objected so much to his canceling the account that she barged into the office and loudly confronted him while he was attending to a patient. He was slow to react, perhaps caught by surprise or embarrassed, but Ms. Cora stepped forward to take charge and single-handedly ushered Johanna out of the office.

Ms. Cora was probably the only woman who felt protective and admiring of Dr. Bartha at this time. She had been one of a dozen women who had applied for the receptionist's job and, according to Dr. Mantia, was hired by Bartha because she reminded him of his late mother, Ethel. Ileana Cora always arrived for work well groomed in tailored attire with a scarf around her neck (Ms. Cora's mother in Puerto Rico made dresses for prominent women), and in addition she was an excellent bookkeeper and adept with the computer.

"Dr. Bartha had a fixation about his mother," said Dr. Alan Winter, one of the two periodontists who rented space in the back. "He would say, 'This is my mother's building,' or 'This was my mother's whatever'—'my mother my mother my mother.'" Dr. Winter mentioned that a photograph of the movie star Anthony Quinn, inscribed to Bartha's mother, hung above Ms. Cora's reception desk, and stored in the basement were the hair dryers that Bartha's mother had used when her beauty salon was there.

"I'm conjecturing," Dr. Winter went on, "and I have no right to do this, but had his mother never had her business here, and had she and he not lived in this building, he might have handled it differently. [That is: instead of taking the building to his grave, he might have put it on the market.] As I said, he had this thing: 'It's my mother's. I can't give it up.'"

One of the reasons he lost the building was undoubtedly due to the courtroom strategy of Cordula's attorney, Donna Bennick, a tiny but formidable blue-eyed blonde in her mid-forties who uncovered and exploited some very damaging evidence during the trial, which portrayed Dr. Bartha as such an unsavory character that the judge eventually ordered him to pay $4 million to Cordula.

The evidence arose out of an argument the couple had during November of 1998; but what was meaningful about this to the attorney, Donna Bennick, was that it provided her with two scraps of paper that Dr. Bartha had torn from a small notebook sometime after the argument; and later, when his wife was not around, he covered the papers with offensive words and drawings and then placed them on the kitchen cabinet where Cordula would sooner or later surely see them. On the paper he had printed: "You Are A Bully!" And next to these words he had drawn the Soviet symbol of the hammer and sickle, as well as a swastika.

Cordula was alone when she discovered his message, and, although confused and quite upset—especially by the swastika and its relationship to her family during the occupation—she did not immediately confront her husband to demand an explanation when he returned home. In fact, she said nothing after removing the scraps, although she did save them and kept them hidden for more than three years. Then, before the divorce trial in 2002, she gave them to her attorney, Ms. Bennick, who later introduced them in court as "Plaintiff's Exhibit One"—which became part of the evidence intending to prove that although Dr. Bartha's mother was half-Jewish, and his maternal grandfather was a rabbi, he himself bore the soul of an anti-Semite.

Shortly after the 1998 argument and her receiving the "Bully" message, Cordula left for the Netherlands for her father's birthday, as she always did in early winter. On being greeted at the airport by her sister-in-law, Cordula mentioned the swastika and indicated that her marriage was over. But during her month-long visit abroad she discovered she had cancer. On returning to New York in January of 1999 and visiting Sloan Kettering, it was confirmed: She had second-stage cancer.

As she would later testify, her husband was "shocked" by the news, and he suddenly began showing signs of concern and affection. He took time off from work on one occasion to join her for a hospital visit, and one evening he surprised her by cooking a special dinner for her. She also recalled the excitement he had shown in telling her that he had just met a physician at Harlem Hospital who had a new cancer treatment that would benefit her.

But there was no follow-up, she went on, and she was "very disappointed." Her husband also refused to participate in the couples' therapy sessions for cancer survivors at Sloan Kettering, she added. He claimed that "he had nothing to say."

In the middle of August 1999—following eight months during which time Cordula acknowledged that her husband had "supported her somewhat"—the couple had another serious argument. Later in their courtroom testimony, neither could precisely recall how the quarrel began or what it was about, other than that it concerned their daughters, Serena and Johanna. "I took the side of Serena and my wife overrode me and took the side of Johanna." That was all he remembered.

As a result of the argument, he and his wife stopped talking for many months. Each day she went to her job and he to his, no longer sharing the marital bedroom at night on the fourth floor. He moved down into the third-floor living room, sleeping on a sofa. He saw their daughters from time to time and they briefly conversed. But it was a broken household that the girls were now part of—although they did not keep this fact entirely secret from some of their friends and acquaintances.

One person with whom Serena discussed this was the sous chef at the Links Club next door. His name was Brian Sugrue. A line cook at the Russian Tea Room before coming to the Links in 1997, Sugrue was a robust, hazel-eyed son of Irish immigrants who stood 5'11", weighed about two hundred pounds, and kept his close-cropped brown hair spiky with daubs of gel. On his left arm was a small tattoo bearing his nickname, "Grue."

He and Serena, also tattooed and with professional aspirations in the culinary world, quickly struck up a congenial relationship, usually chatting along the sidewalk near the brownstone's staircase while he was taking a smoke break from the club's kitchen. Brian Sugrue was a pack-a-day appreciator of Marlboro Lights. Sometimes, for more privacy, he and Serena would meet under the staircase near the entrance to Dr. Bartha's office. Once or twice she gave him a tour of the interior when no one else was around.

Actually, he was already on speaking terms with her father. The two men first met unintentionally one afternoon when Sugrue, puffing on a cigarette while sitting alone on one of the brownstone's lower steps, suddenly heard the sound of the steel door opening, and, turning, he saw Dr. Bartha emerging. Before the doctor could say anything, Sugrue stood up and called to him: "Oh, sorry, I'm blocking your steps."

Not responding, Dr. Bartha kept his eyes focused on his shoes as he carefully made his way down, pausing and taking a breath after each step, holding on to the rail with one hand and a canvas satchel with the other. He wore a blue blazer, a button-up shirt with no tie, and a pair of extra-large-sized khaki pants. Hatless, with his gray hair blowing slightly in the wind and his steel-rimmed glasses balanced on the thick nose of his sturdy face with its solemn expression, he then stepped heavily down onto the sidewalk, almost colliding with the younger man who stood in front of him, holding a burning cigarette down at arm's length.

"Sorry to be invading your space," Sugrue repeated.

Saying nothing, Dr. Bartha regarded him with passive curiosity for a few moments. Sugrue was wearing a baseball cap, checkered trousers, and a chef's white jacket.

"No problem," Dr. Bartha said finally. "You can sit on the steps whenever you wish." The doctor's accompanying smile surprised Sugrue, who had been told by Serena of her father's brusque disposition.

"And so goodbye," the doctor said, with a little wave. "I must be on my way." He stepped around Sugrue and headed toward his car parked at the curb nearby. And from then on, Brian Sugrue took the doctor at his word and laid claim on a daily basis to the brownstone's steps—where, from time to time, he had other brief exchanges with the doctor. It might be references to the weather, or to some minor occurrence in the neighborhood, or to how Sugrue was doing at his job.

The doctor never mentioned that his late father, Janos, had once been a kitchen worker at the Plaza hotel. But when Sugrue later learned of it, he guessed that it might have factored into the doctor's cordiality toward him.

Although Sugrue had expressed regrets to Serena after she had described her parents' troubles, he—and some of his fellow workers at the Links—had already had a close-up view of her family's difficulties, along with times when there appeared to be harmony in the household. From the fourth-floor window of the club's Auchincloss Room, where the members' meals were served during summer months, the kitchen staff would sometimes see the doctor's younger and more slender daughter, Johanna, sunbathing in her bikini on the rear terrace of the brownstone's third floor. At other times, both daughters might be seen standing together at the top of the brownstone's staircase, apparently trying to distance themselves from their parents' noisy arguments within.

One afternoon in mid-October of 2001, Brian Sugrue himself caught a glimpse from a window of Cordula and her daughters leaving the brownstone, and he did not see them return that day, nor the next, nor during all the days and weeks that followed from then on. In fact, Sugrue would never see Serena again. Of course he made no inquiries about this situation during his chance meetings on the steps with her father, nor did the doctor volunteer any information—most often passing by with little more than a nod of recognition. But Sugrue soon concluded that Dr. and Mrs. Bartha were no longer living together.

Chapter 30

D r. Bartha did not want a divorce, but his wife did, and he therefore felt obliged to hire an attorney. He selected one of the leading matrimonial lawyers in New York City, Ira Garr. In his early fifties, Mr. Garr was a refined, slender, soft-spoken individual whose green eyes were framed with wire-rimmed glasses and whose courteous manner made him popular with most of the judges and lawyers he met.

When the Manhattan federal court judge Kimba Wood needed legal representation in ending her fourteen-year marriage to the political columnist Michael Kramer, she summoned Ira Garr. He also stood by Ivana Trump in her divorce from Donald Trump, and he handled the divorce case of publisher Rupert Murdoch following his fourteen-year marriage to his third wife, Wendi Deng.

Even when he himself was a personal participant in such situations—Ira Garr's two marriages ended in divorce—he managed to proceed without any manifestations of rancor between himself and his ex-wives-to-be. The terms were promptly and fairly settled, and, in his first divorce case, his wife trusted him to draft the agreement, which was quickly approved by opposing counsel.

He was introduced to Dr. Bartha by a fellow attorney and friend of Dr. Paul Mantia, the latter experiencing much concern about his mentor's morale and need of legal guidance in the aftermath of the sudden departure of Cordula and the daughters from the brownstone. On October 17, 2001, after she and her daughters had moved briefly to Brooklyn before renting an apartment in Washington Heights, she left a note on a chest of drawers that read:

> *Nicholas, it is clear we cannot live together.*
> *More than two years of no communication seems enough.*
> *All the best for your future. Cordula.*

There actually had been some communication between them during those two years but it had been mostly mean-spirited and accusatory.

In 2000, he had complained bitterly when she refused to file a joint tax return, as they had customarily done in the past. He suspected, not for the first time, that she had been routinely diverting sums of money from their savings into her own banking account registered in the Netherlands, while at the same time she was living entirely on his earnings, which he dutifully deposited into their joint checking account.

During the summer of 2001, while Cordula was on a pro-longed visit to Europe (her father had died there in July), her husband took it upon himself to temporarily rent out the second-floor brownstone space that had been vacant since his mother's death four years earlier. He also removed his wife's name from the joint Chase credit-card account that she had been using. He claimed to be desperate for money, unable to keep pace with the monthly costs of operating the house and paying the taxes—plus his daughters' student loans, the cable and telephone bills, the *Times* daily delivery, the maid, and his wife's trips overseas—with his earnings as a double-shift, and sometimes triple-shift, emergency room doctor, and the small sums that he and his partner, Paul Mantia, were receiving from their newly opened office in the brownstone.

While Cordula was in Europe, he once telephoned to accuse her of being with a lover; and just prior to her trip—in June of 2001—he resumed taunting her in a manner similar to what he had done back in November of 1998, when he pasted scraps of paper to the kitchen cabinet and printed out the words: "You Are A Bully!" and illustrated them with his drawings of the hammer and sickle and a swastika.

He did not repeat "Bully" on this occasion but instead scribbled some difficult-to-read remarks on four torn-out articles from the *Times* (all printed in June of 2001) that he apparently believed reflected negatively on her homeland, the Netherlands, and by extension on herself as a citizen. On each article he also printed a swastika.

One article mentioned that a privately financed 130-foot Dutch ship, *Women on Waves*, was equipped to carry out abortions in international waters near countries where the procedure was banned, adding that the vessel's first port of call would be Dublin.

Another article reported: "Since 1996, the number of young Eastern Europeans, Africans and Asians seeking asylum in the Netherlands has more than doubled . . . China was the largest source of immigration by minors into the Netherlands."

A third article was a follow-up to the *Women on Waves* story, amending that the Dutch abortion shop lacked proper registration and "may sail back to the Netherlands for its missing license, then return to Ireland in July, or it may sail on to South America or Africa to continue its campaign in places where the regulations on abortion are greatly restricted."

The fourth article had nothing to do with the Netherlands; instead it was a profile on President George W. Bush's fifty-four-year-old policy adviser, Stephen J. Hadley, and his efforts "to convince the Atlantic allies and Russia that scrapping the 1972 Antiballistic Missile Treaty for a shared missile defense makes sense for superpowers, former superpowers and skeptical allies."

Since Cordula herself would testify that she was bewildered by whatever his intentions were in posting these news articles with the swastikas, her husband's attorney hoped to find a way for Dr. Bartha to plausibly explain himself, although Ira Garr conceded outside the courtroom that the display of a swastika "was the death knell in Jewish New York City. If you maybe did that some place in the Midwest, they might applaud you." But still, he added: "I do not believe he was an anti-Semite. I don't believe there was any implication of trying to instill fear. It was just a foolish thing that he wrote on those notes."

Ira Garr, himself Jewish, suggested that Dr. Bartha was responding "to something he felt oppressive about the Dutch government," and on the witness stand he guided Dr. Bartha in that direction.

"Did you have any conversations with your wife concerning people of the Dutch heritage being anti-Semitic?"

"Yes," said Bartha.

"What was the substance of that conversation? What did she say to you? What did you say to her?"

"Many of them were anti-Semitic. The husband of the queen used to be a Nazi sympathizer."

"Your wife told you that?"

"Yes."

But when Garr asked Cordula to confirm this, she would only say: "I don't recall."

When he asked her to explain why her husband had written "You Are A Bully," she replied: "I don't understand what this means."

"Dr. Bartha had meant that you were using Nazi tactics toward him," Garr said. "You were bullying him." Getting no response, he continued: "Do you think Dr. Bartha is overly concerned about having enough money to live?"

"I think there would be enough money, if it would be organized differently," she said.

"Did you ever tell him to work less?"

"I live in a situation with a man that you cannot discuss anything with," she said.

Overseeing the courtroom proceedings was Joan B. Lobis, the first openly gay female judge in New York. She was a founding member of the New York City Bar Association's Committee on Lesbian, Gay, Bisexual and Transgender Rights. She would not have been Garr's first choice to preside in this case, for reasons he explained in a pretrial letter to Dr. Bartha on August 12, 2002.

> Dear Dr. Bartha: I appeared in court in connection with the pre-trial conference. It is clear that we do not want Justice Lobis to try the case as she has already formed a negative opinion of you.

But even though Judge Lobis would remain, Ira Garr believed he had a strong case in supporting Dr. Bartha's view that Cordula lacked the legal grounds for a divorce in New York and thus was not entitled to an equitable distribution of marital property. New York was not a no-fault state.

"In order to get a divorce here there are limited grounds," Garr explained. "One is adultery. Dr. Bartha wasn't seeing anyone. One is abandonment. He didn't move out. One is cruelty. Under the statute, cruel treatment is defined as conduct that makes it unsafe or unfit to co-habitate. That's a very high threshold. It almost means you have to have the crap beat out of you. There are two cases: *Hessen* and *Brady*. These are the seminal cases from the court of appeals in the

1970s, and they say you're required to have a high degree of proof of cruelty."

During their nearly twenty-four-year-marriage, there had never been complaints to the police, or restraining orders, or medical evidence of physical abuse. Prior to his "Bully!" posting in November of 1998, Dr. Bartha had done nothing like that in all the years he had known Cordula, beginning in 1973. Never during their long marriage had either spouse so suffered from depression that they were unable to efficiently do their jobs or pursue their daily routines.

"Cordula took care of herself," Garr went on. "She didn't miss vacations. She went several times a year to visit her family in Europe. She moved out after seeing a lawyer, and left Dr. Bartha a letter which says: 'Nicholas, it is clear we cannot live together. More than two years of no communication seems enough. All the best for your future.' There's not a word about abuse here. There's not a word about anything other than she was upset."

On the witness stand, he asked her: "Have you ever been treated for depression?"

"No."

"Never, from 1996 to 2001?"

"No, I'm usually a very cheerful person."

"Mrs. Bartha, why didn't you seek therapy?"

"Because that is not really in our background to do that. And as often as it is used in the United States, you don't go immediately to a psychiatrist. You mostly solve your situation how you deem it fit to do."

When Dr. Bartha was on the witness stand, Garr directed his attention to Plaintiff's Exhibit One—the drawings of the hammer and sickle and swastika, and the words, "You Are A Bully," and asked: "Is there any reason why you left that for Mrs. Bartha?"

"There must have been some kind of argument, and I said, 'You are a bully.'"

"Did she ever bully you?"

"Yes."

"Did you leave that document to impart any type of ethnic slur?"

"No."

"Did you ever discuss this document with Mrs. Bartha? Did she ever mention it to you?"

"Since I don't remember why I put it there, the only thing I can tell you is that there was an argument before, where I probably suffered."

"I show you Plaintiff's Exhibit Two—a newspaper article. It says: 'Dutch ship offers abortions to make Ireland its first call.' The back says Monday, June 11, 2001 . . . and [it] looks like a swastika on the top.

"Did you leave the article for Mrs. Bartha to read?"

"Yes."

"Was there a reason why you did that?"

"Objection," interrupted Cordula's attorney, Donna Bennick.

Garr resumed with Dr. Bartha: "I'll show you Plaintiff's Exhibit Three. Something seems to be cut off . . . Is this your handwriting? Did you ever have any discussion with Mrs. Bartha about any of these three documents?"

"No."

"Did you talk to her frequently?"

"If I didn't see her frequently, I couldn't talk to her frequently."

"She testified that you regularly abused her. True?"

"No."

"Ever hit her?"

"No."

"She alleges in her complaint that you treated her like a slave."

"I don't know what it means."

"On the occasions when you did have an argument, how did it make you feel?"

"I tried to avoid these discussions because it would interfere with my work."

"So you avoided her?"

"I tried to do that."

"Was there any reason you didn't accompany [your wife and daughters] more often on trips abroad?"

"If I wouldn't have worked, we wouldn't have had the money." He added: "My mother-in-law didn't like me."

"Mrs. Bartha complains that you did things on the house and you didn't ask her about what you were doing."

"She really didn't care about the house. She always thought it should be sold because we cannot afford it. And later on, we just didn't talk."

"She wanted to sell the house?"

"All the time."

"Did you ever take an afternoon off from your shift so you could accompany your wife to the [cancer] treatment?"

"I don't know how I could have helped," Dr. Bartha answered. "I just can't tell various hospitals that I'm not going to come in. I was per diem. I didn't have a contract. I don't have medical insurance. Nothing."

None of these excuses were acceptable to Donna Bennick, Cordula's attorney, because she was convinced that Dr. Bartha was guilty of neglecting his wife when she was suffering from cancer. In addition, she believed the swastikas he had exhibited to his part-Jewish wife were tantamount to "cruel and inhuman treatment"—thereby justifying her divorce and her claim to a fifty-percent share of his property and other assets.

"Brutality need not be physical," Ms. Bennick declared, disputing Mr. Garr's argument that Cordula did not bear the marks of a beating, had never contacted the police, had not sought therapy, and had never actually asked her husband to escort her back and forth to the hospital where she was receiving treatment. She had to rely on her daughters and friends, Ms. Bennick continued, "because she knew it was pointless" to seek help from her husband.

Donna Bennick was a fiery, fair-haired, 5'1" native of North Carolina who had practiced law in New York for twenty years, first as a public defender with the Legal Aid Society and then as a matrimonial attorney with a special interest in battered women—among whom she definitely included Cordula Bartha.

It was "psychological torture" for Cordula to remain married to an "ill-tempered bully," Ms. Bennick declared, adding that the only reason Dr. Bartha opposed the divorce was "to save himself from its financial consequences." She went on: "Surely he does not expect this Court to believe, based on the evidence, that the marriage meant anything to him emotionally . . . [It] was merely a supplemental flow of cash necessary to permit him to fulfill his dream of living in an Upper East Side town house."

While Mr. Garr had earlier suggested that Cordula falsely sought sympathy in the courtroom by depicting herself as a Nazi victim—"She was only three at the close of World War II," he said, and yet the "transcript is replete with references to her experience as a Holocaust survivor [that permitted] her to testify to events she could not possibly remember"—Donna Bennick responded: "She truthfully describes herself as an individual of Jewish origin born in the Netherlands in 1942, three years before the end of the war . . . [She] never once referred to herself as a Holocaust survivor despite the fact she was."

The arguments, the counterarguments, the appeals and postponements, the negotiations with regard to spousal maintenance, the equitable distribution of property, and other debatable matters made their way for almost four years through the slow-moving and overworked court system. When the case was finally resolved, in 2005, Cordula gained everything she could have desired.

Judge Lobis granted her a divorce from Dr. Bartha on grounds of "cruel and inhuman treatment." The judge then referred the determination of the financial issues to a judicial official known as a "Special Referee"—in this instance, Marilyn Dershowitz, a sister-in-law of Harvard law professor Alan Dershowitz. Following a hearing, Ms. Dershowitz concluded that while the brownstone was Dr. Bartha's "separate property"—i.e., it belonged to him—she wanted to compensate Cordula for her contributions to this long marriage, and awarded her $1.2 million.

This was unacceptable to Dr. Bartha, and, as a result, his attorney Garr attempted to get the appellate court to negate the Dershowitz judgment as well as Judge Lobis's earlier granting of the divorce. The appellate court, however, affirmed Judge Lobis's ruling while it did concede that Ms. Dershowitz's analysis was wrong; and then, in a finding that absolutely stunned and devastated Dr. Bartha, it held that the brownstone (the doctor's only significant asset) was "marital property"— meaning that its worth would be divided between the doctor and his ex-wife at a later hearing.

Mr. Garr immediately contacted Dr. Bartha to urge an appeal to the court of appeals, New York's highest court, hoping to correct what Garr believed was an example of gross injustice. At this point, however, Dr. Bartha had lost all faith in the system and stopped communicating with his attorney.

Approximately six months later, at a new hearing before Judge Lobis to decide the couple's property division—a hearing that Dr. Bartha refused to attend—Cordula was awarded the sum of $4 million. This figure was arrived at after Cordula's attorney, Donna Bennick, had introduced a real estate appraiser in court who claimed that the brownstone was worth $7 million. Cordula was therefore due $3.5 million, her half of the total. But the court also added another $500,000 in ancillary relief, such as support payments and counsel fees.

Dr. Bartha had stopped paying his lawyer after the divorce was finalized, and therefore he had no legal representation in court to denounce the settlement as excessive and demand a review by the court of appeals. Mr. Garr himself only learned about Cordula's $4 million award because Donna Bennick had telephoned to inform him.

"I tried to reach him, but he didn't answer his phone or my letter," Garr recalled. "I was no longer his lawyer, but that wasn't my big concern. My concern was you have a certain number of days from the decision to file a motion for leave to appeal to the court of appeals. That time was expiring. Then it expired. He had exhausted his remedies. He was stuck. It was like shooting fish in a barrel. Donna puts on an expert: 'What's the house worth?' 'Seven million.' She puts the wife on: 'What do you want?' 'Half.' 'Fine.' He's completely screwed. Instead of having his house, he'll get less than nothing."

Garr went on: "Assuming the house was worth $7 million, its sale would have resulted in an enormous capital gains tax liability. The Bartha family purchased the house for approximately $400,000 in the 1980s and spent more than $1 million renovating it. Therefore, the tax basis would have been $1.4 million. Assuming a 5 percent brokerage commission, which would be $350,000, together with closing costs of approximately $150,000, the gross proceeds of the sale would have netted no more than $6.5 million. However the sale would be subject to a $5.1 million capital gains tax. Assuming a blended federal and state tax rate of 30 percent, the tax liability would have been $1.5 million, leaving the net proceeds at $5 million.

"But Dr. Bartha only owned three quarters of the house," Garr continued, noting that when his mother died in 1997—she and her son had been co-owners up to that point—she willed half of her share to him and the other half to be divided between her granddaughters, Serena and Johanna. And so Dr. Bartha would receive $3.75 million and the girls would split $1.25 million.

"The court, not having been presented with Dr. Bartha's fractional interest in the residence, or the tax ramifications resulting from the sale of the residence, awarded Cordula what she requested. The bottom line is that, due to Dr. Bartha's inability to come to grips with the situation, he was now required to pay his wife $4 million when in fact he would not have realized more than $3.75 million from the sale. Simply stated, she would have received more than 100 percent of the net proceeds of the sale of his separate property residence. Apparently, it was more than he could bear."

Mr. Garr referred to Dr. Bartha's situation as "the saddest case" so far in his nearly thirty years as a lawyer. "We have clients who are, you know, self-important. Wall Street guy comes in, he makes a lot of money, thinks he's smarter than everyone, sometimes he doesn't take your advice. Okay, I don't take your advice. Okay, I understand that. Sometimes you represent a wealthy Upper East Side woman married to someone who's made hundreds of millions and they have a certain entitlement.

"But Dr. Bartha was nothing like that. There were no frills. He was casually dressed all the times I met him—nothing like many of our clients in designer clothing. He wore khaki pants, a simple shirt, maybe a jacket. I always ask litigants to wear a suit and tie to court, and women to wear a modest skirt and not too much jewelry. But when Dr. Bartha appeared before Judge

Lobis, he wore no tie. A jacket, but no tie. He was not about to dress up as a sign of respect for someone in whom he had lost all confidence.

"He was a large man with a gruff exterior," Mr. Garr went on. "But I don't recall, when we spoke, his ever raising his voice, or using foul language. He was a solitary man, distant, almost unapproachable. I guess that's partly why I always called him 'Dr. Bartha,' and he called me 'Mr. Garr.' My clients usually call me 'Ira.' I'm loose with my clients, on a first-name basis, and some of them become my good friends, and we have conversations about many things: books, films, theater, and how did you like Kevin Kline in *Present Laughter*? But Dr. Bartha never talked to me about anything but his case and how the court system was destroying him—and it was. It did fail him.

"But judges make mistakes. It was a wrong decision. I think I could show it to any competent lawyer today, and they'd say: 'But that was separate property. How'd they get there?' Oh, I would have liked to continue the case, and if Dr. Bartha had gotten back to me I'd have told him: 'We're going to appeal. This is incorrect as a matter of law.' But I also would have told him that there are no guarantees. You never know if a judge is going to like you or believe you. And there's no guarantee that the appellate court that has thirty cases a week is going to give adequate time to consider your case thoroughly enough.

"But, as I said, Dr. Bartha had given up. He basically said, 'The system is rigged, it's like Communism was in Romania, and the New York judge is a lesbian who favors Cordula and Donna Bennick, and they're all against me.'"

And these sentiments accompanied Dr. Bartha to his grave a year later and were among the final thoughts found in his computer.

* *Judge Lobis decided to evict me from the house for which my mother, my father and myself worked and paid. My parents and I lost out for the second time . . .*

* *Cordula claimed that she was tormented by the swastika in the kitchen with the New York Times articles, intended for Dutch extremists . . . I do not know why Dutch extremists have to export their social ways to another country . . . As far as Judge Lobis is concerned, the swastika was there to torment Cordula, not to show the thinking of some groups in Holland—one group exporting abortion, the other group importing minors for sexual exploitation.*

* *I survived Adolf and the Iron Guard . . . but this is how [Judge Lobis] treats a senior citizen who is 12.5 to 25% Jewish . . . I think I deserve a $7 million dollar crematorium/ coffin. I worked for it for 65-plus years.*

* *Fascism=Communism=Politically Correct*

Chapter 31

During the final year of his life, Dr. Bartha would continue to chat briefly with his next-door neighbor, Brian Sugrue, whenever they met on the brownstone's steps while the latter was taking a smoke break.

The already stout Dr. Bartha had gotten even heavier of late, it seemed to Sugrue, perhaps exceeding three hundred pounds. The doctor was not only moving slowly and haltingly while gripping the rail for support, but he also was climbing down the steps backward.

One dark and chilly afternoon in February 2006, Dr. Bartha paused for a moment as he reached the sidewalk, and, turning to Sugrue, he said in an offhand manner, "You know, February is the most popular months for suicides." He paused again, then asked: "Do you know why?"

"No," Sugrue replied.

"Lack of vitamin D," Bartha said. "Lack of sunshine."

Without waiting for Sugrue's response, Dr. Bartha turned away and proceeded to trudge toward his parked car. Sugrue gave no further thought to this strange exchange until five months later.

It is quite possible that Bartha had contemplated doing this in February or at some other time in the past. Dr. Paul Mantia remembered entering his office in the Bartha brownstone one morning and noticing that all of his framed medical certificates that had been hanging on the wall were now removed. After walking into Bartha's office next door to report this, the latter at first said nothing. Then, reaching slowly into his jacket pocket for his car key, he handed it to Mantia.

"They're in the back seat of my car," Bartha said.

"What's my stuff doing in the back of your car?"

"Don't ask," said Bartha.

Mantia was perplexed. He stood facing Bartha for a second, waiting for an explanation. Bartha remained straight-faced and silent, so Mantia accepted the key and headed out to scout some of Bartha's favorite parking spaces in the neighborhood. Within a block or so, finding the Toyota Echo, he retrieved the certificates and returned to the office to rehang them on the nails that were still in place. He then donned his white lab coat and sat behind his desk, waiting for the receptionist, Ileana Cora, to bring in his first patient.

In the front office sat Bartha behind his computer. He was wearing a suit and tie, as he always did here and never anywhere else. Owning a private practice within his home was for him a prideful and celebratory experience. Unlike serving in emergency rooms, here it was by appointment only.

When he first purchased lab coats for himself and Dr. Mantia, he had their names in front stitched in red scroll lettering. Normally taciturn if not obstinate, he made every effort to greet his patients with a smile after they had been initially welcomed by the gracious Ms. Cora, whose special skill was in running the office in a manner pleasing to both Dr. Bartha and everyone else, a feat made easier by the recent departure of the not-always-happy tenants who had been renting space in the back.

For almost four years, beginning in 2002, a pair of periodontists—doctors Alan Winter and Alan Pollack, accompanied by their hygienist—had rented the rear area, where they also placed a CAT scan machine for dental implants.

Because of the radiation, their patients had to sit waiting in the front along with the Bartha-Mantia patients, which was okay unless there was a shortage of chairs, in which case there might be murmurings of displeasure expressed by Dr. Bartha.

He and Dr. Winter were often at odds over the air conditioner's temperature setting—even on warm days Bartha insisted that the machine function at a low-energy level—and he also wished to keep the atmosphere around the office devoid of whiffs of perfume, having lately become highly allergic to the fragrance. His patients had been forewarned about this by Ms. Cora, but apparently Dr. Winter had not gotten the word, and in any case this was one of many reasons why he and his partner moved out in June of 2006.

"He was such a difficult person," Dr. Winter said. "He was also irrational at times. Sometimes he'd say, 'I don't want you here anymore,' and finally we said, 'No, we can't deal with him anymore.' If you got to know him, I think there was some humor there . . . When Mantia was there, he'd lighten up a bit. He liked Mantia a lot . . . [but] things had to be his way."

Bartha at this point had been living alone in the brownstone for nearly three years. He lived frugally, cooking with a microwave and hot plate. The tenant who in 2001 had taken a one-year lease in his parents' apartment had departed and not been replaced.

This was probably just as well with Dr. Bartha, whose lack of enthusiasm for renters was suggested years before in a list of conditions he initially submitted to a rental agent: tenants must not have pets, not play music, not smoke indoors, never move the furniture.

Even in his solitude, the irritations of the outside world reached him. With limited success, he closed his front windows in an effort to avoid the smoke filtering in from the grill operated by the food vendors of a super-sized pushcart on 62nd

Street and Madison Avenue. He also stayed away from his terrace because it overlooked the coal-burning pizza ovens that functioned in the outdoor dining area in the back of the Serafina restaurant, on East 61st Street. In his computer he wrote:

Mayor Michael Bloomberg is a customer of Serafina.
Whenever he eats a pizza there it makes the breathing more
difficult for people with respiratory problems. Coal burning
pizza ovens are banned for decades in Rome, Italy, but
restaurants in New York City cannot build them fast enough.

Directly across the street Dr. Bartha observed with displeasure the headquarters of the multi-millionaire businessman and investor Ronald Perelman. On the same block where Dr. Bartha's mother had been forced to close her beauty salon due to presumed zoning violations, Mr. Perelman oversaw his commercial empire.

The Fleming School [35 East 62nd St] was bought by
Mr. Ronald Perelman and is now office space for Revlon.
At 37 E. 62 another office building . . . East 62d Street is a
residential and public-use zoned street. It is not for connected
people.

During the late afternoon of Friday, July 7, 2006, while Dr. Bartha was on duty at Mount Vernon Hospital, in Westchester County, a messenger visited the brownstone office and placed an envelope into the hands of the receptionist, Ileana Cora. It had come from the New York City Sheriff's Office. It contained a final warning instructing Dr. Bartha to vacate his residence. Ms. Cora placed it on his desk, and later in the afternoon she left the office for the weekend.

At this time Dr. Mantia was vacationing in Canada with his wife and nine-year-old son. He was due back to the office at nine o'clock on the following Monday morning, July 10. But less than an hour before he was scheduled to arrive, Dr. Bartha was preoccupied with polluting his place with infusions of gas diverted from a pipe in the basement.

Dr. Bartha was alone in the building when it eventually blew up. To prevent anyone from entering, he had positioned himself at the front window of the reception room of his street-level office. Having already read the sheriff's eviction notice set for Monday, he had contacted Ms. Cora and told her to cancel all of that day's appointments. There was no doubt that he planned to die early that morning in the brownstone that he valued more than his life.

Before dawn he had already emailed to a select circle of individuals, including his ex-wife and Dr. Mantia, a suicide note that he had typed earlier on his computer. It was doubtful that anyone had yet read it as he now stood waiting behind his office window facing the street, having no idea how long it would take for the gas to circulate throughout the interior and achieve its desired result.

Shortly before six thirty, the flow of gas was strong enough to have penetrated the basement and main floor of the building next door, the Links Club, a five-story classical brick structure at 36 East 62nd Street to the east of Bartha's property. The first person to smell gas there was a forty-year-old waiter and native of Ecuador named Jack Vergara, who was on duty to help with the breakfast that would be served to the members beginning at seven thirty

That morning at five thirty, Mr. Vergara had taken the train at the Grant Avenue station near his residence in Maspeth, Queens, and, after exiting about forty minutes later, at 59th Street and Fifth Avenue, he briskly walked three blocks uptown, turned right to cross Madison Avenue, and soon was passing under the green canvas marquee of the sixteen-story Cumberland House co-op, at 30 East 62nd Street.

A few steps ahead, extending across the sidewalk, was a nine-foot-wide driveway that led down to the Cumberland's underground garage; the driveway also bordered the western wall of Bartha's brownstone. As Jack Vergara passed the brownstone and advanced toward the Link Club's entrance, he might well have been among the last of those whom the doctor would see alive.

After entering the vestibule of the Links Club shortly before six thirty and exchanging greetings with the night watchman, Vergara said: "I smell gas." As the watchman shook his head, indicating that he smelled nothing, Vergara hastened past him toward the staircase, and he did not stop climbing until he had reached the kitchen on the fourth floor.

He suspected that someone on the staff had carelessly left the oven on all night; and even though this turned out not to be true, he immediately saw to it that Con Ed was notified and that an urgent request was made for inspectors to come as soon as possible.

Within twenty minutes two inspectors had arrived, along with members of the Fire Department; but although the Con Ed inspectors' handheld detectors registered the presence of gas they were unable to trace its source. Meanwhile, as the kitchen workers were downstairs setting the tables in the third-floor dining room, Vergara told the cook: "We're serving only a cold breakfast today"—meaning that while there would be juice, fruit, cereal, pastry, and hot coffee from the electric machine, there would be no ham, eggs, pancakes, or anything else that was usually prepared on a gas range.

The cook objected: "The chef will be angry when he shows up and sees we don't have the bacon ready," adding that the members would probably also be unhappy with the restricted menu.

"Cold breakfast today," Vergara repeated. He was only a waiter, but in the absence of his boss, the general manager, he was imposing his status as a senior employee. He had been working at the Links Club for nearly twenty years. And so on this morning a cold breakfast was served, and, with him having explained the circumstances to each arriving member, there were no complaints.

It was during the latter part of the breakfast service, somewhere close to eight thirty, that Vergara first heard what he later described as a "big tremor," a loud noise accompanied by a quivering sensation within his body that he initially attributed to the collision of a dump truck outside, or maybe a major malfunctioning of its engine.

However, as he peered down from the fourth-floor window, overlooking the street in front of the club, he saw nothing amiss. Then, after going down to the third floor and looking through one of the side windows, he saw huge clouds of dark dust rising into the atmosphere and then realized, much to his amazement, that the familiar sight of the old brownstone next door, a fixture since 1881, was no longer there.

Crumbled by the explosion, dismantled in size and shape, it was now vaporized within a mirage of cascading chaos, a fiery heap of fallen floors that steadily covered the sidewalk and curb with an ascending mound of charred and splintered remnants of Dr. Bartha's household fixtures and personal possessions — his burned books, his crushed computers, tiny pieces of his shoes, clothing, spectacles, his bed, microwave, eating utensils, bathroom tiles, carpeting, banisters, door knobs, chunks of the half-intact stone stoop, the battered newel posts, the contorted and loosely hinged French-style iron front door — Christopher Gray of the *Times* wrote that it "staggers like a drunk at the top of the stairway." There were also spread throughout the remains of a few of Dr. Bartha's late mother's hair dryers that he had stored in the back of his office as a memento from when she briefly ran a beauty parlor there; and mixed in with the piles of splintered wood there might have been chips from the wainscoting of The Room in which Vincent Astor had once presided over his elite group of espionage aficionados; and amid the several glass-less window frames flung here and there was the one behind which Dr. Bartha had been standing just prior to his body being buried in the avalanche of wreckage.

Completely unaware of the occurring calamity—which would in time injure ten firefighters as well and five passersby, and damage the interiors of thirteen apartments within the eighty-four-unit Cumberland House—was a sixty-six-year-old financier and Links member named Eric Gleacher, who, as Bartha's house was tumbling down, was fully concentrated on soaping himself under a shower in one of the club's guest rooms on the fourth floor. He was staying at the Links because he was getting a divorce and his new apartment was not yet ready for occupancy.

"The two rooms at the Links which are used for overnight stays have not been renovated for many years," Mr. Gleacher said. "They seem right out of the 1960s, reflecting old school WASP gentility. The good news is the water pressure is great. I'm slow when I shower in the morning because I shave in the shower. While I was shaving I heard a loud noise. It sounded like a backfire in a furnace system. I was not concerned, as the noise was not particularly loud and I had been trained in explosive ordnance while on active duty with the Second Marine Division at Camp Lejeune, North Carolina, in the 1960s. I know what a blast from C-4 plastic sounds like, as well as dynamite and hand grenades. This noise wasn't close to the percussion from those explosives.

"I looked out the bathroom window and saw a white unmarked panel truck parked in the middle of 62nd St. directly in front of Ronald Perelman's office. I could see debris in the street and a woman lying on the sidewalk almost at the northeast corner of Madison and 62nd.

"My first reaction was that someone tried to blow up Perelman's office," he said, referring to the frequently litigious and four-times-divorced mogul. "Ronald was a client and a friend with whom I had worked many times. I helped him acquire Revlon in the 1980s and I knew him well. He was thoroughly honest and very tough in his business dealings and, as a result, had made enemies who would like nothing more than to see him taken down a peg or two.

"I dressed quickly and opened the door to my room. Much to my surprise right outside stood a New York firefighter, ax in hand. He told me I'd better hustle down the stairs and vacate the premises. There was broken glass in the front door area and the attendant on duty was cut and bleeding. I picked my way around the debris and crossed to the north side of 62nd Street.

"I immediately saw the flames, which looked ferocious and climbed all the way up the west firewall of the Links, licking the roof after reaching the top. I immediately assumed that the Links building was surely going to be consumed by the flames. Within seconds of that, though, the NYFD demonstrated what it could do. They turned on the hoses and washed the side of the building with water, and the flames fell away with remarkable speed."

Ronald Perelman was not in his office at the time of the incident, but his secretary, seated at her desk, said that the impact knocked her off her chair and the explosive sounds she heard reminded her of when she had lived in Israel and worked for twelve years in the office of the mayor of Tel Aviv. Another employee in Perelman's office, a native of California named

Ashley Stackowski, thought at first that she was in the middle of an earthquake. She did manage to take a photo of the destruction across the street, and it ended up on the front page of the next day's edition of the *New York Daily News* (with a photo credit).

Throughout the afternoon, television-news helicopters hovered over the neighborhood, and although the White House announced that the blast did not appear to be the work of terrorists, Dr. Bartha's notoriety quickly spread around the world via television and the print media. Some headline writers began referring to him as "Dr. Boom." At Camp Fallujah, west of Baghdad, a Marine Corps lieutenant named Renny McPherson saw images of the burning brownstone on the television set in his mess hall, and he immediately emailed his parents, who resided on 62nd and Park Avenue—his father was also a member of the Links—and asked: "Are you all right?"

When Dr. Paul Mantia arrived at the building surrounded by the police vehicles and fire trucks, he was relieved to learn that Ms. Cora had not been inside. Although his office was buried under piles of rubble, he had fortunately made duplicate copies of his medical certificates and kept them at home. Also at home, on his computer, was a message that Dr. Bartha had emailed him an hour or two before the explosion.

Paul, I am sorry, but I cannot put up with this situation any more. I am glad you passed your board recertification. It made my decision easier. I hope your vacation was good.

Dr. Bartha had also emailed two final messages to his exwife. In one he wrote:

Cordula, my further staying alive does not make any sense.
Work as described above is pure punishment. I will lose

my office. Getting sick even in the most optimal conditions is not easy. Alone is certainly terrible.

The other message to Cordula read:

When you read these lines your life will change forever. You deserve it. You will be transformed from a gold digger to an ash and rubbish digger.

After the firemen had recovered Dr. Bartha's unconscious body from the rubble, it was rushed to the emergency room of the New York-Presbyterian Hospital. Almost half of his body was charred with second- or third-degree burns, and during his time in the hospital he was unable to speak or communicate in any way. He died there on July 15, five days after he arrived. On the following week, he was buried in Queens.

"It was a small ceremony for family-only," said the funeral director, meaning that none of Dr. Bartha's close friends (such as doctors Mantia and Nazario, and the computer-servicing Alex Justo) were invited. Cordula did appear at the grave site to lay some white baby roses on the tombstone, but the gravedigger at the Cypress Hills Cemetery told the *New York Daily News*: "There weren't any tears. Nobody was really busted-up . . . A preacher read a short prayer from the Bible, then we lowered the white coffin."

Following the funeral, Cordula (who later bought an apartment outside Manhattan) refused to grant interviews to the press, and this would be her policy from then on. Anyone trying to contact her or her daughters would be contacted by Cordula's law firm and warned about invading the family's privacy.

Although Dr. Bartha did not leave a will, his daughters (who already owned 25 percent of the property) inherited his remaining 75 percent share, along with his posthumous debts—which included his $5,000 hospital bill, a $5,730 tab for the Queens funeral, and the sum of $230,000 that New York City was charging for scooping up the mounds of debris and carting it away in dump trucks.

There were also several lawsuits levied against the estate to cover the costs of property damage to the neighboring Links club and the Cumberland House co-op, as well as the personal injuries to such individuals as twenty-two-year-old Jennifer Panicali, who underwent surgery after being sprayed with shards of glass and bits of splintered wood while walking along 62nd Street toward her summer job with the Parks Department.

Even Dr. Bartha's office manager, Ileana Cora, filed suit against the estate, seeking unspecified damages for "persistent emotional and mental distress" as a result of approaching the building ("key in hand") as it came crashing down. She suffered no physical injury, her attorney explained, but she was offended by the fact that the doctor had earlier instructed her to cancel all appointments for Monday, July 10, "but never warned her not to come to work."

Among the other publicized complaints at this time was an Associated Press story in which one of Cordula Hahn's attorneys, Polly Passonneau, objected to her client being referred to in the doctor's suicide note as a "gold digger," a description that was widely repeated in the media, including in the *New York Times*. The late Dr. Bartha had objected to a fair settlement, Ms. Passonneau said, and thus he suffered "the consequences of his own behavior."

There was also an article in the *New York Post* referring to a wrongful-death suit brought by the son and daughter of a woman who had died due to an overdose of medication issued at the Lutheran Medical Center in 1999. Dr. Bartha was mentioned as one of the physicians involved in the case, which resulted in the hospital agreeing to a settlement fee of $50,000 each to the son and daughter, although the article added that "it was unclear who administered the overdose."

The largest debt owed by the estate was the one that Dr. Bartha chose to not live long enough to deal with: the court-ordered sum of $4 million awarded to Cordula in the divorce case.

No money would be available, of course, until someone bought the lot—which was, in fact, worth more because Dr. Bartha had transformed his brownstone into two thousand square feet of empty space. If he had not made it disappear, his revered 124-year-old building might have sold for around $7 million, which was the sum quoted by the real-estate appraiser who evaluated it during the divorce trial.

But, as an empty lot, it represented a much more lucrative opportunity for real-estate developers—and indeed, within a year of the explosion, a creative and ambitious developer bought the lot for $8.3 million from Serena Bartha, the executor of the estate, and then announced plans to erect on the spot a luxurious five-story town house that would go on the market within a few years at an asking price of between $30 million and $40 million.

The new buyer of 34 East 62nd Street was a glamorous forty-year-old Russian-born blonde named Janna Bullock.

Chapter 32

Leaving behind an unhappy marriage and a young daughter in the temporary care of her mother in Saint Petersburg, Ms. Bullock—whose married name in Russia had been Boulakh—arrived in New York in the early 1990s and settled in the Brighton Beach section of Brooklyn, known for its sizable Russian-speaking population. There she held various jobs, among them working as a clerk in a delicatessen and serving as a nanny in the household of an Orthodox Jewish gentleman who had seven children and a wife in a mental institution.

Later Ms. Bullock was hired as a paralegal and translator by immigration lawyers in Brooklyn whose clients included a Russian economist who in 2000 would become the finance director of the region surrounding Moscow. He was a tall, suave, and bespectacled individual in his late thirties named Alexei Kuznetsov.

When Mr. Kuznetsov was scheduled to visit New York on business, Ms. Bullock's employers dispatched her to the JFK airport to greet him. This greeting eventually led to an affair, and then to a marriage, and within a few years she was running a real-estate enterprise in Moscow and New York whose value she estimated at one point to be as much as $2 billion.

In an article in the *New York Times* it was reported that her fortunes began to rise in 2003 after she began "acquiring vast tracts of land around Moscow to develop malls and homes, and eventually forming a partnership managed by her husband's department."

Beginning in 2005, the *Times* continued, she began buying, renovating, and reselling Upper East Side town houses at great profits—"flipping," it's called in the trade; a good example was the town house at 54 East 64th Street that had been the home of the *New York Observer* weekly newspaper. Ms. Bullock bought the building for $9.5 million in January of 2005 and, after spending about $1 million on renovations, resold it eleven months later for $18.75 million.

Shortly after buying the Bartha property Ms. Bullock said that the new town house would have a limestone and glass exterior, a geothermal heating and cooling system, a bamboo-fenced roof garden, a courtyard waterfall, and a 12 × 36 foot swimming pool in the basement. There would be an all-glass elevator, four bedrooms, a formal dining room, a butler's pantry, a wine cave, and a spa with a steam room.

Perhaps seeking favor with the Links Club next door, Ms. Bullock's architect designed the town house with a recessed entranceway that was likewise set back five feet from the property line, and the fifth-floor roof of the new building would be built back eight feet so as not to intrude upon the mansard roof of the Links.

Still, the Links president, John S. Pyne, was unimpressed after seeing the plans for Ms. Bullock's property. "The design plans bear no resemblance to any building on our block," he said, emphasizing that this area existed within the Upper East Side Historic District—and its membership promptly supported him with a 27–5 vote declaring that the design was "not in keeping" with the neighborhood. Mr. Pyne also pointed out that the town house's facade of limestone was "jarring and overbearing" when placed next to the redbrick construction of the ninety-one-year-old Links club.

Nevertheless, Ms. Bullock continued to promote the desirability of her proposed town house by displaying illustrations of it in Sotheby's real-estate brochure and touting it in the many newspaper interviews that came her way. When a *Times* reporter asked her if buying the old Bartha property presented her with an "image problem," she replied, "I don't want any association with the tragedy. To me it is an empty lot." Her broker added: "Memories are short. Things happen every day in New York. How often can you get a brand new house built on the Upper East Side?"

One day, stepping out of her chauffeured limousine at the curb of 34 East 62nd Street, Ms. Bullock strolled past a chain-linked fence and entered the empty lot wearing a white Valentino suit, a pearl necklace, and black kitten-heeled shoes. Then she sat down, legs crossed and hands clasped, in an Arne Jacobsen Egg chair that her press agent had delivered there sometime earlier, balancing its four-star aluminum base in the dirt not far from the west wall of the Links Club. Surrounded by low-growing weeds, pebbled rocks, spreads of sand, and a few droppings and footprints of rodents, Ms. Bullock posed for a *New York Times* photographer and spoke to a reporter while reclining comfortably within the 20 × 100 foot lot that had not been bathed in natural light for more than one hundred years.

The *Times* article described her as looking like "a socialite or an heiress," adding that she was "ubiquitous on the social circuit." In a later article in the same paper: "There she is at the American Ballet Theatre spring gala wearing elegant black; at a Society of Memorial Sloan Kettering Cancer Center spring ball in white; at a Guggenheim gala in blue."

Reference was also made to her once having ridden a motorcycle from Saint Petersburg to Moscow accompanied by the actors Jeremy Irons and Dennis Hopper, as well as Thomas Kerns, formerly the director of the Solomon R. Guggenheim Foundation. She herself had joined the Guggenheim board in

2007, and it was reported that she possessed a distinguished selection of contemporary paintings and sculptures as well as some late-nineteenth-century Russian artwork. In addition to her homes and holdings in Russia, Manhattan, and the Hamptons, she was said to own an apartment in Paris, property in Switzerland, a yacht, and a hotel in the ski resort of Courchevel in the French Alps.

But her good life went into decline after Alexei Kuznetsov, with whom she had her second daughter, resigned from his government position in 2008 and soon sought refuge in France. Meanwhile an associate of his in Russia was targeted in what the press called a contract murder attempt.

In time, not only Kuznetsov but also his wife were accused in Russia of corruption—partnering in fraud, money laundering, and embezzling at least $26 million in Russian state funds. Ms. Bullock's real-estate development company in Russia was seized and taken over by a rival group that included Vladimir Putin's former judo coach. Her extradition was sought, but U.S. authorities ignored the request, since Janna Bullock was an American citizen.

Her husband claimed publicly that he was forced to resign from his post in Moscow because government investigators had discovered irregularities in his wife's real-estate activities, but she characterized all the charges levied against her as politically motivated and symptomatic of Russian envy. "Just because I did better than others," she told the *Times*, "somebody had the appetite to take it all away from me."

In February of 2012, in a vacant East 80s Beaux-Arts mansion that she was trying to sell, she held a photo exhibition featuring two dozen images of influential Russians—individuals in business, the law, the media, or politics, including Mr. Putin—and the captions accompanying these images were rarely flattering.

"Ms. Bullock has taken on nothing less than the Russian power elite," wrote a reviewer from the *Times*, while the critic from *Art in America* magazine added: "The content in the exhibition reads more like propaganda than fact, and it's likewise difficult to tell whether or not Bullock has been wronged, or if she was complicit in her own downfall."

She was now separated from Alexei Kuznetsov, and would soon become divorced, and she was also struggling to arrange financing for the new town house she planned to build on Dr. Bartha's old property. Her architect blamed the delay on the recession and real-estate slowdown, explaining: "The economic downturn coincided almost immediately with the plans to begin. I think every time there's a glimmer of hope in the economy, it turns the other way." Still, he went on, regarding Janna Bullock's desire to erect a luxury residence at 34 East 62nd Street, her "enthusiasm had not waned a bit."

He said this in 2012. But even a year later, and more than two years after that, the empty lot remained empty and unoccupied—except for the growing weeds, the scampering rats and mice, and occasionally some homeless men who slipped through an opening in the chain-link fence and huddled at night within the northwest corner of the slot. Many neighbors on the block were displeased by this unseemly sight, and few people were more so than the normally patient and mild-mannered sixty-two-year-old James Savage, a bespectacled and studious-looking wealth-management consultant and a Cumberland House board member whose fourth-floor apartment windows, located along the eastern wall of the sixteen-story co-op, overlooked the junkyard.

Before working in finance at such places as Merrill Lynch, James Savage had spent decades within the New York City Police Department, beginning as a cop in 1966 and six years later as a plainclothesman who went on to serve as a trustee of the Patrolmen's Benevolent Association's pension fund, until 1999.

He and his wife, Marie, a blue-eyed brunette whom he married in their native Brooklyn in 1969, had been vacationing in Montauk when Dr. Bartha blew up his brownstone on July 10, 2006. After being flabbergasted by the news, the couple quickly drove back to the Cumberland House, where they soon joined crowds of other residents on the sidewalk behind a police barricade while firefighters were packing up their gear and dump trucks were hauling away piles of crushed masonry and soot.

After receiving word from engineers that the building was safe for occupancy, the residents filed through the lobby and took elevators up to examine their living quarters.

"Our front door was bashed in by firefighters," James Savage recalled. "Our walls and ceilings were black from the smoke. Paint was peeling from the heat of the fire. Our windows were gone, frames and all. It was the weirdest feeling. It was as though we were stepping outdoors. There was broken glass all over. Our apartment was a mess. We found signs of blood in a bathroom. Apparently a fireman cut himself somehow. A box of Band-Aids was left in the sink. We managed to retrieve all the valuables we could carry. But our pet cat, Rosie, was nowhere to be found."

After learning that their cat had been taken by one of the first responders to a nearby animal shelter, James and Marie Savage collected their cat carrier and the $120 in cash that they had left for the cat sitter, and appeared at the front desk of the shelter—only to learn that their cat had just died while being tested for rabies.

"My wife was devastated at the news," he said. "So was I. We returned to our car with the empty carrier. We realized we were homeless. So we decided to drive back to Montauk where we had left our things. This was the first day of our vacation and worst day of our lives."

In the weeks and months that followed, the couple bunked with relatives, stayed at the New York Athletic Club, and then moved into an East Side condominium. In January of 2007, six months after the explosion, their apartment at the Cumberland House was finally ready for them to reoccupy, and as they did so they were greeted by an unexpected bonus. Since Dr. Bartha's building next door was no longer blocking their view, their fourth-floor residence was now bathed in extra light. This was true not only of their space but as well for many of their neighbors.

A half block south, overlooking the rear of Suzanne Newman's millinery, at 27 East 61st Street, streams of supplementary light now reflected upon the heads of people making hats, and next door at the Serefina restaurant the diners on the patio had an unobstructed view of Ronald Perelman's mansion located on the north side of 62nd Street. The horizon was also extended northward for the rear-window beauticians at the Minardi hair salon, at 29 East 61st Street, where Marie Savage was a regular customer.

Having sudden access to the two thousand square feet of added viewing space in New York undoubtedly represented a rare and valuable amenity, but no one could put a price tag on it in an ever-expanding and soaring city in which it so often seemed that the light was on loan.

Marie Savage first became aware of this sometime during 2015, when she began noticing that the clarity of the sky beyond her dining-room window was now being penetrated by a narrow climbing shaft of darkness. Her dining room was in the rear of the apartment, and it was where she sat in the afternoons doing portrait painting, a talent cultivated years earlier at the Art Students League.

The source of the rising shadow was actually five blocks south of the Cumberland House. It was a newly constructed ninety-six-floor condominium at 432 Park Avenue, between 56th and 57th Streets. At a height of 1,396 feet, it boasted of being the city's tallest residential property, but not far away, at 217 West 57th Street, there was under development the 1,550-foot residential-commercial property called the Central Park Tower. It would be second in height only to One World Trade Center, which, thanks to its spire, reaches 1,776 feet. (The Empire State Building, completed in 1931, is 1,250 feet.)

"This is a golden age of construction in American metropolitan areas," said Gian Luca Clementi, a New York University associate professor of economics at the Stern School of Business. He went on to say, being quoted in an article published in the *Times*: "The U.S. is still less urbanized than similar countries, so if anything, we will probably see more and more construction."

The New York City Department of Buildings issued an all-time high 179,320 construction permits throughout the five boroughs in 2017. Earth-moving equipment, towering cranes, and workmen wearing hard hats and tool belts (and speaking different languages) seemed to be everywhere, spread throughout thousands of construction sites and actively engaged within the wall-anchored scaffolding and safety nets of new buildings as well as old ones in need of repair or restoration.

One old building whose outer walls were now lined with multi-decked scaffolding housed the central offices of the New York City Department of Buildings, at 280 Broadway. It's a seven-story mid-nineteenth-century structure that started as a department store, then served for decades as the headquarters of the *New York Sun*, and finally was acquired by the city in 1966. (The defunct newspaper's slogan: "*The Sun* . . . It Shines for All.")

But in 2016 the building's marble facade had deteriorated so badly that it was deemed unsafe for pedestrians, and so a multi-year restoration project was begun. In addition to the suspended scaffolds and safety netting, the site was further protected from falling debris by a sidewalk shed made of steel pipes, beams, planks, and a heavy-duty plywood parapet.

Scaffolding was reportedly a billion-dollar industry in New York. There were more than sixty firms specializing in the trade, and the buildings department had issued permits for the creation of approximately 7,700 sheds. If they were all lined up in tandem, about 280 miles of New York sidewalk would be shaded by sheds. The parapet of every shed was painted green because in 2013 Mayor Michael Bloomberg decided that the color coordinated well with the city's Million Trees initiative and its huge investment in parks.

In the early winter of 2017, Marie and James Savage were horrified by the sight of a green plywood shed going up on the sidewalk next door to their Cumberland House apartment, and also by the presence of several workmen wearing hard hats and toting toolboxes and planks of heavy timber and steel beams into the empty lot at 34 East 62nd Street.

Unbeknownst to the Savage couple, and nearly everyone else in the neighborhood, the lot had been privately sold a year or more before by the Russian-born contessa of flippers, Janna Bullock, to a real-estate development firm in Rye, New York, named the Woodbine Company.

One of the two owning partners at Woodbine, Theodore Muftic, was a stocky, fifty-year-old, blue-eyed blond native of Colorado who graduated from the Harvard Business School in 1992 and was the son of a doctor born in Montenegro. Theodore's politically active mother, born in Oklahoma, ran unsuccessfully for mayor of Denver in 1979.

The other partner at Woodbine was Francis Plummer Jenkins III, a preppy, dark-haired six-footer in his midforties who was born in Tarrytown, New York, and, after graduating from Suffolk University in downtown Boston, earned a master's degree in business at the University of London.

It was Jenkins who did most of the face-to-face negotiating with Janna Bullock, and, having been reminded by his attorney of her compatibility with Russian oligarchs, he attended each meeting wearing a fine suit and tie accessorized with an Hermes scarf and a borrowed Rolex watch.

He ultimately convinced Ms. Bullock in 2015 to sell her lot for $11.95 million. Even though she had acquired it for $8.3 million in 2007 from the Bartha estate, she was not happy with her profit margin on this occasion. But her resources and bargaining power had been greatly diminished in recent years following the financial scandal in Moscow involving her and her imprisoned ex-husband, so she assented to Woodbine's final offer—which marked at least the twelfth time since the late 1880s that this small but desirable residential space had been transferred from one owner to another.

Chapter 33

The building was first advertised for sale during the spring of 1882, for the price of $10,000, by a pair of developers named Joseph B. Wray and Samuel P. Bussell. At the same time they built two adjoining, and similarly priced, neo-Grecian brownstones at 32 East 62nd and 30 East 62nd. These two would be demolished in the late 1950s to make room for the sixteen-story Cumberland House co-op, which took its address as 30 East 62nd.

The first buyer and occupant of the brownstone at 34 East 62nd, according to a *Times* article written by the architectural historian Christopher Gray, was a fruit dealer named Charles H. Parsons, who in 1884 moved and remained there for nearly ten years before selling it in 1893 for $45,000 to John S. Robinson. The latter might have then experienced bad times; in any case he unloaded the property a year later for $28,500 to one Peter Brady, who just as quickly passed it on for the same price to another buyer, Oliver J. Wells.

Wells was a Brooklyn attorney and later a municipal court judge who had served as an infantryman in the Union army during the Civil War. He and his heirs maintained ownership of 34 East 62nd Street for more than half a century, finally selling it in 1952 for $60,000 to a real-estate investor in Yonkers, New York, named Vatcho Kobouroff, a native of Bulgaria.

Between 1952 and 1975, Kobouroff retained control of the building, but, like Oliver J. Wells and his inheritors previously, he sometimes leased out the brownstone to prominent New Yorkers who were often mentioned in the press and it was sometimes noted that they resided at 34 East 62nd Street.

Among the early leaseholders during the Wells family owner-ship period was a gallant 6'3" individual named Walter Gibbs Murphy, an importer of champagne and son of Thomas Murphy, a state senator who had been collector of the Port of New York during the presidency of Ulysses S. Grant. The younger Murphy was an avid golfer, sailor, and competitive marksman who won some amateur shooting matches, including one in Monte Carlo. He never married, which might explain why in later years access to the 34 East 62nd address fell into the hands of his relatives within the Aldcroft and O'Kane families.

In 1930, for example, there was an article in the *Times* society section that began:

Mr. and Mrs. Richard Bradbury Aldcroft of 34 E. Sixty-second Street have announced the engagement of their daughter, Miss Elena de Rivas Aldcroft, to Robert Fisher Kohler, son of Mrs. Emil Kohler of 830 Park Avenue and New Canaan, and the late Mr. Kohler.

Miss Aldcroft is a member of an old New York family and of the well-known de Rivas family of Cordoba and Madrid, Spain. She is the great-granddaughter of the late Thomas Murphy, a leading merchant in New York in the '60s, who was a close friend of Presidents Lincoln and Grant.

In 1939 there was another *Times* piece on its social page with this lede:

Mr. and Mrs. Thomas Francis O'Kane of 34 East Sixty-second Street entertained with a buffet supper last night in their home for their daughter, Miss Helen Marcia O'Kane, who will leave soon to make her home in Hartford, Conn., while studying there for a year.

During this time Vincent Astor and members of The Room were meeting periodically in the unmarked suite on the parlor floor, while another distinguished tenant renting in the building was the industrialist Siegfried Bechhold, whose company during World War II developed the Sherman tank.

It is unclear when exactly the brownstone was converted from primarily a one-family dwelling into a tenant building, but it is known that sometime after Vatcho Kobouroff took over from Oliver Wells's inheritors in the early 1950s he created ten half-floor apartments, between the basement and top floor, and provided each with a bathroom, a refrigerator, and a gas range.

One of his tenants who fell behind in her $225 monthly rent during the late 1950s was named Virginia McManus, although elsewhere she identified herself as Karen Moore and other names as well; and Vatcho Kobouroff, believing she was a prostitute, one day padlocked her door and took her to court, complaining to the judge of the ongoing "influx of masculinity" leading up to her third-floor apartment.

The judge ruled that he had a right to the unpaid rent but admonished him for locking her out and denying her access to her clothing and other personal property. "One must not take the law into his own hands," said the judge. "Justice is indispensable in our society and its importance is so great that even those who are evil-minded are entitled to its consideration."

In 1976, Vatcho Kobouroff sold 34 East 62nd Street for $256,000 to Joerg Klebe, a Berlin-born, New York–based investment banker in his midthirties who, among other enterprises, headed the Agate Realty Corporation at 666 Fifth

Avenue. Mr. Klebe kept the brownstone for four years and then sold it to the Bartha family in 1980 for $395,000.

A little more than a quarter of a century later, Nicholas Bartha would turn the building into the empty lot that Janna Bullock would sell in 2015 for $11.95 million to Woodbine's Theodore Muftic and Francis Jenkins, who in turn would hire an architect to transform the lot into a luxury town house that it was hoped would sell for at least $30 million.

The architect was named Henry Jessup. He was a lean and agile man in his midsixties who stood 6'2", wore tortoise-shell glasses, cut his gray hair short, and kept his comments brief and to the point.

As a young teenager growing up in Greenwich, Connecticut, Jessup earned summer money by painting the houses of people who lived in the area, and sometimes they would ask him to fix the garage door, or replace the shutters, or even enlarge upon parts of their property.

Learning as he went along to master the skills of carpentry and also bring mature shape and form to his childhood preoccupations—"I was always drawing and painting as a kid"—Jessup started a construction company at nineteen that would pay for his four-year tuition at Brown University, in Providence, Rhode Island, which he entered in 1970 as an art-history major.

He had not yet decided to become an architect. In fact he then had "no clue" about his future goals, and so, after high school and before entering college, he spent eight months touring Europe on a bright yellow motorcycle he bought in London for about $600 and rode as far as Turkey and Greece. His parents had separated when he was thirteen, and while he divided his upbringing agreeably between the two of them, he mainly measured himself against his own expectations.

After leaving Europe he brought his motorcycle home and used it for a while before going off to Providence, where, in addition to his studies, he played for Brown University's highly touted soccer team well enough to be offered, after graduation in 1974, a contract in the American Soccer League with the Rhode Island Oceaneers.

Although he never made more than $500 per game, and far less in later years as a semi-pro player, Henry Jessup continued playing soccer until he was forty years old—by which time he was the father of two daughters and married to a woman from New Jersey who, when he met her, was an aspiring screenwriter and young actress with a few small parts in Hollywood films and a dancing role in the 1977 Broadway revival of *The King and I*. They were married in 1984.

Jessup's decision to attend the Columbia Graduate School of Architecture, from which he graduated in 1978, had been encouraged by a satisfied customer (an architect) for whom he had once built a house in Katonah, New York. In the nearly forty years since then, most recently working out of his office on lower Broadway, he completed approximately five hundred projects of varying sizes in different parts of the world. These countries include Australia, Costa Rica, Spain, Germany, and France—although a vast majority of his clients lived in New York City or the Tri-State area.

One exception was a financier from Vermont named Peter Novello, who, in 2008, paid $10.8 million to buy a century-old six-story brick town house at 21 Beekman Place and later hired Jessup to gut the place and redo the thirteen-room building from top to bottom. Jessup designed a new entrance with a covered portico of limestone and, on the roof, a pergola and garden. In between, he ordered new windows, new staircases, three fireplaces, and additional brickwork and cornices, and he excavated the cellar to add a gym.

But just as the construction work on the town house was completed and the furniture was about to be installed, the owner suddenly died in Vermont at the age of fifty-six. "I was shocked and saddened that he was never able to enjoy the place and convince his family in Vermont to spend more time with him in it," said Henry Jessup.

A year later, in July of 2013, Novello's heirs sold the property for $34.35 million to the state of Qatar—a record price at $4,754 per square foot for a twenty-foot-wide Manhattan town house. One result of this transaction was the increased awareness by New York developers of Jessup's work, and soon he was hired by Woodbine's Francis Jenkins and Theodore Muftic to redesign a town house for them on East 64th Street, and then another on East 66th Street, and finally to design an entirely new building on the lot at 34 East 62nd Street.

"He's the best architect I've ever run into," said Muftic. "Most architects are trying to strive for that picture that makes it into *Architectural Digest.* He just wants to do a building that all the tradesmen respect him for and that the client likes."

"There are a lot of architects that push the boundaries of the art world," Jessup said, "but I'm not one of them. I'm a professional. I do what I say I'm going to do. Because I have this construction background, I can be pretty realistic about everything that's going on. And so apparently that combination of factors has served me well, in terms of clientele."

Among the first things he did after accepting the 62nd Street commission from Woodbine Company was to produce a computer-generated image of the town house he had in mind and then estimate what it would cost to complete and what type of client might buy it.

Since current rules mandated that no building on the block could have apartments, Jessup and the two owners believed that their proposed five-story town house might serve as an ambassadorial residence or consulate, or it might appeal to some of the wealthy people from China, Russia, or such Middle Eastern countries as Qatar, the latter of which, in addition to Novello's property, had earlier spent many millions buying other town houses in Manhattan.

"The original design was geared toward this," Jessup said. He explained that in the preliminary sketches of the town house he had designated a "separate staff entrance, which is essential for many Middle Eastern cultures," and also "large entertainment rooms with possible staff services in the cellar to accommodate a possible sale to a diplomat." Finally, he and the owners contemplated changing the address from 34 East 62nd to 32 East 62nd because 4 is not considered to be a fortuitous number in Chinese culture.

But in subsequent months, as the shifting real-estate market in New York produced fewer international buyers—partly due to less favorable tax regulations and tighter capital controls in China, Russia, and elsewhere—Jessup reshaped his floor plans in anticipation of American ownership. For example, he eliminated a service-staff-oriented entertainment room that might be needed by a diplomat and replaced it with a large family kitchen.

Regarding the exterior, Jessup foresaw his imagined town house in the Beaux-Arts tradition, but he also wanted it to blend in somehow with the two very divergent architectural styles that stood on each side of his work-in-progress. On the west side was the sixteen-story, brick-built 1950s Cumberland House co-op, with its lower two floors fronted by Indiana limestone. On the east side was the century-old neo-Georgian Links Club, which in Jessup's opinion was a "really beautiful representation of a historic building."

To the degree possible, Jessup believed that he could bridge the gap with the Cumberland House by designing a brick wall on the western side of his town house that overlooked the co-op's nine-foot-wide parking ramp and matched the Cumberland's bordering brick wall. He also hoped that his future town house's facade of creamy white French limestone might co-mingle with the Cumberland's Indiana limestone base, although Jessup conceded that the co-op's type of limestone somewhat resembled concrete.

He had an easier time imagining compatibility with the Links Club, believing he "paid homage" to it in providing his town house with a mansard roof and copper dormers that were harmonious with the historic building next door. He also sketched into his design such visual enhancements as cornices, dentils, and quoins, which are decorative edges of masonry giving the impression of clamping the corners of a wall.

Still, he insisted, he was designing his town house for "today," as a building that at first glance might pass for historic but was actually "historically derivative," meaning that while the scale, proportions, and materials were based on classical precedent he remained ever mindful of being contemporary — demonstrating this, for example, by fronting his building with black casement windows made of steel instead of wood, as "a nod toward a more modern feel that we want the place to have."

There were a total of fourteen openings on the front of his proposed town house—two on the fifth floor, which would be a pair of arched copper dormers set into a mansard roof of black Vermont slate tiles; three windows on the fourth floor, all capped by a cornice with dentils below; three windows on the third, where the shape of the building was designed to have a bow front; and on the second floor would be three French doors opening onto a Juliet balcony with a metal railing.

On the first floor he had two windows overlooking the sidewalk, and to the east of the windows would be the town house's simple modern entrance, a plain door painted black, flanked by metal railings, and reached after climbing two very low-set, squatter-discouraging granite steps, the lower step being two inches high, and the upper step three inches high—a major example of downsizing when compared with the almost eight-inch-high, nine-step staircase that Dr. Bartha took with him in 2006 and thus deprived the Links's sous chef of a favorite hangout during smoke breaks.

When an architect such as Henry Jessup designs a building that he calls "historically derivative," he is conceding at the same time the existence of historical works worthy of derivation, and, in his opinion, many of these were created in New York between the late 1880s and early 1900s—a period he calls "the heyday of town house construction."

Among the architects from that era that he said inspired him were Charles A. Platt, who in 1907 designed Sara Delano Roosevelt's town house in the East 60s; Chester Holmes Aldrich and William Adams Delano, who in 1916 created the Colony Club for women on Park Avenue and 62nd Street; and Mott B. Schmidt, who in 1927 built Vincent Astor's town house on 80th Street between Park and Lexington Avenues.

Astor lived there when he was a frequent visitor to 34 East 62nd Street to meet with his fellow members of The Room, and Jessup decided to cover the front of his coming town house with the same type of limestone that Astor's architect had used nearly a century earlier, which Jessup himself associated with prestigious projects. It is called French Roche.

Jessup would obtain his supply from a quarry in Euville, a village in northeastern France, and then have it delivered, tons of it, to a factory in Corgoloin, located it the eastern center of the country, where, during the next five or six weeks, it would be cut to size and be shaped to conform to what Jessup had specified earlier in his construction drawings. His illustrations would show not only what his finished town house would look like, but they would also single out and enumerate each and every chunk of limestone that would cover the front of the building. This would amount to a total of approximately three hundred pieces, ranging from a cornice that might weigh six hundred pounds to a smaller example of decorative molding, or a windowsill, or roof coping, which might weigh anywhere from fifty to a hundred and fifty pounds.

After all the chunks of limestone had been fabricated to Jessup's specifications at the factory in Corgoloin, they would be wrapped, packed, and dispatched to the port city of Le Havre, where, in twenty-foot shipping containers, they would be forwarded to a terminal in Staten Island. The cargo would spend about fourteen days at sea. Trucks in Staten Island would later take it into Manhattan.

Each of the three hundred pieces would be marked by a number (which would match the number appearing on Jessup's construction drawing) in order to help the workmen on 62nd Street who would later receive the limestone and then carefully hoist it, hang it, bracket it, and finally interlock it into a predetermined numbered space within the building's steel-fronted frame. For the workers it would be like doing a jigsaw puzzle with variously shaped cuts of limestone.

The cost of all the limestone would be nearly $500,000. The amount of money needed to complete the entire building—material plus labor—would be $5 million. The target date to finish the town house was expected to be no later than January of 2018.

But before any of this would happen—indeed, even before Jessup would place his order for the limestone in France—he had to devote full attention to the tedious and time-consuming task of getting permits from the Department of Buildings for everything he hoped to accomplish. This also required, among other things, sharing his construction drawings with the Upper East Side Historical Society and the Landmarks Preservation Commission in the hope of obtaining their support. At the same time, he was hiring expeditors, engineers, and lawyers to help him deal with the DOB's many zoning and structural restrictions as well as concerns with the plumbing, electricity, sprinklers, and the new elevator that Jessup had designed for use between the basement and the fifth floor. (The old brownstone did not have an elevator.)

Jessup would also have to assure the Department of Transportation that the sidewalk and street would be repaired if damaged during the construction period; and have to consult with the Department of Environmental Protection regarding water connections to the street, and the Department of Energy prior to any drilling of the structural pilings, and the Fire Department to confirm that there would always be roof access in case of an emergency.

Chapter 34

A typical pedestrian strolling past a construction site has little idea that such architects as Jessup must spend nearly a year on paperwork before the first nail of a carpenter is hammered into timber or the first gallon of concrete is funneled out of a mixer truck. And it is probably also true that few individuals pause and ponder that perhaps under each newly poured concrete foundation there exists a potter's field of terminated and conventional people who long ago inhabited and enjoyed that space as part of a farm, or a park, or a friendly front porch, or a room with a view, or some other desired and desirable place now landmarked in obscurity.

The Greeks built on top of Phoenician temples, and the Romans built on top of Greek temples, and thus it has gone thereafter. And now in New York, Henry Jessup was planning to put a town house on top of Dr. Bartha's ashes.

Yes, it is true that everywhere there are street signs, plaques, statues, buildings, and transportation hubs reminding us of the departed noteworthy: Carnegie Hall, LaGuardia Airport, George Washington slept here, Herman Melville lived here, Dylan Thomas drank here, John Lennon died here.

But in order for the name of an ordinary person long deceased to remain in print within the voluminous and dusty files of the Department of Records and Information Services, at 31 Chambers Street, it would help if that person had once owned a piece of property.

This might partly explain why owning property mattered so much to Dr. Bartha. World wars arise from disputes about land and property rights, and indeed Bartha's family in Romania had lost its land to the Nazis and Communists during the 1940s. And perhaps it is why, much later in New York, Dr. Bartha went to war with his ex-wife, and her attorney, and the judge, and finally with the sheriff who nevertheless prevailed, and exiled him into homelessness, and left him an all but forgotten New Yorker whose name endures in the city files and press records today principally because he once owned property that he believed was worth dying for.

The plot of Bartha's story is about a 20 × 100 foot plot of land not much longer, and not as wide, as a tennis court. But while it is merely a dot on the map of the Upper East Side it is, no less than anywhere else, marked by the footprints and fingerprints of multitudes of diverse people who, since colonial times, have represented the will and ways of the larger city along with its propensity for differences and disagreements over politics and property.

It is likely, if not entirely verifiable, that the soil under Bartha's brownstone was acquired at some point during the late 1700s by a prominent Irish-born New York printer, publisher, and property owner who, during the Revolutionary War, became controversial because he had shifted his allegiance from the American rebels to the occupying British. His name was Hugh Gaine.

Born into a struggling family near Belfast around 1726, he was employed as a printer's apprentice in Ireland for about five years; and then, in 1745, at the age of eighteen or nineteen, he arrived alone in New York. He soon found work as a journeyman printer for James Parker, the official printer of New York province, who, years before in Philadelphia, had been mentored and befriended by Benjamin Franklin.

Hugh Gaine continued under Parker for seven years—from 1745 to 1752—and then went on his own, eventually becoming very successful in downtown Manhattan not only as a printer of official documents and decrees, and as the publisher of a weekly newspaper called the *New-York Mercury*, but also as the proprietor of a bookshop and general store named the Bible and Crown.

In his three-story building in Hanover Square, south of Wall Street, he filled his shelves and bins with an eclectic selection of merchandise: books of all kinds (Bibles of the Old and New Testament, Fielding's *Tom Jones*, Montesquieu's *Letters*, Pope's translation of Homer's *Iliad*, John Pomfret's poetry, school texts, and a variety of almanacs, printed in both English and Dutch); household and office supplies (stationery, quills, ink, wafers for sealing letters, lead pencils, corkscrews, playing cards); and, in addition, other sundries that might appeal to customers' needs and desires (doeskin gloves, cotton hose, boots, shoes, London razors and straps, scissors for trimming horses, body powder, patent medicines, musical instruments such as fiddles, flutes, and fifes, lottery tickets, and also tickets to concerts and the theater).

He was a great supporter of (and, indeed, paid the rent for) the John Street Theatre, which, until it closed in 1798, after thirty-one years, was the first and only theater in Manhattan. Among those performing on stage was Eliza Arnold, mother of Edgar Allan Poe.

Gaine was also involved with civic and philanthropic organizations, including the New York Society Library and New York Hospital, and he served as a vestryman at Trinity Church. There, in 1759, when he was about thirty-two, he celebrated his marriage, which eventually produced three children.

While he joined other New York newspaper publishers and printers in expressing displeasure at some of Britain's policies, such as the Stamp Act in 1765, he nevertheless advocated restraint and continuing respect for the Mother Country, and this no doubt encouraged his British hosts in 1768 to appoint him the public printer of the province of New York, a profitable position from which James Parker had retired years earlier.

Gaine now began enlarging his property holdings, purchasing a six-thousand-acre farm in upstate New York in 1770, and a few years later he bought into a partnership at a paper mill in Long Island. But when the war began in 1775, and with British troops about to attack New York, Gaine sought to save himself and his family from danger by moving to the rebel-controlled city of Newark.

He had remarried in 1769 following the death of his first wife, and, having fathered two more children in addition to the earlier three, he had a large household for which to care, and he was eager to be on the winning side of the war. It was his belief that the Continental Army would inevitably drive out the British.

Meanwhile his property in Hanover Square—his Bible and Crown shop, his living quarters, and his printing operation—had been taken over by the invading British, and their pressmen assumed control over his newspaper (which he had recently renamed the *New-York Gazette and Weekly Mercury*) and turned it into a decidedly pro-Tory publication.

A year later, with the British occupation ongoing and the Continental Army in retreat, the Tory authorities promised amnesty to anyone pledging loyalty, and one individual who agreed to these conditions was Hugh Gaine. His decision was of course widely ridiculed within the rebel community of Newark and elsewhere; Anthony R. Fellow, in his book *American Media History*, describes Gaine as a "Turncoat Editor" and "Opportunistic Irishman."

While he was welcomed back to New York by the British, he no longer held the title of public printer; and although he regained control of his property and his newspaper, his editorial authority was scrutinized from above. This did not appear to offend him. He remained a loyalist throughout the eight-year period of British occupation, although not an outspoken one, ever wary of being singled out by zealots formerly associated with the Sons of Liberty, a secret society of patriots who during the revolutionary era had chapters spread throughout the thirteen colonies.

When the British were finally driven out in 1783 and New York City came under rebel control, Gaine removed the word "Crown" from his store sign, ceased publishing his newspaper, and counted his blessings. He still had his book business and considerable wealth to his name, however tarnished, and during the remaining two decades of his life he took full advantage of the opportunities available to people with money in a new city consisting of vast amounts of uncultivated land that required investors and developers.

When he arrived as a teenager in 1745, Manhattan's population was about eleven thousand, with nearly everyone clustered downtown close to the water and traveling along some of the same cobblestone roads that the Dutch first laid down a century earlier. In 1783, though the population had risen to about thirty thousand, the downtown area remained an overcrowded center of civilization, while for miles to the north—from about 23nd Street and Madison Square all the way up to Harlem—it was largely an abandoned wasteland sharing its unaffiliated space with swamps and underdeveloped forests and outspread farms with grazing animals and horse-cart lanes over what had been Indian trails.

This was not yet taxable territory, but if it were made more habitable and marketable, it would potentially be a major source of income for a city needing funds for public improvements. Somewhere between the 1780s and 1800, Hugh Gaine bought some land for investment purposes in what today would be part of the Upper East Side, including 62nd Street between Park and Madison Avenues.

But in those days buying land uptown was an ambiguous undertaking. Despite the best efforts of surveyors and their chain bearers, boundaries were often imprecise. Draftsmen made errors. The details shown on maps might be misrepresentative or merely approximate.

Also, being a surveyor then was a difficult and dangerous occupation. Casimir Goerck—who in 1785 personally charted great stretches of territory at the behest of municipal authorities and was producing an amended city layout a decade or so later—died in 1798, while in his midforties, due to yellow fever prompted by the numerous mosquito bites he received while working long hours in the filthy and swampy places he was exploring.

At the same time the city was selling lots ranging in size from about five to nine acres that were four-sided but not rectangular. Consequently, the uneven edges sometimes led to disputes over property lines between adjacent owners.

According to public records, something like this occurred in the East 60s in the early 1800s between Hugh Gaine and one of his nearest neighbors—the scion of a prominent merchant family, Peter P. Van Zandt. During the Revolutionary War, Van Zandt had served as a major in the Continental Army. He was active in the Dutch Church and a member of the state assembly. He had inherited his land from his father, Johannes Van Zandt, who in earlier times had become engaged in quarrels with other property owners elsewhere and been cited by authorities for frequently encroaching upon and laying claim to property that he did not own.

But before Hugh Gaine's dispute with the younger Van Zandt had been resolved, Gaine died in 1807, at the age of eighty-one. In 1812 Peter Van Zandt himself was dead, at eighty-two—but not before his land, and that of every property owner in the city, had been dealt with in ways that finally brought added clarity and preciseness to the often misunderstood map of Manhattan.

What produced this change was the so-called Commissioners' Plan of 1811, which was based upon some of Casimir Goerck's earlier recommendations and, in the words of the architectural historian Christopher Gray, writing in the *Times*, "made Manhattan's streets an iron fist of right angles."

Except for allowing Broadway to continue pursuing a wavering course through the center of town, most of the rest of the city's sprawling space was sculpted into a rectilinear grid system consisting of twelve parallel north-south avenues that were crisscrossed by 155 east-west side streets. The grid of 1811 covered two thousand blocks and extended for about eleven thousand acres, and the commissioners believed that it would encourage the creation of smaller and smaller lots, which in turn would make them easier to buy, to sell, and to build upon.

In time this would happen, but decades would pass before real-estate developers would emerge to lure homeowners to this area. Just because the streets were clearly marked on a drawing board did not mean that people would live on them, especially since there was still no reliable means of public transportation between uptown and downtown. It was a rare case when someone who bought property actually intended to put a house on it. More often than not they were speculators, people like Hugh Gaine, who bought the inexpensive acreage and held on to it in the hope that someday a rising economy and population would increase its value.

One notable exception was William Stephens Smith, who—married to one of President John Adams's three daughters—

was planning to construct a mansion on the land he had purchased in 1795 near the East River and 61st Street. But then he and a few of his acquaintances were indicted by a federal grand jury for violating the recently introduced Neutrality Act. They had supported a movement attempting to free Venezuela from Spain. Although Smith was found not guilty, he never built his mansion, and after selling his property in 1796, he moved upstate to Lebanon, New York. However, a carriage house that he did build on 61st Street still exists and is currently in use as a museum.

In 1816, more than nine years after the death of Hugh Gaine, his heirs sold his still undeveloped property to an individual named Henry Dickers, who held on to it for a while before releasing it to the city, which in 1823 sold it along with other land to an elite merchant downtown on Pearl Street named John Mason.

After making his fortune in dry goods and leading a bond drive in support of the U.S. government during the War of 1812, John Mason began buying land with a voracious appetite almost rivaling that of his older contemporary John Jacob Astor. While the latter was consuming much of the Lower East Side and Times Square area, while spending little to improve it, Mason was directing his interests farther uptown and would eventually own much of the space that extended from 53rd Street to 64th Street, between Fifth and Park Avenues. Some of what he bought had formerly belonged not only to Hugh Gaine but to Peter P. Van Zandt and other landholders as well.

At this time John Mason was also a shareholder of the Chemical Bank, on the way to becoming its president, and in 1832 he began operating the New York and Harlem Railroad along a route that would later be paved over by parts of Park Avenue. Whenever the boilers of his trains malfunctioned, he would summon his horses.

Mason did not live long enough to see the Upper East Side transformed into a luxurious district favored by the socially prominent and wealthy. He died in 1839, at sixty-six. But one of his daughters would eventually build a white marble chateau on the northeast corner of Fifth Avenue and 57th Street and become one of the area's trendsetters.

She was Mary Mason Jones. Her husband, Isaac Jones, whom she married in 1818, succeeded her father as president of the Chemical Bank. At the time of the marriage the couple resided in a house she owned downtown on Chambers Street. Before that she and her two sisters owned three adjoining houses on lower Broadway at Waverly Place, in which the entertainment rooms could be opened to one another whenever it was necessary to accommodate a ball or other large social event.

A grand-niece of Mary Mason Jones was the novelist Edith Wharton, who, as a young girl in the mid-1870s and early 1880s, would sometimes visit her rich aunt, who moved into the chateau at 1 East 57th Street in 1870. Mary was then a widow in her sixties. Her husband had died in 1854, leaving her with three children. According to 1880 census data, Mary was living in the chateau with one of her daughters, a granddaughter, and five servants. The residence was alluded to in Edith Wharton's 1920 novel, *The Age of Innocence*, in which a character based on Mary appears as Mrs. Manson Mingott:

It was her habit to sit in the window of her sitting room on the ground floor, as if watching calmly for life and fashion to flow northward to her solitary door . . . She was sure that presently the quarries, the wooden greenhouses in ragged gardens, the rocks from which goats surveyed the scene, would vanish before the advance of residences as stately as her own.

In actual fact, Mary was never an isolated socialite in downtrodden territory waiting for life and fashion to flow northward to her solitary door; indeed, even before she decided to build her chateau in 1867, several among her set had already moved uptown, and her younger sister Rebecca was on the way.

Rebecca's inheritance of two city blocks consisted of 55th and 56th Streets between Fifth and Park Avenues, and, assisted by an architect, she designed a row of eight Fifth Avenue houses made of olive-colored Ohio limestone that she hoped would suggest the spirit of a Parisian boulevard. After claiming a corner house for herself, she would sell or rent the other houses to friends and acquaintances, following a plan that Mary had already initiated a year earlier on Fifth Avenue between 57th and 58th Streets.

Mary's development, called Marble Row, was more architecturally elaborate than her sister's, conforming in style to Mary's own corner house, at 1 East 57th, which was inspired by the palace of Fontainebleau. But both sisters were financially successful with their real-estate investments, and among Mary's distinguished tenants (at 745 Fifth) was Dr. Charles Leale, who as a surgeon in earlier years had worked at a hospital in Washington and was the first to arrive at Ford's Theatre to treat the fatally shot President Lincoln.

With the completion of Central Park in 1873, property values north of 59th Street rose by 200 percent. Between the 1860s and 1880s, largely due to the influx of immigrants, the population of Manhattan increased from about 800,000 to more than 1 million. Many immigrants were among the 20,000 Central Park workers who provided the muscle that moved the rocks and shoveled the soil and planted more 270,000 shrubs and trees.

In earlier years, the city evicted several hundred squatters and shanty dwellers who had long lived along the rocky outcroppings, with their pigs and goats, within areas extending from 59th up to 106th Street, bounded by Fifth and Eighth Avenues. In its final stages of completion, Central Park's northern edge touched upon 110th Street and its scope encompassed 843 acres. During winter afternoons visitors skated on lakes that had once been the site of swamps.

In 1881, Mary Mason Jones died in her chateau at the age of ninety. Her sister Rebecca had died two years earlier. Within twenty years, as their heirs and other wealthy people moved further uptown, 57th Street and its surroundings were taken over by commercial enterprises. Replacing the demolished residential properties of the Mason sisters and other patrician families were office buildings, banks, department stores, fashionable shops, and boutiques.

During Mary's heyday as a social doyenne, her corner neighbors on 57th Street and Fifth were named Whitney, Huntington, and Vanderbilt. More than a century later, her former home address of 1 East 57th Street would be inherited by Louis Vuitton's luxury goods store. The other three Fifth Avenue corners would be occupied by jewelers—Van Cleef & Arpels on the northwest corner, Bulgari on the southwest corner, and Tiffany on the southeast corner—and south of Tiffany would stand Trump Tower.

Chapter 35

The year of Mary's death marked the start of the construction of what a century later would become Dr. Bartha's brownstone. The 20 × 100 foot plot at 34 East 62nd Street, together with other land, had been bought in 1881 by the partnership of Samuel D. Bussell and Joseph B. Wray. The construction crew they hired to erect the five-story residence did not fortify it with a concrete foundation, possibly because the land then was rocky enough to support the structure. Or maybe in that time and place the regulators were not very particular, especially since the city was so supportive and needy of uptown development.

In any case, in the spring of 2016, after the architect Henry Jessup requested and reviewed a soil report, he decided that the lot at 34 East 62nd Street was too sandy and incapable of holding a house in place, and therefore it was essential to provide a concrete foundation.

The first step was to remove all the sandy soil, litter, and other refuse from the lot, requiring several men with shovels and another man sitting in the cab of a hydraulic digging machine, which has a claw that can hoist about a hundred and fifty pounds of material in a single scoop. The material the men and machine collected was deposited into a dumpster twenty-two feet long and parked at the curb; when full, this was replaced by an empty dumpster delivered on a flatbed truck.

Two weeks were spent loading the dumpsters with waste. What was deposited weighed in total about nine hundred thousand pounds. With this gone, there was a hole in the ground eighteen feet deep. Eventually this low-level and flattened terrain would become the locale of a basement and cellar, but first it was invaded by a pile driver that, one at a time, pierced and buried twenty-four concrete piles into the surface. Each pile was thirty feet long and nearly a foot thick.

The twenty-four piles were spaced four to a row across the width of one end of the lot, and it took six rows of four to cover the entire lot. Then the lot was overmounted with pile caps, which are hollow troughs placed horizontally over the rows of pilings and filled with steel rods for reinforcement before being inundated by tons of flowing concrete delivered by two trucks.

One was a mixer truck, the other a pump truck. The latter had a boom supporting a rubber hose that could reach across the sidewalk and extend over the entire lot and, in a day's time, pour seventy-two thousand pounds of concrete down upon it—but not before the workmen had snaked through some drainpipes and conduits for electrical wiring.

After the poured concrete was spread out and smoothed over by men using long-handled tools, and after it was dry enough to be walked upon, which might take more than a week, the foundation floor was finished.

Next came cement-block walls enclosing the four sides of the basement and cellar floors, and, after steel beams were installed horizontally to support the basement's roof, that roof helped to prop up the tier above—and, in turn, lend support to the four higher levels to follow within this five-story steel and wooden structure on the rise. The upward thrust was covered on the outside by scaffolding, and erected on the sidewalk was a green plywood shed to protect pedestrians from falling tools and debris.

Since the town house was being built within a historic district, regulations demanded that its owners—in this case, the Woodbine Company partnership of Theodore Muftic and Francis Jenkins III—provide and pay for the distribution of vibration monitors to be affixed to the exterior of all buildings within ninety feet of the construction site.

These monitors, not much larger than smoke detectors, carried wireless sensors that were intended to warn neighboring owners if their buildings were being adversely affected by what was going at 34 East 62nd Street. Ten buildings were requested to have at least one monitor, and those approached were the Links Club, Cumberland House, Ronald Perelman's mansion across the street, and seven other properties within the ninety-foot radius. The monitors were to function throughout the duration of the town house's construction. The cost to Muftic and Jenkins for this precautionary measure would be about $75,000.

The sums paid in salaries to all the workers participating in the project—those responsible for the carpentry, painting, wiring, plumbing, brick and steel work, et cetera—came out of the pocket of a veteran contractor named Steve Mark, a vigorous and meticulous individual in his early seventies who enjoys a longtime reputation in New York for producing the best work at the best price and, as a result, is often hired to oversee as many as half a dozen or more construction sites at the same time, which is why he is a longtime millionaire.

Steve Mark is a blue-eyed, gray-haired, trim and bespectacled man of 5'9" who bears the craggy windblown look of a road cyclist, which, in a way, he is. He travels from job to job each weekday on his bicycle, peddling from the town house he owns in the East 70s to various parts of the city, sometimes as far south as Greenwich Village, but more likely within the Upper East Side, where, since 1978, he has built or renovated hundreds of single-family homes and mostly duplex and triplex apartments located within multi-story cooperatives.

The architect Henry Jessup joined him on some of these projects, and it was Jessup who recommended to the owners that Mark take on 62nd Street. Whereas Jessup's salary as the town house's architect was about $400,000, the cost of hiring Mark was $800,000, which is his standard fee for such a single assignment. In addition, the owners advanced Mark $5 million to cover the costs of the building's materials as well as the payroll of approximately 150 workers and the bonuses that he frequently adds.

That he can both be generous to others and profitable to himself testifies to his budgeting abilities (he is the son of an accountant) and to the fact that he knows from personal experience the value of manual and skilled labor—and, indeed, he can use every implement in a toolbox at least as well as anyone in the construction gangs he oversees around the city.

When he was thirteen, and growing up in East Meadow, Long Island, his parents hired a contractor to build an extension on their house, but the man disappeared midway through the project. And so young Steve borrowed some tools from his uncle Max, who was a plumber, and more from a neighbor who was an electrician, and, with some guidance from both, managed to complete the extension.

From then on he kept a small workshop in his parents' garage and from there he once used his burgeoning skills as a carpenter to repair a leaky wooden sailboat and made it sufficiently seaworthy for gliding through Long Island Sound.

At school he was found to have a high IQ but was also labeled an underachiever and lazy, disappointing his mother, who was a teacher; yet he was otherwise very motivated and reliable when it came to holding jobs after school and during summer vacations. One summer he worked at a corner luncheonette on Broadway and Nassau Street delivering orders and helping in the kitchen, where he particularly enjoyed the camaraderie of the diverse group of fellow employees, which he would later re-experience as a construction boss.

During another summer he worked in an accounting office under the supervision of his father. His father, born in New York as Morris Margolies, had graduated from law school but, according to his son, "couldn't find work at a law firm until he changed his name from Morris Margolies to Murray Mark." But he so disliked his work as a lawyer that he eventually shifted to accounting.

Both of Steve Mark's parents were the children of Jewish immigrants. His mother's kin were Austro-Hungarian and her father, Harry Strauchler, ran a fruit and vegetable stand in the Bronx. His paternal grandparents were from Poland, and his father's father, Joe Margolies, owned a coffee shop in the Bowery. Steve's mother, Roslyn, was an elementary school teacher and served for thirty years within the city's public school system.

Steve received a degree in accounting in 1968 from Adelphi University in Garden City, Long Island, attending school at night while holding jobs during the day, including one at a ski shop in Great Neck. He devoted some of his earnings toward flying lessons, and after graduation from Adelphi he enlisted in the air force, planning to attend an officers training school for pilots.

But while based in San Antonio he became injured while playing recreational football, and after his recovery at a military hospital he dropped out of the program. His interest in flying continued, however, and he currently owns a single-engine propeller plane that he flies for pleasure whenever he can get his mind and body away from his construction business. In his plane he ventures as far north as Canada and southward into Florida.

After his discharge from the air force he married a young woman he had known from school, and he single-handedly remodeled the couple's first home in Flushing and their second in Larchmont, sharing it with their two daughters.

For two years he ran a bath and kitchen remodeling business at the A&D Building in Manhattan, on East 58th Street, and then with much encouragement and a few loans from some of his wealthiest customers, he started his construction business. Within four or five years, he had a working crew numbering between eighty and ninety men, and as many as nine project managers, all of them women.

"Women are so much better managing projects than men," he said. "They have no egos. Or, if they do, they don't bring them to work every day." The managers' mission was to provide him with logistic and liaison support, splitting their time between his office and the job site while making sure that everything was operating on schedule, on budget, and that harmony prevailed among the suppliers, workers, architects, consultants, and clients.

One of his project managers is his daughter Rebecca, a married woman in her thirties with two children. His other daughter, Alissa, also married with two children, is a gastroenterologist. Both daughters are from his first marriage, which lasted twenty years. In 1992 he remarried and has two daughters and a son, all of them currently in college. His son also has a pilot's license and sometimes flies with him on weekends.

Steve Mark and his crew finished working on the 62nd Street town house in late December of 2017, spending a little more than a year on the job. Fortunately, none of his workers experienced fatal falls or serious injuries, and, except for the tardy delivery of the windows, all of the subcontractors fulfilled their obligations on time.

After it was completed and the scaffolding was removed, there was a sense of relief and contentment expressed by those living in the area. Now there was an end to prolonged traffic jams and honking horns caused by delivery trunks and machinery blocking the street, and finally pedestrians were no longer walking between vertical steel pipes and through the dim light imposed by a sidewalk shed.

The officers of the Links Club, who a decade before had been so condemning of the modernistic mansion that the Russian woman, Janna Bullock, had proposed for 34 East 62nd Street, now welcomed Henry Jessup's historically derivative design as compatible with their own neo-Georgian building.

Most of the co-op owners within the Cumberland House are also satisfied with the new town house. These include James and Marie Savage, whose fourth-floor apartment overlooked the job site and had endured a year of noise and flying dirt while the couple observed nearby, through their windows, the sparks of welding torches, the mist of steel particles rising from circular saws, and the hoisting of insulation panels, air-conditioning units, and chunks of limestone.

The daily clamor reminded James Savage of when he lived in Bay Ridge, Brooklyn, during the early 1960s and his neighborhood was invaded by workers building entranceways to the soon-to-be completed Verrazzano-Narrows Bridge. But he also remembered living next to the filthy rat-infested empty lot at 34 East 62nd Street for a decade, and so this new town house was a desirable replacement.

The next step was for the owners to sell it, so Theodore Muftic and Francis Jenkins contacted the Sotheby's real-estate office on East 61st Street and listed their town house for

$32.5 million. A full-page ad showing the building appeared in the *New Yorker* magazine, and there were articles in newspapers with such headlines as: "Former Upper East Side Blast Site Will Give Way to $32.5 M Beaux Arts-inspired Mansion," and "Manhattan Townhouse Built on Site of Gas Explosion Asks $32.5 Million."

But during this period, from late 2017 through 2018, there was a slump in the housing market, prompting Muftic and Jenkins to reduce the asking price to $27.9 million. Even so, it remained unsold. As a *Wall Street Journal* article explained in November of 2018: "New York is facing the convergence of several large economic forces: an oversupply of new condos, a drop in international buyers as some countries impose capital controls, changes to the tax law that cap state and local deductions, and rising interest rates. There is also a shift in taste from uptown to downtown."

Early in 2019, with the town house still empty—a headline in the *Wall Street Journal* read: "Slump in Housing Market Deepens"—the owners were obliged to take on an annual expense of $80,000 on taxes and maintenance fees, which includes security, washing the windows, and excluding bugs and rodents from the premises.

While disappointed by their inability to sell, Muftic and Jenkins remained confident that sooner or later they would make a deal. "We could sell this building within a day or two if we'd accept something in the high teens," Jenkins said, meaning around $18 million or $19 million. But he and his partner found this unacceptable. And so the blue sign that the Sotheby's real-estate agents hung in front of the town house—"Newly Built Mansion For Sale"—was still hanging nearly three years after the completion of its construction.

Hoping for a better financial outcome, the partners in late 2019 switched real-estate agents from Sotheby's to Douglas

Elliman. But as another two years passed without producing a sale, the displeased owners became increasingly negotiable. Finally, in October of 2021, the *New York Post* reported exclusively that the "Dr. Boom mansion" had finally found a buyer, a man who resided in the Chicago area named Marcus Lemonis. The negotiating agent at Douglas Elliman, T. Roger Erickson, confirmed that the town house had sold for $18.2 million.

Mr. Lemonis, who refused to grant interviews, was described as a Lebanese-born, twice-married, forty-seven-year-old entrepreneur who, among other endeavors, produced a reality series for CNBC called *The Profit*. Since he was unwilling to comment, it is unclear whether Mr. Lemonis and his wife intend to sell their residence in the Midwest and relocate full-time to New York, or whether they would commute back and forth. But it is a fact that, while they spent huge sums throughout 2022 into 2023 renovating the interior of their new acquisition, they had yet to inhabit it as their domicile.

During this period when it continued to be unoccupied, Dr. Bartha's onetime divorce lawyer, Ira Garr, happened to walk by one Saturday afternoon after shopping with his girlfriend at the Hermes store on the corner of Madison Avenue and 62nd Street. Mr. Garr does not live in the neighborhood and so had rarely frequented it since the days when he used to visit the brownstone and urge Dr. Bartha to make concessions to his divorced wife, to avoid endless hours of aggravation and the soaring costs of litigation.

In a way, Mr. Garr could sympathize with his stubborn and inflexible client, understanding how the doctor had been so emotionally attached to his home site that he could not, under any circumstance, abandon it—or allow his former wife, who never enjoyed living there, to share in any of the revenue from its enforced sale. Like the lawyer in Melville's story who cared about Bartleby while being confounded by him and ultimately unable to help him, Mr. Garr now stood for many moments lost in his own thoughts. Finally, his girlfriend nudged him from behind and asked: "Is something wrong?"

"No," he said, after a pause, "but I was just thinking that this is the place where a client of mine once had a brownstone."

He then reached out, took her arm, and resumed walking.

"Yes, this is where it was," he said, "and the sad thing is that all he had to do was settle the case, and he might be living in that old brownstone today. It would be worth $12 million today. He'd be made in the shade."

His confused girlfriend turned toward him and asked: "What are you talking about?"

"Oh, it's a long story, " he said. "I'll tell you some other time."

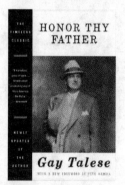
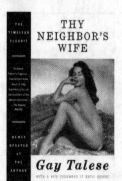